STRANGE BRIGHT BLOOMS

STRANGE BRIGHT BLOOMS

A History of Cut Flowers

Randy Malamud

REAKTION BOOKS

For Vipin and Narendra Gupta,
my second parents

Published by Reaktion Books Ltd
Unit 32, Waterside
44–48 Wharf Road
London N1 7UX, UK
www.reaktionbooks.co.uk

First published 2021
Copyright © Randy Malamud 2021

Printed and bound in India by Replika Press Pvt. Ltd

A catalogue record for this book is available from the British Library

ISBN 978 1 78914 401 7

CONTENTS

INTRODUCTION

'O Tiger-lily,' said Alice, addressing herself to one that was
waving gracefully about in the wind, 'I wish you could talk!'
  'We can talk,' said the Tiger-lily: 'when there's anybody
worth talking to.'

LEWIS CARROLL, Through the Looking-glass[1]

Flowers, free designs, lines aimlessly intertwined and called
foliage: these have no significance, depend on no determinate
concept, and yet we like them.

IMMANUEL KANT, Critique of Judgment[2]

'**M**rs Dalloway', Virginia Woolf's novel famously begins,
'said she would buy the flowers herself.'[3] Of course she
would: why would anyone surrender the most pleasant part of
the day to someone else? The flowers will decorate Clarissa's
lavish fête that evening, a hoity-toity gathering of people whose
company she doesn't especially enjoy, as the culmination of a
day that promises (and delivers) other assorted unpleasantness.
Those who share Mrs Dalloway's passion for buying flowers are
precisely the sort that Lewis Carroll's Tiger-lily will find 'worth
talking to', so I invite fellow floraphiles to follow along into
these strange, bright crowds of flowers and hear what they have
to say to us.

1 What do flowers tell us?
Illustration from Lewis
Carroll's *Alice's Adventures
in Wonderland* (1911).

Flowers grace our lives at moments of celebration and despair. 'We eat, drink, sing, dance, and flirt with them,' writes Kakuzō Okakura, an early twentieth-century artist and scholar, in *The Book of Tea*, his treatise about *chadō* – 'teaism', the Japanese ceremony – and *chabana*, the flower arrangement featured in a tea room.

> We wed and christen with flowers. We dare not die without them. We have worshipped with the lily, we have meditated with the lotus, we have charged in battle array with the rose and the chrysanthemum. We have even attempted to speak in the language of flowers. How could we live without them? It frightens one to conceive of a world bereft of their presence. What solace do they not bring to the bedside of the sick, what a light of bliss to the darkness of weary spirits? Their serene tenderness restores to us our waning confidence in the universe even as the intent gaze of a beautiful child recalls our lost hopes. When we are laid low in the dust it is they who linger in sorrow over our graves.[4]

Flowers brighten our homes, our parties and our rituals with incomparable notes of natural beauty, but the 'nature' in these displays is tamed and conscribed. If flowers are valued as luxuriant emblems of nature, they are also extensively acculturated by the time they get to their audience of sellers and buyers, artists and lovers, celebrants and mourners. One of the strangest things about these strange, bright blooms is that they have been transplanted (or, if you will, trans-un-planted) into a context far removed from their native environs.

We might recreate their verdant original landscape in our heads, mocking up imaginary shimmering meadows in a shadow-world

2 Odilon Redon, *Vase of Flowers (Pink Background)*, 1906, oil on canvas.

inspired by the domesticated cut flowers with which we have bedecked our surroundings. Conversely, we might feel heroic about having rescued these fragile floral specimens from their dull, lonely fields. We preserve them from the indignities of insects, weather and remote insignificance as we arrange them, just so, in a precious vase on an extraordinary mantelpiece. This bouquet becomes the focal point of the loveliest room in the house, in the heart of the cosmopolitan metropolis, with a precise symmetry, or a studied asymmetry, featuring colours, quantities and varieties that we have judiciously curated: the best and the brightest.

3 A Hindu bride and groom will exchange elaborate flower garlands that symbolize love, prosperity and piety.

In the first case, we use the flowers to regard ourselves as being closer to (and more integrated with) the natural world; and in the second, we select a small sample of natural beauty from out of the totality of nature – which can be a bit overwhelming and messy! – to be more effectively enjoyed in smaller, domesticated arrangements that serve as a microcosm, or, as an English professor might say, a synecdoche, of the world's gardens.

Flowers have specific identities – some distinct expression is conveyed by a rush of roses, a sheaf of lavender, a handful of early spring daffodils or midsummer sunflowers – as well as more generic cultural and commercial contexts: wedding flowers, corsages (and their ancestors, nosegays, posies and tussie-mussies), Valentine's Day bouquets, funeral wreaths, Hawaiian leis, Maypole crowns, sachets, Hindu *jaimala* (matrimonial) garlands. We have created a forest of industries and customs that require flowers: almost always, more flowers – prettier and more perfect, a greater variety of species – than our personal gardens or windowboxes could possibly provide. We might want summer roses at Christmas or frangipani in Fitzrovia: floral desires that are temporally or geographically impossible, except . . . they're not. Everything has its price.

The fashions of flower arrangement and floral accessorizing might initially seem relatively straightforward, variations on a theme. But the deeper we dig, the more varied and contradictory resonances emanate from the strange, bright blooms. If we assume that flowers always make everything prettier, unfortunately, we are wrong: floral scenes can be ironic, corrupt and sometimes even darkly misanthropic.

To cut a flower, or pay someone else to do so, is to stop that flower from growing – to kill it, technically – knowing that it will remain pretty just briefly before withering and becoming unsightly, worthless. 'The flower smiles in the vase but no longer laughs,' writes Malcolm de Chazal,[5] and Okakura laments the tragedy of the cut flower more severely in *The Book of Tea*:

Tell me, gentle flowers . . . are you aware of the fearful doom that awaits you? Dream on, sway and frolic while you may in the gentle breezes of summer. To-morrow a ruthless hand will close around your throats. You will be wrenched, torn asunder limb by limb, and borne away from your quiet homes to be imprisoned 'in some narrow vessel with only stagnant water to quench the maddening thirst that warns of ebbing life'.[6]

(The horror! The horror!)

Investigating the ethics of cutting flowers – an intervention which might, admittedly, seem petty – we may surmise that aficionados believe they can appreciate and make better use of the flower in a vase, a restaurant, a celebration or some other human design than the flower can on its own in the soil. The poet Rabindranath Tagore, in this spirit, advocates harvesting a flower before it goes to waste: 'Pluck this little flower and take it, delay not! I fear lest it droop and drop into the dust.'[7] Bringing home a bouquet or three is a decadent luxury; we don't need the flowers, we *want* them. There is an imperious sense (perhaps subconscious, perhaps not) that we deserve to have such flowers simply because we crave them and we can afford to have them grown, harvested and delivered; therefore, they must be ours. We are monarchs of all we survey. In a similar vein, some carnivores rationalize their dietary preferences by arguing that the lucky cows raised to become their hamburgers wouldn't have had a life at all were it not for meat-eaters generating an economic incentive. Nature should be grateful that people have taken a commercial interest in her wares.

However, if it seems that a daisy's premature demise is the worst of it, there are weightier concerns to consider in terms of our appetite for flowers. It is not widely recognized that flowers are implicated in perpetuating the hegemonies of race, class and privilege. Floral crops are farmed mainly by poor people of colour for rich white consumers. The industry poses toxic health risks to the growers and exacts an environmental toll (borne disproportionally in the poorer societies where the flowers are produced rather than in the wealthier societies where they are enjoyed) that belies the simple, natural purity we would prefer to enjoy in a resplendent urn of larkspur. The artificial light, heat and water, along with fertilizer and pesticides, required to produce flowers

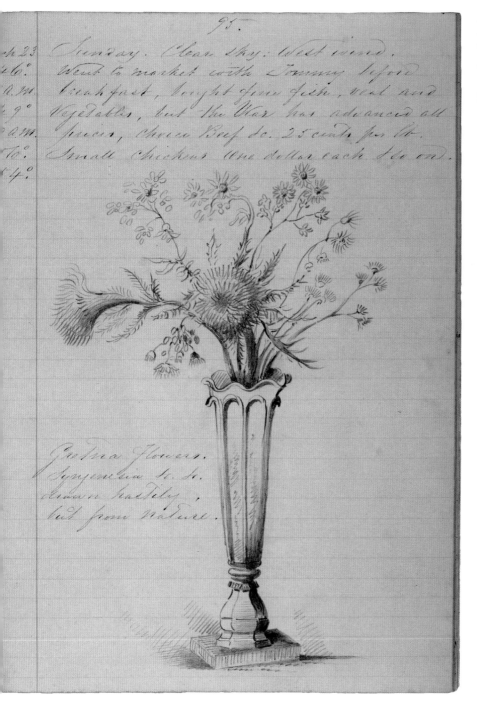

4 A vase of flowers always delights: Thomas Kelah Wharton's simple yet sublime diary sketch of 'Gretna [Louisiana] flowers, Syngensia etc. etc., drawn hastily, but from nature' (1860).

in Africa and South America for shipment to Europe and North America in temperature-controlled cargo trucks and planes produce sizeable CO_2 emissions – tens of thousands of metric tonnes for a single holiday's inventory – while exhausting scarce resources. (The good news is that some producers and customers have begun promoting more sustainable ways to satiate consumer appetites.)

Moral complications notwithstanding, the infectious allure of flowers, their stimulating aura, colours, smells, shapes, and semiotic and symbolic associations, is indefatigably enchanting. It is miraculous how powerfully these flowers, which we integrate into our constructed worlds, spread pleasant feelings, reminders that despite so many indications to the contrary, life can actually be quite beautiful. 'A flowerless room is a soul-less room,' writes garden designer Vita Sackville-West, 'but even one solitary little vase of a living flower may redeem it.'[8] Sackville-West was an intimate companion of Virginia Woolf, and her passion for flowers exemplified their connection.

Flower power also works on a much larger scale than Sackville-West's 'little vase'. Amid the coronavirus pandemic in 2020, self-fashioned guerrilla florist Lewis Miller's blooms provided a dose of comfort and beauty as he sneaked through New York City, in the middle of the night, creating enormous ornate 'flower flashes'. The heart-shaped installations variously comprising peonies and gerbera daisies, lilies, rhododendron and roses, delighted those who happened upon them: 'This is the most beautiful thing I've seen in a long time,' one passer-by noted. '"During good times, flowers are awesome, we all know that," Miller said. "But now more than ever we need flowers in the city. Who isn't looking for a little joy?"'[9]

Despite occasional patches of weedy ambivalence, I undertake this book mainly because I love surrounding myself with crowds of flowers and I hope to attract crowds of readers to join me. There is no floral scene I find as deeply satisfying and emotionally rejuvenating as the one promised in the first sentence of *Mrs Dalloway* and consummated soon after, as we follow Clarissa 'pushing through the swing doors of Mulberry's the florists'.

> She advanced, light, tall, very upright, to be greeted at once by button-faced Miss Pym, whose hands were always bright red, as if they had been stood in cold water with the flowers.
>
> There were flowers: delphiniums, sweet peas, bunches of lilac; and carnations, masses of carnations. There were roses; there were irises. Ah yes – so she breathed in the earthy garden sweet smell as she stood talking to Miss Pym who owed her help, and thought her kind, for kind she had been years ago; very kind, but she looked older, this year, turning her head from side to side among the irises and roses and nodding tufts of lilac with her eyes half closed, snuffing in, after the street uproar, the delicious scent, the exquisite coolness. And then, opening her eyes, how fresh like frilled linen clean from a laundry laid in wicker trays the roses looked; and dark and prim the red carnations, holding their heads up; and all the sweet peas spreading in their bowls, tinged violet, snow white, pale – as if it were the evening and girls in muslin frocks came out to pick sweet peas and roses after the superb summer's day, with its almost blue-black sky, its delphiniums, its carnations, its arum lilies was over; and it was the moment between six and seven when every flower – roses, carnations, irises, lilac – glows; white, violet, red, deep orange; every flower seems to burn by itself, softly, purely in the misty beds; and how

she loved the grey-white moths spinning in and out, over the cherry pie, over the evening primroses![10]

So many flowers, so emotionally and aesthetically satisfying. Woolf sketches, in the background of this scene, the flowers' larger eco-system (the moths beloved by both Mrs Dalloway and Mrs Woolf, the earthy aroma, a summer sun giving way to cool evening air), hints of human kindness drawn out by floral influence, and other simple pleasures (clean linen, cherry pie, muslin frocks) in a quiet ecstasy ignited by this jungle of flowers. Miss Pym keeps the blooms, jars and jars of them, always replenished, always available to make a bit more tolerable the prospect of enduring a day in a crowded city and an evening with catty acquaintances.

Mrs Dalloway's party represents a moment of connection, rubbing up against friends and relations, and some strangers. If the party won't be perfectly idyllic, with its necessary small talk and nervous-making, Clarissa determines to do the best she can, especially amid the chaos of Europe in the years after the First World War (and the coinciding influenza pandemic, which afflicted Clarissa and Woolf herself) when many people were dead and others were shell-shocked, psychologically ruined. The flowers serve to support and enhance the evening's activities: to decorate the party, to diffuse beauty and life and festivity, to help sublimate the pain of the world.

Woolf sets life among flowers in league with her sister, Vanessa Bell, and their Bloomsbury Group colleagues Roger Fry, Duncan Grant, Winifred Gill and Dora Carrington among others, who painted dozens of canvases (and tables, cabinets, tiles and walls) full of the same sorts of breezy, uplifting flowers that Woolf word-paints here, affirming the same faith in their salvational power to improve the state of our homes and our minds. The 'Bloomsberries' filled their rooms with flower paintings along with pillows, rugs, cups, tapestries and other accessories.

For Woolf and her artistic colleagues, flowers are not a backdrop, not merely decorative; they are coexistent with us in our world as repositories of sense and life, in all their beauty and in all their fragility. Clarissa's parties are tedious; her friends and mopey teenaged daughter undependable; her husband well-meaning but remote; and the melodramatic beau from her youth emotionally draining. But brilliant flowers flourish transcendently (as they did in all the Bloomsbury Group salons, where Omega Workshops decor brimmed with flower designs by Fry, Bell, Grant and many others) as emblems of life at its best – a celebration of our spectacular existence, however tenuous all the rest may be. Experiencing the flowers is a part, possibly one of the most important parts, of experiencing the world in which we live. All we need to know about Clarissa's beloved friend from the past appears in one floral tableau:

> Sally's power was amazing, her gift, her personality. There was her way with flowers, for instance. At Bourton they always had stiff little vases all the way down the table. Sally went out, picked hollyhocks, dahlias – all sorts of flowers that had never been seen together – cut their heads off, and made them swim on the top of water in bowls. The effect was extraordinary – coming in to dinner in the sunset. (Of course Aunt Helena thought it wicked to treat flowers like that.)[11]

Remember the prim red carnations 'holding their heads up' in Mulberry's; here, the modernist revolution is enacted as a battle of flowers when Sally – unconventional, bisexual, invisible to the aristocracy – decrees: off with their heads! Her iconoclastic flower arrangement betokens a new day.

Woolf's flowers, beautifully erect in one scene and beautifully emasculated in another, exemplify an agonistic force. Examining both sides of the coin will generate a rich exploration of how vividly flowers – simultaneously natural and unnatural – inhabit our lives, and how we use them to express such important ideas about love and passion, family and community, ritual and beauty. Some of these flowers' inherent elegance endures despite us (despite our obsessive cutting and fussing and comodifying and decontextualizing and decapitating and fetishizing and botanically manipulating), and some does not. The flowers we gather are compelling, attractive . . . and may also turn out to be less beautiful, less ideal, than they first seemed. They invite us to admire them in settings premised upon artificiality, quite distant from the ways in which they grow naturally or in industrial floriculture. T. S. Eliot writes about 'the look of flowers that are looked at',[12] which is precisely what I will try to capture in a profusion of vantage points and varieties as inspired by Clarissa Dalloway's exuberance in Mulberry's, where she has gone to buy the flowers herself.

Strange, bright crowds

'Strange, bright crowds of flowers': Emily Dickinson's phrase typifies her sense that the realm of nature is at least as spirited and interesting as human society, and probably more so. Now acclaimed as one of America's greatest poets, Dickinson (1830–1886) was little known during her lifetime. Highly unconventional and idiosyncratic experimentation infused every aspect of her poetry, from form, rhyme, metre, punctuation and lineation to aesthetics and philosophy, resulting in an imaginatively unfettered oeuvre: surreal, feminist, deconstructive, queer and postmodern are some (anachronistic) categories that describe Dickinson's poetic vision, and her flowers are at the centre of this vision.

I have plucked the 'strange, bright' descriptors that blossom in this book's title from her poem describing a flower that embodies profoundly sublime importance: energy, exploration, animation, rumination, force of will.

> As if some little Arctic flower
> Upon the polar hem –
> Went wandering down the Latitudes
> Until it puzzled came
> To continents of summer –
> To firmaments of sun –
> To strange, bright crowds of flowers –
> And birds, of foreign tongue!
> I say, As if this little flower
> To Eden, wandered in –
> What then? Why nothing,
> Only, your inference therefrom![13]

What an incredibly expansive flower-odyssey unfurls in this 57-word poem: flowers of the world, unite. From the coldest to the warmest place on earth, to territories where flowers and birds are as expressive, as busy, as essential as (usually) only people are, to a spiritual expanse, the Garden of Eden, a mythically perfect place, or near perfect, for flowers and nature. Dickinson's protagonist – a flower! – casually and easily goes everywhere, adventuresome, self-confident, empowered. Its ambition and fearless dynamism seem to mirror human conquests and imperial expeditions, but the flower doesn't maraud or pillage, doesn't upheave the places through which it travels.

Dickinson connotes the actual ecological movement of flowers (for example, as seeds may be spread across thousands of miles by migrating birds), but her poem also brings to mind the myriad gatherings and transpositions of flowers – the circulation, the figurative movements of symbols and traditions across time and culture – that take place in the kinds of social and commercial iterations I will explore: think of stems of statice grown in Kenya and shipped to Kraków.

'As if': the poem's first two words inform that it describes not a literal botanical phenomenon but an imaginative one: it is a freeplay fantasy of a single flower's boundless agency and significance. It is *as* if Dickinson's remote Arctic flower is everywhere, always: cold and hot, north and south, grounded and aloft, past and present, sacred and ordinary, solitary and in a crowd. This flower traverses both physical and metaphysical realms of space, time, morality (from Edenic simplicity to postlapsarian complexity), and cultural consciousness.

Offhandedly but provocatively, Dickinson floats a question at the poem's end – 'What then?' – asking what we do with flowers, how they matter in our world (or perhaps it is *their* world, and *our* task is to determine how we matter there). How do we reckon with them (and they with us)? What are the terms of our engagement? Concluding her brief-but-vast account of how her flower surmounts the world, the poet wonders, What's the point? What does this mean? – and just as flippantly answers, 'Why nothing, only, your inference therefrom'.

Thus charged, I shall proceed to draw out a strange, bright, crowded array of flowery *inferences* (responses, suggestions, hypotheses, interpretations, provocations, extrapolations, queries, flat-out guesses), as Dickinson prompts: inferences about where all these blooms in the world – real and painted, musical and poetic, romantic and political – come from, and where they go, and how they get there, and what they signify. What is their value? How do we understand and describe their beauty? What beyond 'mere beauty' makes flowers so endlessly fascinating? What psychological or archetypal appeal? What magic? What evolutionary or biophiliac pull? What spiritual compulsion leads Christians to venerate the Rosary (crown of roses), Hindus to worship with a *puja* (flower act) in which marigolds, hibiscus and jasmine mediate between divinity and humanity, Buddhists to glorify the lotus as their central metaphor for enlightenment, and Muslims to worship prostrate on a *sajjāda* (prayer mat) that often features profuse rosette-form patterns of tulips, hyacinths and carnations? Dickinson makes it seem vital, more important than anything else we do, to infer such things and many more from flowers. A flower is a delight, a gift, a literal and spiritual article of beauty; and it is also an invitation to investigate.

Although Dickinson's little flower wanders through Eden, I will pay scant attention to that prominent Garden, and, for that matter, to gardens in general. (It's not a categorical exclusion: a few might crop up here and there – a foolish consistency is the hobgoblin of little minds.) I mean no disrespect to people who raise their own flowers, but I am primarily interested in the *product* of such gardens – the cut flowers, that is – as opposed to the *process* of gardening. If it seems like an egregious detachment to eschew gardens, that is precisely my point: most of the human engagements with flowers explored herein are premised on

6 This 16th-century silk and wool prayer mat from an Istanbul workshop features an enormous array of flowers in intricately interlaced patterns. The arch-shaped design symbolizes a mosque's *mihrab* (prayer niche), identifying the rug's religious purpose.

detaching those flowers from their gardens, and from their (literal and figurative) roots.

Although my subject-matter is closely related to gardening, there is a subtle yet significant distinction. Gardeners are in it for the long haul, whereas the flower-loving consumers I will analyze demand full floral glory immediately, without the work. For them (or, more accurately, for us), acquiring flowers is a shortcut to beauty without the required investment of time, labour or the cultivation of botanical expertise. Of many wonderful testimonies to the pleasures of gardening, Penelope Lively offers a representative example in her horticultural memoir *Life in the Garden*:

> We garden for tomorrow, and thereafter. We garden in
> expectation, and that is why it is so invigorating. Gardening,
> you are no longer stuck in the here and now; you think
> backward, you think forward, you think about how this
> or that performed last year, you work out your hopes
> and plans for the next. And for me, there is this abiding
> astonishment at the fury for growth, at the tenacity of
> plant life, and the unstoppable dictation of the seasons.[14]

This lively engagement Lively describes – with seasons, time past and future, biological and ecosystemic energy – is considerably abridged, if not altogether suppressed, when one simply goes out and buys the flowers, or paints a still-life, or even looks at one. The time-scheme is compressed from cyclical eternality to immediacy. To put it plainly: someone else does the dirty work. The flowers that have been detached from their gardens will not go to seed or replace themselves; they will not appear in the same place next year, though their identical duplicates will likely appear in the same florist's bucket next week, where they may be purchased again. The bought bloom, the cut flower, the commercial commodity, may hint at this wonderful ecological force Lively describes – 'the fury for growth' – but that is mostly shorn away; it's not our problem. The flower-users I examine here are in it for short-term bliss, which may well be antithetical to the *quidditas* of flowers; if so, so be it. It wouldn't be the only thing in nature we reconfigure to be more convenient for us. (If you have a yen for giraffe-spotting, are you more likely to visit Africa or your local zoo? Do you usually swim in an actual lake or an unlovely concrete pool?)

Gardening is place-based: one gardens in one's home or school playground, one's community or allotment. The activity and the flowers are tied to the land, grounded. Flower buying is mobile, global, placeless – or, what may amount to the same thing, hyper-geographical. The orchid that now preens in my vase was in the Philippines or Peru only a few days ago. Gardening takes place mainly outdoors; my flowers 'live' (figuratively, though not biologically) inside. Gardening is ecological; cut flowers are business.

My strange, bright crowds of blooms comprise flowers in culture, flowers in the imagination: divorced from gardens, isolated from their ecological cycles and not especially useful except as they affect us. Flowers in symbol, myth, song, poetry and art, in ritual, fashion, ceremony and spirituality, are not so much flowers *per se* as they are *our* flowers. This book will explore what we do with flowers, and what we think of flowers. There is significant human cultural value added (or sometimes, certainly, value subtracted) from the floral specimens that are on display here. 'Come play in the dirt again,' my local gardening store advertises. But we won't get our hands dirty with these flowers, which are resituated ('wandering', in Dickinson's account) as they are reimagined.

What is a flower?

What exactly is a flower? 'The word, as used in normal speech, is imprecise,' writes James Cullen, a horticultural taxonomist famous for his six-volume *European Garden Flora*, which identifies 16,000 species of cultivated ornamental flowering plants.

> The 'flower' of a dandelion is, in fact, an inflorescence (a collection of flowers forming a coherent whole). Flowers vary greatly from species to species, and it is difficult to find a definition that covers all the cases which occur. Possibly the best that can be done is to say that a flower is usually borne at the top of a long or short stalk (the pedicel), or, if stalkless, has its insertion on to some other organ and contains either one or more female sexual organs (carpels) or one or more male sexual organs (stamens) or one or more carpels together with one or more stamens . . .[15]

There's more, but I'll stop there. No disrespect, but I'm glad I'm not writing this kind of analysis (and I presume you're glad you are not reading it). Botanical phraseology is 'cryptic and not to be mastered without study', writes the naturalist Henry Salt in *The Call of the Wildflower*. 'When, for example, we read of a certain umbelliferous plant that its "cremocarp consists of two semicircular-ovoid mericarps, constricted at the commissure" . . . we probably feel that some further information would be welcome.'[16] Scientific discourse can easily seem offputting, even ugly – and what a shame. Flowers are magnificent, and flower language should be eloquently resonant, which is what I'll aspire to provide here. I turn to John

Tab.873

Tragopogon pratensis.   Wiesen-Bocksbart.

7 What is a flower? This 19th-century botanical illustration anatomizes *Tragopogon pratensis*, known in German as *Wiesen-Bocksbart* and in English, variously, as Jack-go-to-bed-at-noon, meadow salsify or showy goat's-beard.

Ruskin for a more mellifluous definition than botanists provide: 'Flowers seem intended for the solace of ordinary humanity;'[17] and consider also Ralph Waldo Emerson's bon mot, 'Earth laughs in flowers.'[18] Oliver Wendell Holmes writes, 'The Amen! of Nature is always a flower,'[19] and for good measure, Emily Dickinson offers a typically incisive and obscure pronouncement (which serves perfectly well as a précis for this book): 'Bloom – is Result – to meet a Flower.'[20]

On the subject of language, I've encountered delightfully peculiar flower names during my research. My top-ten list of favourites includes bastard toadflax, corn-cockle, sneezewort (aka sneezeweed), flowering spurge, Brazilian Dutchman's pipe, goat's rue, goosefoot, grass-of-Parnassus and snake's-head fritillary. And the winner: impudent lawyer – which I enjoy giving to the woman I love (who is, obviously, an impudent lawyer) on the rare occasions that my florist has it in stock. Such florid phantasmagorias, as pleasing to the ear and mind as they are to the eye and nose, are incomparably preferable to *Campanula portenschlagiana*, *Lamprocapnos spectabilis* or *Linaria acutiloba* (better known as Dalmatian bellflowers, bleeding heart and that impudent lawyer). They say a rose by any other name would smell as sweet, but . . . *Rosa rubiginosa*? *Rosa dumetorum*? Possibly not.

Botanical dialect, with all its taxonomic hierarchies, orders and groups, embodies one way to describe the essence of these flowers; I choose instead to wander down the path of art, myth, folklore and symbolism. Sometimes, if infrequently, I am entranced by the scientific vocabulary: the rhizomes, stipules and petioles are all Greek to me, but I try to remember that this arcane language and method of detailed classification does parallel the more cultural and aesthetic perspectives I bring to my flowers (or, as botanists denote them, 'angiospermae'). It has been amusing to learn such intriguing terms as 'ptyxis', which describes how young leaves are packed in the bud. I doubt I will use it much over the course of my writerly career, but look: I just did.

Attraction to flowers may offer some evolutionary advantage, psychologists believe: 'flowers show where fruits can grow', so floraphiles would be better able to predict 'future food supplies and possibly a better place for rearing progeny'.[21] For botanists, the flower's function is generating seed for reproduction: 'The real business of flowers is sex,'[22] which surely inflects why we are drawn to them, and why they give us pleasure. It may not be blatantly obvious, this sensual charm of flowers, but neither is it invisible. The floral forms, textures, pigments, smells and symmetries we find so entrancing evolved to attract pollinators, who are likewise entranced, thereby ensuring the continuation of life. Subtly, modestly, flowers arouse a passion that is not unrelated to human sexual delight. Pistils, stamens, nectaries, ovules and pollen do not broadcast a flagrantly erotic tableau (at least not to people – bees, butterflies, birds and bats would beg to differ); subconsciously, however, we probably perceive botanical seductions with at least some faint frisson. Indeed, some people *do* experience a more rampant floral sensuality: Japanese photographer Nobuyoshi Araki explains, 'Flowers are all erotic in my eyes. They're all Eros. Once you realize that they're all reproductive organs, they begin to look like dicks and cunts.'[23]

E. O. Wilson, a champion of sociobiology and biodiversity, put forth the concept of biophilia, which proposes that people must be attached to the world beyond ourselves: we need to nourish our bodies and souls with constant affirmations of our interconnections in the web of life (and the notion of a 'web of life' aligns fairly closely with what Dickinson and I denominate as 'strange, bright crowds'). 'Our love affair with flowers is ancient and visceral,' writes gardener Debra Prinzing.[24] We have always felt compelled to reach out to them, to flowers and rivers and nature at large, and nature, too, reaches back to us in a feedback loop. With our techno-industrial capabilities and manias, we may delude ourselves in the belief that we are separable from the rest of the world: apart from nature rather than a part of nature. We fantasize that we can wall ourselves off from the bugs and bears and pollen and weather and other presumptive threats to our habits and preferences, but I think this is wrong. Global warming shows that as a species *Homo sapiens* isn't really all that sapient in terms of understanding of how we fit in with the rest of our ecosystem. I prescribe, as a corrective, a devout attention to the splendours of flowers and our interactions with them: it may help temper our anthropocentric (human-centred) perspective, even if just in small measure.

Horrible beauty: *Fleurs du mal*

Flowers bring out the best in people, except when they don't. Sometimes people love flowers so much that they love them to death. Superblooms, a phenomenon propelled by social media, conjoin strange crowds of people and bright crowds of flowers, with unpleasant results. A wet year following a drought produces ecstatically blooming fields, as happened at California's Lake Elsinore in 2019, where hills were covered with Day-Glo orange poppies. But flowers

> are being trampled, despite efforts by park rangers to keep people on trails and walkways. 'Look at those people. They're stepping all over the poppies,' a park ranger said. The spectacular sight is creating a bit of a traffic nightmare . . . with cars backing up as much as 20 miles at times.[25]

People pick lots of flowers at a superbloom – in their infinitude, there seems to be a limitless supply. Visitors, some dragging camera tripods, pose for pictures crouching in the middle of the field, and some even fly in on helicopters, causing significant damage when they land right on the flowers. Crushed wildflowers can no longer produce seeds and procreate. Off-trail strolls cause long-term soil damage, hindering the bloom for future seasons. An Ontario sunflower farm 'was forced to close its property to the public for good after it was ruined by Instagram photographers', Molly McHugh writes. '"I can only describe it as like a zombie apocalypse," one of the family farmers said of the deluge.'[26]

Tulip festivals, sunflower fields, cherry blossom season and other floral wonders precipitate such invasions with increasing frequency. It's not the world's greatest tragedy, probably not even in the top fifty, but it's a shame people can't be more considerate. It doesn't, to my mind, suggest that people have cultivated the ideal appreciation of flowers in our world when a particularly incredible display of them triggers such thoughtlessly narcissistic behaviour. 'Lake Elsinore's superbloom has become a symbol of the destructiveness of Instagram culture,' writes McHugh. 'The pursuit of the perfect photo leads some onlookers to treat the outdoors like a disposable, replaceable backdrop.'[27]

When hordes of people descend on a superbloom, hiking blogger Casey Schreiner complains, 'they're not necessarily outdoorsy people who understand the ethics of Leave No Trace. They just see an article in the LA Times about all these beautiful wildflowers, and they go out there to see it.' He finds it 'particularly troubling when those photos come from influencers with massive followings who are signaling to their audience that rolling around in a field of poppies is acceptable behavior'.[28]

Everyone likes flowers. Consummately alluring, they add wholesome pleasure to whatever scene they embellish and inspire kindness, gratitude and serenity from their admirers. Do they have a downside? I would suggest, I hope not too cynically, that there is a downside to everything. Nothing, at least nothing valuable, can

8 The lavender petals of Fremont's phacelia erupt in a 2017 superbloom at Carrizo Plain, California.

be unilaterally good and pure: everything is subject to misuse or ruination.

Vase mit Blumen is a nice, simple flower painting, isn't it? Pleasant, colourful, not earth-shatteringly moving but a completely satisfying array of zinnias, or perhaps dahlias.

Well, guess what? It was painted by Adolf Hitler.[29] How do you like it now?

Hitler wanted desperately to be an artist but twice failed the entrance exam to Vienna's Academy of Fine Arts. He seemed to like flowers a great deal, painting them copiously. When he was imprisoned after his 1923 attempted coup, he 'wanted for nothing ... there were flowers' in his cell.[30] ('Flowery dell' – Cockney rhyming slang for a prison cell – is obviously ironic: jail is the last place one would expect to find flowers.) As a young insurgent, Hitler recounts in *Mein Kampf*, 'we emphasized our convictions by wearing cornflowers,'[31] which were Kaiser Wilhelm's favourite. According to legend,

9 Adolf Hitler, *Vase mit Blumen*, 1912, watercolour.

when the Kaiser's great-grandmother, Queen Louise, fled from Napoleon's invasion of Berlin, she hid in a field blossoming with the intense blue flowers and kept her children quietly distracted by weaving cornflower garlands with them.[32]

Pan-German nationalists sported cornflowers in the nineteenth century, and after Austria banned the Nazi party sympathizers wore the flowers as a secret symbol to recognize each other. A far-right political party in modern Germany, Awakening of German Patriots (AdP), has resurrected the cornflower in its visual messaging.

Flowers for Hitler is the memoir of a young girl growing up in the Third Reich who was chosen to give Hitler flowers during a parade. Ilse Dorsch was four years old on a warm Munich day in 1934. Dressed in a festive dirndl, she and her mother went for a walk and came upon a large crowd. They took their place at the back to see what was going on. Ilse wended her way forwards and 'stood on the edge of the curb next to a large man in a brown uniform. He was holding a bouquet of flowers.'

'There he is! It's the Führer!' someone in the crowd shouted enthusiastically and every head turned . . . Two blocks down, a slow moving line of vehicles had appeared from around a corner. In the lead car – a black Mercedes convertible – a man, also dressed in a brown uniform, stood and extended his right hand out and up. The crowd cheered and returned the salute. I remember the large man standing next to me glancing around as if he were looking for someone. I soon found out he was looking for a lady or girl to present the flowers to the man in the car. Not knowing what any of this meant at the time, I stretched my arm out in salute like those around me were doing. When the lead car got close to where we stood, the man standing beside me smiled at me, leaned over, and handed me the flowers. 'Here, little one, give these flowers to the nice man standing in the car.' Then he nudged me out into the street. As I walked into the street, the standing man saw me and his car stopped. I walked up to the car and the standing man with a funny little mustache and blazing blue eyes leaned over and took the bouquet with one hand and patted me on the head with his other hand. Adolf Hitler said to me, 'Thank you, little girl, someday you are going to be a brave and proud German woman.'[33]

It's not the flowers' fault: I do not believe they possess free will. But it is, clearly, an indication that flowers can be used in the service of evil, and that we might be wise to guard against this possibility. Enjoy them, but not uncritically. Sometimes, perhaps, problematize them. I will try my hardest to make sure neither I nor my reader like flowers any less by the end of this journey, but that we appreciate, even more keenly than we do now, their power and their hold over us.

In *Les Fleurs du mal* (1861), Charles Baudelaire's flower imagery serves tropes of decadence that are disturbing and sometimes disgusting. A paradigm of the sordid, anti-social *poète maudit* (cursed poet), Baudelaire subverts the aesthetic presumption, as expressed in Kant's *The Critique of Judgement*, that flowers embody objective natural beauty. In 'A Carcass', for example, the title object is described with 'its legs raised in the air',

Burning and dripping with poisons,
Displayed in a shameless, nonchalant way
Its belly, swollen with gases.

herzlichste
Glückwünsche

The sun shone down upon that putrescence,

As if to roast it to a turn,

And to give back a hundredfold to great Nature

The elements she had combined;

And the sky was watching that superb cadaver

Blossom like a flower.[34]

In art, Baudelaire writes, 'what is horrible becomes beauty.'
Joris-Karl Huysmans's 1884 *À Rebours* (*Against Nature*) recirculates
Baudelaire's tradition of sickly floral corruption: his protagonist
obsessively adores gruesome and deadly flowers, which looked

> as though consumed by syphilis and leprosy, for they
> exhibited livid surfaces of flesh veined with scarlet rash
> and damasked with eruptions. Some had the deep red hue
> of scars that have just closed or the dark tint of incipient
> scabs. Others were marked with matter raised by scaldings.
> There were forms which exhibited shaggy skins hollowed

by ulcers and relieved by cankers. And a few appeared
embossed with wounds, covered with black mercurial
hog lard, with green unguents of belladonna smeared
with grains of dust and the yellow micas of iodoforme.

Surveying his macabre conservatory, Huysmans's narrator reflects,
'nature had been reduced to copying the inner membranes of
animals, to borrowing the vivid tints of their rotting flesh, their
magnificent corruptions.'[35] As a perverse exercise, look at a flower
and describe it in the mood of depravity that Baudelaire and
Huysmans embrace. It is a strange and sobering experience: I tried
and was unable to do it myself – it just didn't make sense.

Baudelaire, Friedrich Nietzsche and Hitler 'were most lucid,
most frank, and most eloquent about painting evil and presenting
it in its florified garb', writes the philosopher Clare Ortiz Hill. They
'understood that the rawest evil could be presented in attractive
trappings and they proved to be exceptionally perceptive about
the seductiveness of evil'. Baudelaire 'labored to "extract beauty
from evil" and to express this in poetic form'.[36] Far from the norm
– the exception that proves the rule, I'd venture – Baudelaire's
florification is splenetic, louche.

Nietzsche avidly read Baudelaire, and Hitler was familiar
with Nietzsche, reiterating in his own writing the philosopher's
idea of 'great men'. Twice Hitler gave flowers to Nietzsche's sister,
Elisabeth Förster-Nietzsche: in 1932 he sent roses to the German
premiere of a play (by Benito Mussolini) she directed, and in 1934
he personally gave her a floral wreath – 'To a Great Fighter' – for
Nietzsche's grave. Baudelaire knew that 'approached from the right
angle, anything, including what is most execrable, could be made
attractive. Discovering terrible beauty in what is most abhorrent'

was his forte. "'Your flowers of evil," Victor Hugo once wrote to him, "shine and sparkle like stars".'[37] Object lesson: watch out for flowers from tyrants and degenerates, whose strange, *dark* blooms are capable of perverting even the most beautiful and innocent aspects of life.

I return where I began, to Virginia Woolf's world, for a last word to redeem flowers from fascist appropriation. Virginia's husband, Leonard, wrote in his memoir about a scene from the final days of pre-war peace.

> They were the most terrible months of my life, for, helplessly and hopelessly, one watched the inevitable approach of war. One of the most horrible things at that time was to listen on the wireless to the speeches of Hitler – the savage and insane ravings of a vindictive underdog who suddenly saw himself to be all-powerful. We were in Rodmell during the late summer of 1939, and I used to listen to those ranting, raving speeches. One afternoon I was planting in the orchard under an apple-tree iris *reticulata*, those lovely violet flowers. Suddenly I heard Virginia's voice calling to me from the sitting room window: 'Hitler is making a speech.' I shouted back, 'I shan't come. I'm planting iris and they will be flowering long after he is dead.' Last March, twenty-one years after Hitler committed

11 Title page for a limited edition of Baudelaire's *Les Fleurs du mal*, with illustrations by Carlos Schwabe (1900).

> suicide in the bunker, a few of those violet flowers
> still flowered under the apple-tree in the orchard.[38]

Flowers present a bulwark against the folly of the world and the cruelty that emanates from its most egregious non-floral life forms. As Leonard Woolf testifies, they are surprisingly useful in their apparent uselessness and powerful in their seeming fragility. Despite their ephemerality, they endure.

1

FLOWERY WRITING

What favourite flowers are mine, I cannot say –
My fancy changes with the summer's day.
W. H. DAVIES[1]

I hide myself within my flower.
EMILY DICKINSON[2]

As if there weren't enough strange, bright crowds of flowers in the world – that is, actual blooming, living (or recently cut) plants – there is quite a passel of poems about them as well.

In addition to poetry, certainly, many plays, novels, films and songs also include floral components, or at least seem to. Roses, lilies or azaleas may appear prominently in titles, but often such nominally flowery works end up off in the weeds. *Flowers for Algernon, Our Lady of the Flowers, Flower Drum Song, Send Me No Flowers, The Black Orchid, The Scarlet Pimpernel, Red Azalea, White Oleander, Purple Hibiscus, Black Narcissus, Flowers in the Attic, Lilies of the Field, Steel Magnolias, The Perks of Being a Wallflower, The Effect of Gamma Rays on Man-in-the-moon Marigolds, Please Don't Eat the Daisies* and 'A Rose for Emily' are all texts that invoke flowers insubstantially, comprising a crowd insufficiently strange and bright for my purposes. Some kind of heavy-handed horticultural metaphor (aha!) might blossom perfunctorily near the end after readers had all but forgotten the floral foreshadowing, but otherwise the magnolias, marigolds and orchids have little work to do in these texts apart from sitting prettily on the title page and perhaps in the cover's graphic design.

Mark Twain, wondering how Buffalo, New York, got its name, muses: 'I don't know why, unless it is because there are not any buffaloes there.'[3] By the same logic, flower-titled stories and songs often unfurl to reveal that there are not any flowers there. The world is filled with absent floral references that recall Twain's buffalo: Carnation condensed milk has nothing to do with carnations except for the name and logo. Indigo flowers are completely irrelevant (except for branding) to the upscale Hotel Indigo chain, or the Indigo Girls band, or IndiGo Airlines – and what a tease, I think. How frustrating that such strikingly luxuriant flowers fail to materialize in the lobby, or the lyrics, or the airplane cabin, of enterprises so named; someone needs to hire a floral consultant! There is nothing remotely floral about the Toyota Corolla – a 'corolla' is a whorl of petals, sometimes free from each other (as with daisies) or sometimes, as with orchids or petunias, fused together to form a tube – or such sports cars as the Lotus or Clover. The automobile with the most striking flower power is, of course, the vw Beetle, which included a *Blumenvase* (bud vase) on the dashboard. This feature first appeared in the 1949 model[4] and

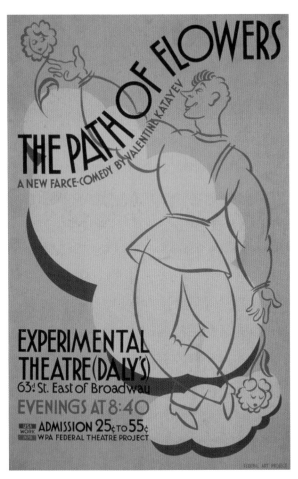

12 *The Path of Flowers*, a 1936 theatrical satire on the meanderings of a 'pseudo-Communist', has nothing at all to do with flowers.

endured until 2012, when management determined its presence marked the Beetle as a 'chick car', removing the offending accessory to encourage a more masculine market.[5]

Umberto Eco chose his novel's title *The Name of the Rose* hurriedly and arbitrarily 'because the rose is a symbolic figure so rich in meanings that by now it hardly has any meaning left', he writes. 'The title rightly disoriented the reader, who was unable to choose just one interpretation'. (Scrupulously postmodern, Eco believes 'a title must muddle the reader's ideas'.)[6] Emily Saliers gives a similarly unflowery explanation for why she and Amy Ray called themselves the Indigo Girls: 'we needed a name and we went through the dictionary looking for words that struck us and indigo was one.'[7] After watching *The Purple Rose of Cairo*, *Late Chrysanthemums* or *Honeysuckle Rose*, viewers might find themselves humming Neil Diamond's 'You Don't Bring Me Flowers', a song that is actually about guilt, not flowers. (Incidentally, purple roses, while they do exist, are rare breeds and difficult to grow; if someone sells you a purple rose, it is almost certainly a white rose that has spent a day in water spiked with purple food colouring.) Other gratuitous flower songs include The Rolling Stones' 'Dead Flowers', about heroin, not flowers, and Marie Osmond's 'Paper Roses', about emotional falsity, not flowers. Buttercup, from The Foundations' 'Build Me Up Buttercup', is a pet name for an undependable girlfriend, botanically meaningless.

But poems are prone to deliver the flowers they promise, responsibly and reliably. Flowers seem at home in poems, which might be considered the literary equivalent of vases. What point does this poetic floriculture serve? Often it simply (and resplendently) presents paeans to flowers. 'Si hortum in bibliotheca habes, deerit nihil,'[8] Cicero writes: If you have a garden and a library, you have everything you need. Flower poetry brings blossoms into books, satisfying both of Cicero's passions at once by stocking libraries that are comprised of gardens.

Dylan Thomas celebrates botanical energy with a flurry of floral fricatives: 'The force that through the green fuse drives the flower / Drives my green age,'[9] W. B. Yeats juxtaposes his resonant symbolic flower with his similarly resonant Celtic mythos: 'Red Rose, proud Rose, sad Rose of all my days! / Come near me, while I sing the ancient ways.'[10] A line of pentameter demands poetic economy: every word must count, every syllable richly vital. Three of the first ten syllables are 'Rose' and the same line concludes the poem, leaving readers with a half-dozen stems, Rose by Rose (crowned with a capital R to ensure that we get the point). The metrical arrangement of these Roses is comparable to the literal display of flowers arranged in a vase, or composed in a painted still-life. As with florists and painters, poets, too, group their 'raw materials' in a certain way for a certain desired effect: the shapes, the colours, the forms, the impressions, and the unquantifiable metaphysical stimuli inherent in a fistful of blooms take on a patterned presentation as artists in various media arrange their flowers. For Yeats, each rose is highlighted in the stressed syllables of the opening and closing lines' first three iambic feet. The title, 'To the Rose upon the Rood of Time', offers – what else? – a bonus Rose, an efflorescent lagniappe, seven for the price of six.

H. D.'s flowers are stylized, minimalist. A pioneer of the Imagist literary movement, her name itself (Hilda Doolittle became H. D. when she embraced the aesthetic of compression) reflected the idea that concentration revealed the essential nature of things. In poems from her 1916 collection *Sea Garden*, she stands in quiet, mystical awe of the sea poppy's delicate intensities – 'Beautiful, wide-spread,

/ fire upon leaf, / what meadow yields / so fragrant a leaf / as your bright leaf?' – and the sea violet's subtle power: 'Violet / your grasp is frail / on the edge of the sand-hill, / but you catch the light – / frost, a star edges with its fire.' Her sea lily draws strength from its turbulent surroundings: 'slashed and torn' by gusts and waves where land meets ocean,

> scales are dashed from your stem,
>
> sand cuts your petal,
>
> furrows it with hard edge,
>
> like flint
>
> on a bright stone.

> Yet though the whole wind
>
> slash at your bark,
>
> you are lifted up,
>
> aye – though it hiss
>
> to cover you with froth.[11]

These flowers are 'arranged' in ways that highlight poesis, a term describing the crafting of words in verse and the ways they bear the marks (the sounds, imagery, patterns, associations) of their maker and their genre. The details that, in real life, comprise *botany* – leaf, petal, stem, texture – are here translated, modified and trans- formed, to produce a parallel *textuality*. Consider the depiction of a flower in art, where the visuality of the canvas makes it easier to see (and to realize that we are seeing) Picasso's angular composition of a vase with blooms, van Gogh's brushstrokes in the sunflowers, O'Keeffe's flamboyant petals, Warhol's bright brash forms and so on, in the expressive painterly texture each artist uses to present

13 Sea poppies (*Glaucium flavum*), featuring the fragrant, fiery, bright leaves H. D.'s poem extols.

Glaucium luteum Scop. 1864.

each flower. In flower poems, too, we can detect, albeit more subtly, the writer's voice and perspective. It helps to realize that a flower poem is always implicitly ekphrastic: that is, a linguistic rendering of a visual image. When reading a flower poem, try to conjure up the picture that the poet has crafted in words, and think of that image as twofold: comprising both the original subject (the actual flower that the poet must be observing or imagining) as well as the poet's unique tropes and styles, her fingerprints.

In 'The Métier of Blossoming' (1999), Denise Levertov presents an amaryllis:

> steadily up
> goes each green stem, smooth, matte,
> traces of reddish purple at the base, and almost
> imperceptible vertical ridges
> running the length of them:
> Two robust stems from each bulb,
> sometimes with sturdy leaves for company,
> elegant sweeps of blade with rounded points.
> Aloft, the gravid buds, shiny with fullness.[12]

Levertov's poetic study of the flower emerges from her meticulous lyrical attention to its growth and development, its firm structure ('robust', 'sturdy', 'rounded points'). Descriptive observations – 'vertical ridges', 'shiny with fullness' – combine with more subjectively celebratory appraisals: 'elegant', and in the next stanza, once the métier of blossoming has occurred, the flowers sit 'triumphantly at the summit / of those strong columns, and each / a Juno, calm in brilliance'. Levertov shows methodically how to regard this flower – how to anatomize and poeticize it in the same moment – while modelling the expansive wonderment readers may reap from this flower-observing consciousness she illustrates.

The word 'métier' in Levertov's title has a connotation that seems intriguing, but also askew. Flowers don't actually have callings and specializations, do they? They just blossom – naturally, unconsciously, automatically. Or, we wonder (and don't even pick up a poem without setting aside a block of time to indulge luxuriant meandering through a meadow of interpretive possibilities):

47

is the point of 'métier' to unsettle our received ideas by under-cutting narcissistic assumptions that only people have jobs and talents in the world? Perhaps we could better appreciate our own (non-central) place in the ecosystem by looking also at what sort of 'work' its other constituents provide, what sorts of careers are staffed by snails, glaciers and orchids. If an amaryllis's professional charge is blossoming, Levertov reminds us it performs this

14 Imogen Cunningham's 1933 photograph *Amaryllis* reflects the robust and sturdy botanical structure, supporting the gravid bud aloft (partly out of frame), shiny with fullness, which Denise Levertov, too, highlights in her poem.

assignment with unfailing proficiency and dependability, meriting outstanding annual (and perennial!) performance reviews.

These small bouquets from Yeats, Thomas, H. D. and Levertov provide a select few representatives of the countless blossoms that fill the fields of literature, as each writer cultivates his or her own small patch of poetry's strange, bright crowds of flowers. These poets capture a flowery spirit in relatively straightforward and sincere texts: they are not troubled, ironic or anxious (as, we might be surprised to discover, some other flower poems are). People who like flowers will like these flower poems and vice versa: these wordsmiths are preaching to the choir. They share a basic directness in diction and imagery, requiring little extravagant artifice, in their poems that sensibly, eloquently, describe each flower's essence.

Dancing with flowers

Other flower poetry is more complex. Emily Dickinson, at the centre of my poetic garden, creates botanical word-visions that are profoundly cunning, strategic, confusing. 'A Flower will not trouble her, it has so small a Foot.'[13] What engrossing poetry – and what could this possibly mean? 'I dared not meet the Daffodils – / For fear their Yellow Gown / Would pierce me with a fashion / So foreign to my own.'[14]

As I begin moving down the path towards Dickinson's strange, bright blooms, I want to embrace the potential complications of flower poems: reading between the lines, digging beneath the surface, hesitating to take these specimens at face value however compelling their faces are.

Poets may *use* flowers, opportunistically, for their own figurative agendas – as vehicles for poems that are less precisely about

49

flowers per se and more broadly about love, romance, perfection, imperfection, loss, devotion, spirituality, seasonality, eternity, ephemerality. Such poems are more about people than they are about flowers: our concerns and values, our perspectives and interests. Some flower poems emphasize human perceptions of the natural world's lifeforms and processes as opposed to depicting the world and its energies on their own terms. Is this anthropocentric aesthetic an appropriate and respectful use of flowers, or does it exploit them, burdening them with a weight they are not meant to bear? A mere flower, when plucked to render a figurative function, may get trampled as poets romp around in more lyrically stanzaic fields after harvesting a few token blossoms.

Are literary lilies, lilacs and lady's slippers imperfect because they are, at root, deflowered? As keenly as a poem may evoke a flower, still, it must lack some significant component of the actual hue, aroma, shape, feel and biota. Poetic flowers, flowers of language, are not alive. They are intellectualized flowers; flowers removed from flowers. They may educate and entertain, seeding new ways to think about flowers and about the world in which flowers bloom (and wilt), but for those of us who value authenticity and immediacy they may seem somehow deficient, artificial, even perverse. Why bother writing or reading poems about flowers when we have ... flowers?

Is Yeats committing the dreaded 'anthropomorphic fallacy'? Is it affected, even absurd, to describe a 'proud Rose, sad Rose', when these flowers lack such human emotions as pride and sorrow? People used to make the same critique against animal poetry if non-human characters showed a range of emotion and sentience that, as we flattered ourselves, people alone had the intelligence to deploy. It turns out we were completely wrong about that: see, for example, Jeffrey Masson's *When Elephants Weep: The Emotional Lives* of Animals.[15] Poets and painters often recognized other animals' broad capacity for thought and feeling, sharing these insights with their audiences via 'anthropomorphic' art, well before the animal behaviourists and zoologists figured it out.

So what about flowers – have we underestimated them too? It is hard to imagine how an orchid *couldn't* feel pride; how a crocus that has had the misfortune to bloom before a deep frost *wouldn't* experience fear. (Emily Dickinson imagines what flowers think about cold weather: 'Apparently with no surprise / To any happy Flower / The frost beheads it at its play – / In accidental power.'[16] They expected the frost, she ventures: they were ready for it. Perhaps she is right.) Do flowers feel pain when we cut them? Can they tell when we coddle or ignore them? I don't know how much they care about what I have to say, but I am certainly not the only floraphile who talks to foxglove and freesia, both growing and vased.

Researchers are learning that there's more going on with our flowers than meets the eye. Despite their apparent sedentary and passive lifestyle, 'in fact, plants have evolved sophisticated perceptual abilities that allow them to monitor and respond to a wide range of changing conditions.' Examining such phenomena as how carnivorous plants capture prey, how flowers respond actively to visits by pollinators and how they perceive herbivorous threats, Mark Mescher and Consuelo De Moraes write in the *Journal of Experimental Botany*,

> We are only beginning to understand the full range
> of sensory cues that mediate such interactions and to
> elucidate the mechanisms by which plants perceive,
> interpret, and respond to them. Nevertheless, it is clear
> that plants continually gather information about their

environments via a range of sensory modalities and actively respond in ways that profoundly influence their interactions with other organisms.[17]

Flowers can hear the sounds of pollinators and respond by making their nectar sweeter, bioacoustics researchers have discovered.[18] And when living plants are stressed, they emit ultrasounds to communicate their feelings.[19] 'Plants can behave in remarkably animal-like ways,' says Heidi Appel, who studies plants' responses to animal vibrations. 'If plants can hear, what are their ears?' asks Ed Yong.

> It's the flowers themselves . . . lasers show that the primrose's petals vibrate when hit by the sounds of a bee's wingbeats. If they covered the blooms with glass jars, those vibrations never happened, and the nectar never sweetened. The flower, then, could act like the fleshy folds of our outer ears, channeling sound further into the plant.[20]

While I am unqualified (as a humanist) to extend this kind of botanical research, I am superbly qualified (as a humanist) to disseminate my *intuitions* about how flowers engage and communicate with the other lifeforms, including us, in their biota. My evidence is flower poetry, flower paintings, flower customs and so on. The deep, passionate interest I share with the crowds of poets, artists, revolutionaries and other flower fans cultivated in this book presumes some kind of interactive relationship between people and flowers.

The best flower poetry, the most powerful, incisive, durable floral aesthetic, demands a dialogue, an emotional, intellectual and aesthetic encounter, between an individual artist and an individual flower, and on a larger scale, between human culture and the enthralling sphere of botany. Whether consciously or subliminally, writers and artists who depict flowers are enacting – and imploring their audiences to enact in tandem – a dance with them, and it is a mutual dance: it takes two to tango. (Dancers, of course, receive flowers after they perform. The ballerina Anna Pavlova had a rose named after her, and more recently Polina Semionova, too, is the namesake for a rare hybrid of rehmannia.[21]) These dances with flowers transcend detached observation or possession; instead, they engage with flowers, plunging into the ephemeral yet cyclically eternal celebration of peonies and gardenias, chrysanthemums and irises.

A host of golden daffodils

I didn't fully appreciate the splendour of William Wordsworth's flower poetry until I finally visited England's Lake District myself. I had once regarded his poetic daffodils as histrionic, even a bit facile. They became real and compelling for me only as I traipsed through the hills and rills bedecked with indescribably vivid daffodils – 'indescribable' for me, that is, but obviously not for Wordsworth, who blazed this path with his 1807 poem:

> I wandered lonely as a cloud
> That floats on high o'er vales and hills,
> When all at once I saw a crowd,
> A host, of golden daffodils;
> Beside the lake, beneath the trees,
> Fluttering and dancing in the breeze.

(*A crowd*: I wonder if Dickinson was channelling Wordsworth's bright crowd of flowers when she cultivated her own?)

After my excursion to visit the same daffodils Wordsworth had seen, albeit at a two-hundred-generation remove, I came to understand why these flowers moved him to inscribe them in poetry. Perhaps his lyric was somehow imperfect because the poem alone did not consummately convey to me the intensity of these flowers. But, on the other hand, his words were intriguing enough to convince me, along with crowds of many other pilgrims, to wander among the Cumbrian daffodils myself, so perhaps that makes him completely successful: I think it does.

They were astonishing flowers. How could he not have joined his voice with theirs to celebrate, for poetry aficionados everywhere, the richly moving experience that his encounter with the daffodils inspired? Did he even somehow, metaphysically, share with them some kind of symbiotic ecstasy of daffodility? 'Ten thousand saw I at a glance, / Tossing their heads in sprightly

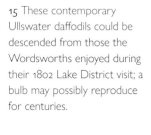

15 These contemporary Ullswater daffodils could be descended from those the Wordsworths enjoyed during their 1802 Lake District visit; a bulb may possibly reproduce for centuries.

dance.' (Ten thousand! Fortunately, Romantic poetry, however sub-lime, did not have the viral reach of today's social media, or else Wordsworth might have precipitated a superbloom invasion.) I imagine that the flowers' 'sprightly dance' mirrors Wordsworth's own dance along the littoral paths when he was actually in their presence; then, after the fact, his poem functions as a reprise of his dance with them, his dance for them – and his choreography for our dance with them.

A poem is forever: 'So long as men can breathe or eyes can see', Shakespeare's sonnet 18 declares, 'So long lives this, and this gives life to thee'[22] (and while Shakespeare's 'thee' refers to the young man he loved, the sentiment is easily enough adapted to denote a flower that has been preserved in verse). It is as if the daffodils and their celebrant are still dancing, and dancing together, in a poetic *always*. The terpsichorean energy of the floral experience moves in the poem as Wordsworth moved (along the same trail I followed two centuries later), geographically and emotionally, around Glencoyne Bay, Ullswater, with his sister, Dorothy, stroll-ing from Eusemere back to their Grasmere residence, Dove Cottage.

> For oft, when on my couch I lie
> In vacant or in pensive mood,
> They flash upon that inward eye
> Which is the bliss of solitude;
> And then my heart with pleasure fills,
> And dances with the daffodils.[23]

Dorothy's *Grasmere Journal* records her own response, which also includes dancing, to the scene:

When we were in the woods beyond Gowbarrow park
we saw a few daffodils close to the water side. We fancied
that the lake had floated the seeds ashore and that the
little colony had so sprung up. But as we went along there
were more and yet more and at last under the boughs of
the trees, we saw that there was a long belt of them along
the shore, about the breadth of a country turnpike road.
I never saw daffodils so beautiful they grew among the
mossy stones about and about them, some rested their
heads upon these stones as on a pillow for weariness and
the rest tossed and reeled and danced and seemed as if
they verily laughed with the wind
that blew upon them over the lake, they
looked so gay ever glancing
ever changing.[24]

16 Whether in a poem, by a lake or from a mail-order catalogue, daffodils evoke indefatigable exuberance.

As I danced with these daffodils, I believed them to be (at least at that particular moment) the most beautiful flowers I had ever seen, affirming the brilliance of Dorothy's and William's descriptive detail in capturing both the flowers themselves and also the experience of seeing the flowers. On the other hand, though, I reflected that these flowers have a metaphysical radiance that transcends language: to 'write' these flowers is arguably to reduce them; even, to profane them. Why not just let them live, and enjoy their brilliance? *That*, truly, might be the most intense homage to them, rather than trying to compete with their beauty through poetry in an attempt to 'capture' them (even if only figuratively, literarily). I have written elsewhere about non-human animals, broaching a similar ethic: let them be; leave them alone.[25] Don't kidnap animals from their habitats and resituate them in little cages near where we live just because it's convenient for us. Don't abrogate their image and their authenticity, don't dissipate their brand, by naming cars and sports teams after them. Don't always be using them, or we'll use them up. Try to understand and respect their integrity in their own untrampled habitats. It seems domineering, overweening, to look at nature's creatures, both fauna and flora, with a voracious appetite predicated on the obsessive perspective people have cultivated as we trek through the world with all its glories: what can you do for me? What can we make out of you?

A last glance towards the Romantics: Lord Byron's letters unfurl a flower poem that never was. An admirer writes:

> Miss Pepper presents her compliments to Lord Byron,
> begs he will excuse the liberty she takes in troubling
> him, particularly as she comes as a petitioner – she
> is painting a collection of flowers & wishes to have a
> verse of four or eight lines to every flower – if Lord
> Byron would oblige her, and send her one, she would
> consider herself & collection highly honoured: she
> takes the liberty of writing a few names of flowers –
> that his Lordship may select which he pleases.

She suggests a dozen flowers – including convolvulus, heliotrope, sweet pea, amaryllis, heath and jonquil – from among which he might choose one to poeticize. There is no evidence that Byron

57

ever responded to her, or that he was inclined to write poems to order; still, one is impressed by Miss Pepper's moxie.[26]

'I hide myself within my flower'

A poet who features flowers profusely must spend a great deal of deliberate contemplation about precisely what these flowers are and how they might best be transposed into verse; she might well feel some uncertainty, some anxiety, that *her* flowers, however ornately worked, cannot be as fulsome as actual flowers. How does the poet transplant a primrose or periwinkle from where it grows into the lines of a poem? How does she render the bright, scented, three-dimensional flower on paper – in the book? Does she feel some compulsion to compensate for the absence of the actual flower in her poetry, and to implant sensory, emotional and biophiliac connections through her words and images to make up for the missing flower-ness? Unlike a writer, a painter can recreate at least some of this botanical absence: not the smell or feel, but the colour, form and context can be conveyed on canvas. Doing so in verse is more complicated: it is, simply, harder to *see* flowers in a poem than in a painting.

Getting flowers in books takes many forms. One interesting method is simply, literally, putting flowers in books: that is, pressing them. I'm not sure why this went out of style, but in centuries past it was a popular way to create keepsakes, giving flowers a much longer presence in the world than they would otherwise have: less beautiful than nature's unmolested flowers in their reduction from three dimensions to two and the diminution from brighter to paler hues, but if pressed carnations are not quite as brilliant as their initial living incarnations, still, they are not too shabby. (Carnations are actually not ideal candidates for pressing because of their puffy thickness – it takes more time and preparation than it does for, say, a pansy – but it can be done. Microwave ovens help, especially with bulkier flowers like carnations, perhaps signalling that it is time to revive this tradition; it would be wonderfully retro.)

Ancient Greeks and Romans collected pressed flowers for scientific reference, preserving and archiving botanical knowledge. When I buy an antiquarian book, it will as likely as not include a pressed flower. I cannot know its special meaning – that secret vanished with the presser – but there was probably some reason for saving it, memorializing a flower-giver and an occasion. Putting a flower in a book (both literally, when it is pressed, and figuratively, when it is poeticized) means that the flower will in some sense 'live' as long as the book does.

Almost none of Emily Dickinson's poetry was published during her lifetime: she copied out her poems longhand, collecting them in forty sewed booklets called fascicles (which also happens to be a botanical term for a cluster of leaves, flowers or roots growing together from a base) that she left in a drawer for her family to find and manage after her death. She never profited from her writing, but if she *had* submitted invoices, what would her poems cost?

> I pay – in Satin Cash –
> You did not state – your price –
> A Petal, for a Paragraph
> Is near as I can guess –[27]

Writing is like flowers, I think – constantly – as I read Dickinson's poetry. Or even more succinctly, her writing is a flower: a Petal for a Paragraph. But before entering the central hothouse of Dickinson's flower poetry, let us whet our appetites and prepare our vision by attending to the pressed flowers in her elaborate herbarium, which shows the interconnection between her flowers-in-books and her flowers-in-poems.

Dickinson assembled her herbarium between the ages of nine and sixteen (1839–46), before she began writing the poetry that appears in our contemporary editions (though there must be some undiscovered flowery juvenilia, I feel certain, that coincided with her work on the herbarium). This project shows that she thought long and hard about putting flowers in books – that is, by physically attaching actual flowers to paper – before she began doing this imaginatively, poetically. Her herbarium was like an apprentice-ship for collecting and presenting the flowers in her poetry. A close study of this volume (its 66 digitized pages feature on Harvard's Houghton Library website[28]) provides excellent preparation for a close reading of Dickinson's botanical poetry. The herbarium's pro-fuse variety of flowers, which foretells the profuse variety of her flower poems, overlaps considerably with the poetic corpus. 'So important were flowers to Emily Dickinson,' writes Judith Farr, 'so knowledgeable was she about botany, that the key to a successful reading of an individual Dickinson lyric can depend on one's knowledge of the background and identity of a plant or flower or of weather and climatic conditions.'[29]

Both the herbarium and fascicles display Dickinson's flowers methodically collected, preserved and arranged. Both involve learn-ing about flowers and cultivating that knowledge widely; both suggest that the more flowers one knows, the richer is one's picture of the world. 'Her poems, like her flower garden, were a means of creating order and beauty,'[30] and the herbarium, too, manifests order and beauty. It is 'beautifully arranged, bound in leather with a green

17 This page of Dickinson's herbarium includes specimens of *Mimulus ringens* (Allegheny monkey flower), top; a large Queen Anne's lace, centre; *Prunella vulgaris* (heal-all), bottom left; and Venus' looking glass, bottom right.

Dianthus virgens. 13. 2.

Prunella vulgaris. 13. 1.

Campanula speculum. 5. 1.

Chaerophyllum annuum. 14. 2.

fabric cover embossed in a floral pattern', writes Marta McDowell. 'It looks like an expensive photo album.'

> Many girls making herbaria would have used single sheets put together 'loose leaf' in a portfolio, a simpler and cheaper way to collect dried plants. Emily collected a specimen of each plant, over four hundred of them, then pressed and dried them between sheets of blotting paper . . . Each specimen is carefully mounted with strips of gummed paper and neatly labeled in her best penmanship. The layouts are lovely; on many pages Emily offset a single large specimen with several smaller ones. Sometimes the arrangements are whimsical, two daisies crisscrossed at the bottom of a page like swords supporting a coat of arms. Others are vigorous, three stems of aralia fanned out over a tripartite leaf of hepatica.[31]

Her pressed plant project embodies 'an elegy for time, composed with passionate patience, emanating the same wakefulness to sensuality and mortality that marks Dickinson's poetry', Maria Popova writes. The book's labels 'punctuate the specimens like enormous dashes inscribed with the names of the plants – sometimes colloquial, sometimes Linnaean – in Dickinson's elegant handwriting'.[32]

The herbarium specimens are real flowers, though they are not growing. They are not completely natural, one could argue, as they are transformed (selected, cut, preserved, arranged, named and labelled) in this collection, but still they are, I'd say, *pretty natural*: like her poems. They show Dickinson's meticulous attention to the details and attributes of flowers. Her methodical study of botany and herbalism at Amherst Academy is evident: the herbarium's scholarly and scientific components complement the aesthetic achievement it represents as a foundation for her poems. Many writers kept 'commonplace books' for pasting in odds and ends and gathering scraps (proverbs, reading notes, drafts of ideas) that they would develop into poetry: I consider Dickinson's herbarium exactly such a pre-text. She obviates any qualms I might have about poetic flowers – my concern that something corporeal and essential has been stripped away from the real flower as it is poeticized – because of her parallel, complementary canons of actual flowers (living as well as pressed: she was an active and devoted gardener) and poetic flowers. Would it be unreasonable to compel every bona fide flower poet to do some kind of comparable preparatory module?

Flowers and writing are closely connected for Dickinson, even facets of a single symbiotic object: a flower-text, or text-flower. Her poetry 'was often enclosed in letters pinned together by flowers, or in bouquets that made the poem concealed at the flowers' center and the flowers themselves one message'.[33] Was she sending flowers along with her poems, or poems along with her flowers? The flowers that accompanied her poems sometimes added meaning to them or explained them. Her flower poems approach the condition of flowers as closely as it is possible to do in writing: small and lovely; subtle elements of an intricate larger ecosystem; impermanent, yet embodying enduring beauty.

My *Strange Bright Blooms* presents a field of flowers under the primary influence of Emily Dickinson, whose guidance I mark not just with a title snipped from her poetry but also with my own iteration of her flower-poetic spirit. I adapt and recycle her pure, basic awe; her idiosyncratic complexities of perception and interpretation; and the devout sense of floral prominence and infinitude that infuses all her writing: flowers are everywhere, and they are important. My 'inference therefrom' is that people would be well-advised to think about flowers deeply, and to live our lives in ways that are suggested by their lives. I want to discover what sorts of wisdom Dickinson's strange, bright crowds of flowers can provide to strange, bright crowds of people.

First of all, Dickinson's hundreds of flower poems are, pardon the platitude, extraordinarily flowery: light, delicate, freshly intoxicating and always lovely to read, even the fourth – or fifteenth – time. We notice immediately that her rhythm and metre, her language, her punctuation, her point of view are all . . . off: odd, unconventional, even, sometimes (according to the discourse of poetry before she left her mark on it), possibly unpoetic. Or so it seems, to the uninitiated reader. We come to appreciate that she is stretching the bounds of poetry with poems that are not artificed, not 'man-made' in the way that most poems had been. Eschewing rules and conventions of poetic syntax, her verse is more organic than the tradition that preceded her, more sensory, more elusive, more beautiful and passionate, more evanescent – which is to say, more flowery.

Dickinson's poems present botanical words and terms, but also the methods and sensibilities of botany. It's not just that the poems are about flowers, but, more fundamentally, the flowers in her poems do what flowers do: they blow in the wind, shed their petals, feed bees, flourish in fields. She is highly attuned to the full-blown flower-ness of flowers, not dazzled by their merely symbolic associations, like some other poets.

Some of her poems are *simply* (though they are never actually simple) celebrations of flowers – albeit with idiosyncratic grammatical construction and quirky orthography. Names of flowers and flower parts are often capitalized; I have no problem with that. Strange words (unexpected, unfamiliar, unconventional) recurrently adorn her poems, befitting the *strange*, bright crowds.

> The Dandelion's pallid tube
> Astonishes the Grass,
> And Winter instantly becomes
> An infinite Alas –
> The tube uplifts a signal Bud
> And then a shouting Flower, –
> The Proclamation of the Suns
> That sepulture is o'er.[34]

A florid narrative describes how Dandelions appear and bloom, signalling the end of winter. 'Sepulture' –figuratively connoting the frozen earth – is a strange word meaning 'entombment', as in a sepulchre (a tomb). The Suns – calling forth Spring's Buds and Flowers – Proclaim the end of Winter's sepulture, its entombment in hibernation. ('Suns' are plural, perhaps, to connote sunny day after sunny day? Or for some other reason?) The 'pallid tube' recalls the amaryllis's sturdier stem in Denise Levertov's poem: as we move through crowds of flowers, I like to collect these kinds of details to compare and contrast, noting recurrent themes and tropes. Certainly it is accurate, in gardens as well as in poems, that amaryllis stalks are significantly stronger, harder and greener than dandelion stalks. In visual art it would be more immediately apparent how a stalk would compositionally organize a canvas: a line dividing the painting in some way would direct the viewer's eye towards the flower. In a word-picture like this, even if one doesn't notice the compositional construction as forcefully as in a paint-picture, still, the poet's lines, forms and structures do similar work, laying out this compact, vivid scene and arranging the flower portrait exactly as Dickinson intends for her readers to perceive it.

She does not stint on exuberant ecstasy when flowers are in play – hence this poem's Astonishment, its Proclamation, its shouting. I don't recall any other poetic accounts of shouting Flowers, but as soon as I encountered Dickinson's I realized that of course flowers shout: how remiss of every other flower poet not to acknowledge this. (Henry David Thoreau – her fifth cousin, once removed – had a deaf ear: he demurs, 'One of the most attractive things about the flowers is their beautiful reserve.'[35]) The 'signal Bud' resembles the 'inference therefrom' in Dickinson's poem about the Arctic flower. Flowers *signal* things to people (and in many other ways besides shouting), from which we should hazard lots of *inferences*. Don't just look at flowers: think about them; listen to them; be inspired and guided by them; give yourself over to them. Be alert. Take notes. Follow their signals.

'Strange, bright crowds of flowers' – and also bees, flies and clover, horses and butterflies, hills, fields, suns and winds: all are enchanted with a potent charge of the inspirational power that courses throughout Dickinson's poetry. Flowers stand out as presences, touchstones, practically even characters, that spark transcendental visions – paradoxically, both elusively diminutive and at the same time boundlessly sublime.

> The lovely flowers embarrass me.
> They make me regret I am not a Bee —[36]

She wishes she were a Bee because that creature would more naturally and intimately (than a person), sniff and swoop around in the flowers, moving methodically from bloom to bloom. Indeed,

Dickinson deserves honorary membership in the guild of Bees, making good use of the flowers, productively and transformatively, as well as any apiary creature. ('When "Landlords" turn the drunken Bee / Out of the Foxglove's door – / When butterflies – renounce their "drams" / I shall but drink the more!'[37])

If being a Bee is the ideal way to approach flowers, she also offers an exemplum of how *not* to engage with flowers:

> I pull a flower from the woods –
> A monster with a glass
> Computes the stamens in a breath –
> And has her in a 'class'![38]

Look with your eyes, not with mechanical optical instruments. Don't tally their parts. Don't analyse them: appreciate them holistically, directly, naturally. Don't dissect them microscopically. Don't be a monster. The action described in the first line seems to be Dickinson's self-inscription in this poem: that is, she merely plucks a flower. The 'monster', by contrast, makes it a field of study – fetishizing, overintellectualizing. What about the ethics of the speaker's pulling the flower from the woods, if that is indeed what she does in this poem, and which she did in fact do regularly as she composed her herbarium and attached blooms to letters? What about her own poetic 'inspection' and anatomization of flowers, her figurative and aesthetic studies? Does she lay herself open to charges of hypocrisy here? I suggest we just give her a pass on that.

18 Published posthumously in 1890, Dickinson's poems feature these Indian pipes, also known as corpse plants (one of her favourite species), on the cover. ("Tis whiter than an Indian Pipe – / 'Tis dimmer than a lace – ', one poem begins.)

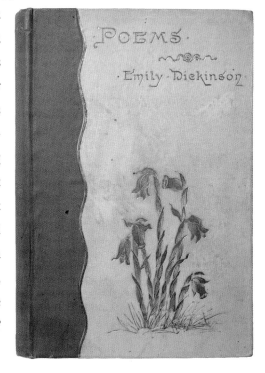

POSTER BY FEDERAL ART PROJECT W.P.A. IN OHIO

Dickinson maintains that bees have a better claim on flowers than people, because they use them; they need them (*they*, bees, use and need *them*, flowers – but also vice versa):

> Perhaps you'd like to buy a flower,
> But I could never sell –
> If you would like to borrow,
> Until the Daffodil
>
> Unties her yellow Bonnet
> Beneath the village door,
> Until the Bees, from Clover rows
> Their Hock, and Sherry, draw,
>
> Why, I will lend until just then,
> But not an hour more![39]

19 *Borrow* flowers, Emily Dickinson urged, in the same spirit as a U.S. New Deal poster urging people to admire blooms without cutting them.

I buy lots of flowers myself, not without equivocation about commodifying botanical products and the ecological toll of this commerce. (And if they are indeed as sentient as botanists are beginning to realize, then I may even have blood on my hands, figuratively speaking . . . or at least sap.) In my guiltiest twinges, I hear Dickinson narrating the poem's first two lines in my head as I purchase my rapacious bouquet.

Who, precisely, is 'I' in 'I could never sell', I wonder? God? Nature? Dickinson? Poetry? Perhaps some combination of all these. This 'I' character refuses to allow someone to buy and own the Daffodil, to cut the flower, to remove it from where it belongs with the Bees who feast on its liquor. But we may *borrow* the

Daffodil (Dickinson underlined the word in her manuscript) for a few minutes, until the Bees arrive to stake their just claim to it. Borrowing means looking at the flower without taking it, and without disrupting the processes of life. We may do this out in the field, and we are also doing so as we read this poem. The speaker acknowledges that we may want the flower, but the poem lectures – or 'signals' – the would-be buyer about how flowers function as part of their native environment. Anything more disruptive than borrowing the flower would harm this ecosystem.

Another encomium about borrowing flowers comes from *The Book of Tea*, where Kakuzō Okakura provides an account of ancient poets and philosophers who anticipated Dickinson's reticence to remove flowers from where they grow and live:

> The ideal lover of flowers is he who visits them in their native haunts, like Taoyuenming, who sat before a broken bamboo fence in converse with the wild chrysanthemum, or Linwosing, losing himself amid mysterious fragrance as he wandered in the twilight among the plum-blossoms

20 Bee: *sine qua non.*

of the Western Lake. 'Tis said that Chowmushih slept in a boat so that his dreams might mingle with those of the lotus. It was the same spirit which moved the Empress Komio, one of our most renowned Nara sovereigns, as she sang: 'If I pluck thee, my hand will defile thee, O Flower!'[40]

There are nearly as many Bees in Dickinson's poetry as there are Flowers, which makes perfect sense botanically and demonstrates her verse-garden's ecological precision, modelling balance and what we now call sustainability:

> Auto da Fe – and Judgment –
> Are nothing to the Bee –
> His separation from His Rose –
> To him – sums Misery –[41]

For a Bee, the flower is the world: stem to stern, alpha and omega. It seems reasonable to draw the inference therefrom that the same single-minded devotion holds true for the poet. 'Often she spoke of the written word as a flower,' Judith Farr writes, and 'spoke of a flower when she meant herself'.[42] Dickinson sees herself as flowery, flower-like, ensconced (like a Bee) in a flower:

> I hide myself within my flower,
> That, fading from your Vase,
> You, unsuspecting, feel for me –
> Almost a loneliness.[43]

She famously avoided Amherst society: the woman in white, the recluse, the brilliant poet who did not publish. Hiding in flowers seems like Dickinson's way of retreating into what she sees as the more satisfying realm of nature. Her flowers stake out ontologies for the larger world:

> The Lilac is an ancient shrub
> But ancienter than that
> The Firmamental Lilac
> Upon the Hill tonight –
> The Sun subsiding on his Course
> Bequeaths this final Plant
> To Contemplation – not to Touch –
> The Flower of Occident.
> Of one Corolla is the West –
> The Calyx is the Earth –
> The Capsules burnished Seeds the Stars –[44]

There are Lilacs and then there are heavenly Lilacs, which is to say, Lilacs writ large: the Firmament imagined as if Stars were Seeds and the Earth were the Calyx (the protective layer around a bud enclosing the petals). Unsurprisingly, a poet focused intently on flowers looks at the large universe around her and sees . . . flowers, extrapolations of flowers, flower-like systems of life. Another tableau that situates the poet as a bridge, or a medium, between the small flower and the large world is this one:

> The single Flower of the Earth
> That I, in passing by
> Unconscious was – Great Nature's Face
> Passed infinite by Me –[45]

All flowers are in some sense one 'single Flower' just as all people are human, with consequent commonalities. Another poem where flowers expand into larger worldly tropes reads, in its entirety:

> Where Ships of Purple – gently toss –
> On Seas of Daffodil –
> Fantastic Sailors – mingle –
> And then – the Wharf is still![46]

This lyric is surreal, impossibly absurd, and yet at the same time, thanks to poetic licence (and especially Dickinson's hypercharged enactment of that licence), completely graspable once our vision acclimates to her Fantastic botanical cosmos. The sketchy narrative – tossing, mingling and then stillness – might describe anything from a simple scene of flowers doing their thing to global conquest: not military or imperial conquest, but floral conquest. Sewn together in unpublished fascicles, her flowery poems embody vast, omnipotent bundles of life and art. Empowered by the innovative energy of the Arctic flower, the Flower of the Earth, the Firmamental Lilac, the Daffodil tied in her yellow Bonnet, the Dandelion's signal Bud, and all Dickinson's other botanical fabulations, there is no better way to navigate the world than setting sail on Seas of Daffodil. What she does with flowers, what she sees in flowers, is in no way (as her work was once regarded) flippant or demure, trivial, diminutive or cute. On the contrary: 'To be a Flower, is profound / Responsibility –'[47] and Dickinson, hiding herself within her Flower, spent her life fulfilling this Responsibility in a monumental garden of poetry that blossomed with floral profundity.

Brownish now

Dickinson's flowery writing is so sharp and economical, so precise and incisive, that it is hard to reconcile with the use of the colloquial phrase 'flowery writing' as a pejorative descriptor. The *Oxford English Dictionary* definition – 'full of fine words and showy expressions, florid; full of elaborate or literary words and phrases' (usage examples begin with Shakespeare's *Measure for Measure* and continue through the nineteenth century) – has a connotation somewhere between merely descriptive and mildly critical. 'Elaborate' diction is not necessarily the worst thing in the world. In current usage, though, the term is more strongly condemnatory: an online thesaurus offers synonyms including 'flamboyant, convoluted, high-flown, high-sounding, overblown, overwrought, highfalutin, fancy-schmancy'.[48] Apparently, flowery writing is now *verboten*: I wonder why. Does it reflect a change in our sensibility towards writing, or towards flowers? It seems odd that flowers connote negative value: wouldn't everything be better if it were more flowery? But perhaps this aligns with a twentieth- and twenty-first-century poetic sensibility that is more dubious about the perfection of flowers, and the conviction that flowers help alleviate the world's ailments. Are poetic flowers losing their lustre?

There are individual counterexamples, such as Ezra Pound's 'In a Station of the Metro' (1913), a delicately compact Imagist poem in which floral fragments describe the world, and stand for the world, as poignantly and confidently as in Dickinson's poetry. Pound's apparition, as he describes the tableau, counterpoises another crowd (he uses that specific word), like Dickinson's 'strange, bright crowds'. His is a crowd of people ('faces'), but also, by poetic equivalence, a crowd of wet petals on a black bough. It is as if the people are, strangely, transformed into flowers. Pound doesn't explicitly colour the petals of this strange crowd bright but I think they are – sharp pink dogwood, in my mind, to counterpoise the black bough.[49]

Conventional poetic flowers once embodied a fairly pure and stable idealism, a tradition rooted in Dante's mystical, celestial white rose. The Virgin Mary presides over this flower of perfection at the culmination of *Paradiso*: its petals are the souls of the faithful, and angels buzz around it like bees. The modern poetic flower is more constricted: sometimes ironized, often quintessentially flawed. Flowers serve as emblems of their times and ours is an imperfect age. In modern poetry there are few of the kinds of flowery firmaments or seas that Dickinson conjured (although H. D.'s *Sea Garden*, glimpsed earlier, offers another outlier), and Dickinsonian self-enflowering is rare. Resisting the too-easy allure of flowers, modernists tend to regard them more suspiciously and cynically than previous generations of poets. Flowers, like so many other aspects of the world around us, are cracking up, breaking down, losing ground.

Looking at newer, lesser flowers, I will examine representative arrangements from Philip Larkin, Sylvia Plath and T. S. Eliot (and the astute reader will sense already that this is headed into a thicket). Larkin's mid-century poetry captures a mood of dissipated grandeur. As the commonplace bromide has it, the sun has set on the British empire (and without sun there can be no flowers). The Second World War seems like a Pyrrhic victory as the UK remains mired in stagnation in its aftermath. 'Church Going' (1955) opens with a panoramic yet irreverent sweep around a church the speaker has just entered, a scene that includes an offhand but cutting floral reference:

Once I am sure there's nothing going on
I step inside, letting the door thud shut.
Another church: matting, seats, and stone,
And little books; sprawlings of flowers, cut
For Sunday, brownish now; some brass and stuff
Up at the holy end; the small neat organ;
And a tense, musty, unignorable silence,
Brewed God knows how long.[50]

The poem typifies Larkin's ambivalence about modernity: on the one hand, he dutifully re-enacts centuries of English tradition by church-going, but he is also ringing the death knell for the institution he finds outdated. There is no hyphen in the title, so the poem is not so much about church-going as about 'church *going*' (that is, becoming obsolete, disappearing), an assessment bluntly expressed in the first-line spoiler, 'I am sure there's nothing going on.'

The church Larkin visits has the accoutrements that once comprised a cathedral's sacred space. But now it is just 'another church', nameless and somewhat tedious in its generic predictability. ('God' – ironic if not profane as invoked here – appears nowhere else in the poem.) It still contains all the things churches have always had, but they have become diminutive, unspectacular, indistinct. Bibles and hymnals are now, for Larkin, 'little books'; the apse, where the clergy sits and the altar is located, alongside the radiating chapels of the chevet, is simply 'the holy end', filled not with such ceremonial, celebratory artefacts as crucifixes, candlesticks and chalices, but merely 'some brass and stuff'.

And the flowers: sanctuaries have always featured floral arrangements adorning services, holidays, weddings and funerals. The seasons are marked by Easter lilies, Christmas poinsettias, chrysanthemums for All Saints' Day, roses to commemorate martyrdom, crocuses (the first flowers to emerge from the wintry ground) as a sign of resurrection, along with so many other symbolically resonant blossoms that comprise an ecumenical 'language of flowers'. The natural serenity of flowers, their celebratory reminder of the world's and God's grandeur, had always served as straightforward Christian trappings. (Flowers are similarly common in mandirs, synagogues, Buddhist temples and monasteries, and Shinto shrines; cut flowers are less common in mosques, though still sometimes present, but Islamic houses of worship frequently feature lavish floral designs in their decor.) Generally furnished through the community's contributions and coordinated by volunteer parishioners who compete fiercely for the honour of supervising the display, floral baskets and altar arrangements are stalwart tokens of the traditional churchly milieu. Puncturing traditions, Larkin takes sharp aim at the flowers in a voice that seems tired and quietly understated, the tone that broadcasts his most acute critiques. Like just about everything else he sees in the world around him, these church flowers have been drained of their vitality and lie faded, impotent, as testimony to atrophied spiritual lives. *Flowers going* is a constituent element of *church going*.

The specific descriptors of the flowers' physical appearance are stinted: 'sprawling', 'brownish'. Of indeterminate species, these flowers are several days past their prime, which in itself suggests that Larkin is in the wrong place at the wrong time. If he wanted to see a vital community and ongoing traditional worship, he might have tried to pop in on Sunday morning. If the poem is set on, say, Thursday afternoon, what does he expect? The flowers are wilted now, their stems flaccid and minimally functional – failing their métier, as Levertov would note, of holding blossoms

proudly erect. But presumably the flowers were fresh for Sunday's worship services, when it mattered. Perhaps Larkin himself bears at least some of the culpability for the lacklustre floral experience his poem describes?

21 Church flowers on Sunday: nothing brownish or sprawling here.

In rosier flower poems from the past, detailed and colourful floral palettes blossom front and centre. Here, 'brownish' – Larkin cannot even commit to a definite, clear-cut brown, but just 'ish' – dulls the tradition of happy flower-poems. If normal bright, fresh flowers demarcate a festive and functional event, then their antithesis succinctly invokes, in this tightly packed image of one unfortunate arrangement past its sell-by date, disappointment and exhaustion.

Flowers are great, until they're not. The greatness is transitory; Britain, too, was once seen as great, before the decline and fall that Larkin's poetry narrates. One doesn't hear much, before modern poetry, about the unbeautiful aspect of flowers. Of course flowers have always gone brownish eventually, but who needs to think about that, and what would it profit a poet to highlight this mundane truth? Just throw the flowers out when they start to sprawl, or, as I do, toss them the day before, when wilting seems imminent, so you do not even have to see them in their impending decrepitude. Pre-twentieth-century poets, Baudelaire and his ilk aside, hardly ever depicted derelict flowers; William Blake's 'O Rose thou art Sick', an exception that proves the rule, presciently anticipates modernism.

I appreciate Larkin's flowers despite myself: I think they embellish and expand the discourse of these strange, bright crowds. Thinking about 'Church Going', whenever I see flowers, especially in a spiritual venue, that are *not* sprawling or brownish, I appreciate their freshness a bit more than I otherwise would; I don't take it for granted.

Troubling tulips

One assumes that a gift of flowers will comfort a sick person, but Sylvia Plath, an autobiographical 'confessional poet' who foregrounded her psychological anguish, explodes this supposition in 'Tulips' (1961). It is perhaps the most unpleasant flower poem ever. Plath's unrelenting cynicism – a stream of violent emotion, conflict and despair – implicates even an innocuous bouquet of flowers. 'The tulips are too excitable, it is winter here,' she begins the poem inspired by her own hospitalization. 'I didn't want any flowers, I only wanted / To lie with my hands turned up and be utterly empty. / How free it is, you have no idea how free.' Like Larkin, but more vehemently, Plath disparages the flowers:

The tulips are too red in the first place, they hurt me . . .
Their redness talks to my wound, it corresponds.
They are subtle: they seem to float, though they weigh
    me down,
Upsetting me with their sudden tongues and their color,
A dozen red lead sinkers round my neck.

And she feels threatened by them: 'Nobody watched me before, now I am watched. / The tulips turn to me, and the window behind me.' She is overcome, like a shadow 'Between the eye of the sun and the eyes of the tulips, / And I have no face, I have wanted to efface myself. / The vivid tulips eat my oxygen.'[51]

'In joy or sadness, flowers are our constant friends', Kakuzō Okakura writes in *The Book of Tea*,[52] but Plath disagrees. Intended to soothe, these flowers instead unsettle the speaker's mind and leave her traumatized. They intrude into her pain, her fragile self-awareness. Presumably they came from someone who meant to cheer the convalescent patient by reminding her of supportive friends and family, but she wants to be left alone: she has had too much of other people. Flowers signify regeneration, and psychologists have found 'a connection between flowers and positive emotions . . . people get better quicker in hospitals if exposed to flowers';[53] but perhaps this patient rejects an optimistic prognosis. She could be offended by the gift-giver's facile implication that she will soon flower again herself.

'Tulips' is highly imaginative, and that imagination seems at least borderline neurotic as the speaker narrates disturbing fantasies about voraciously cruel, devious flowers that harass her, attack her, drain her, suffocate her. Flowers don't really do this, at least not usually. Audrey Jr from *The Little Shop of Horrors* (directed by Roger

Corman in 1960, with numerous film and stage remakes) rivals
Plath's tulips: a nightmare hybrid between a Venus flytrap and a
butterwort, she feeds on human blood, especially partial to any
dismembered corpses that come her way. If flowers really were like
Audrey Jr – greedy, manipulative, egotistical – I wouldn't want
them in my hospital room either. Plath's floral ferocity resembles
Corman's gory cult classic when she writes, 'The tulips should be
behind bars like dangerous animals', imagining them 'opening like
the mouth of some great African cat'.[54]

Red tulips in particular have a violent legacy: I wonder if Plath
knew the twelfth-century Persian fable told by the poet Nizami
about a man's desire for an unattainable princess. The lover, Farhad,
would win his beloved Shirin if he could cut through the mountain,
allowing a stream to flow through the rock. But when he had almost
accomplished his task he received the (false) message of her death
and threw himself off the mountain. Among the blood-drenched
rocks below, red tulips sprung to life.[55] Marjane Satrapi recalls this
legend in *Persepolis 2*: 'It's said that red tulips grow from the blood
of martyrs.'[56] Another unsettling tulip that could have influenced
Plath appears in Robert Browning's 1855 poem 'Up at a Villa – Down
in the City': 'The wild tulip, at end of its tube, blows out its great red
bell / Like a thin clear bubble of blood.'[57]

'I didn't want any flowers' – is this something that a person
might really feel? Had botanical pioneer Luther Burbank been able
to argue the point with Plath (an improbable encounter as he died
six years before her birth), he might have offered his pleasant
apophthegm in rebuttal: 'Flowers always make people better, happier, and more helpful; they are sunshine, food, and medicine to
the mind.'[58] But Plath insists: 'They weigh me down . . . A dozen red
lead sinkers': an incredible (to me) refutation of the light, happy

beauty that flowers so naturally radiate. As hard as it is to imagine having this feeling myself, I can force myself to consider the possibility (it would be a dull world if we were all alike) that someone else might be offended, disturbed, by something that is supposed to be – and that everyone else supposes to be – incontrovertibly harmless. Perhaps a poet like Plath – disruptive, uncensored, radically noncompliant with constrictive social expectations for women – would be especially reticent to buy into such time-worn traditions as bringing flowers to lift a frail patient's spirits. Perhaps she is wise to the fact that flower-givers may intend their beautiful present to flatter a woman, or deceive her, or manipulate her. The simple fact that everyone else enjoys flowers wholeheartedly might provoke her to lash out against them: a contrarian instinct courses through her poetry.

What do poets see in flowers? The case of Wordsworth vs Plath demarcates the endpoints of the continuum. They make us happy, he posits; they do not, she replies. What precipitates the paradox of flowers that don't inspire joy? Is it their fault, or ours? Perhaps it is relevant that today's apples, cherries and tomatoes, bred for homogenous efficiency, taste blander than they did only a generation ago; and flowers, bred for longevity and commercial durability, have also lost a sensory splendour. Their smells are not what they used to be. (Florists now use synthetic aerosol sprays to make their shops smell flowery.[59]) So it is actually possible that flowers have devolved and contemporary poetry reflects this diminution. But the greater part of the burden is likely on us: people have changed. We are not able, as we once were, to be so easily uplifted and inspired by flowers. Perhaps this is because we are smarter now (and not prone to be hoodwinked by a pretty diversion); or, equally possibly, because we are stupider. Perhaps the once-instinctual thrill of flowers has become banal because, thanks to cheaper air transport, global pathways of commerce and mass supermarket floral produce, we have too many flowers and we have become jaded; perhaps flowers are simply one of those things that once brought easy and universal pleasure yet, for whatever reason, don't work as well now.

Emily Dickinson, too, contemplated flowers that might not convey the expected pleasure:

> So gay a Flower
> Bereaves the Mind
> As if it were a Woe –
> Is Beauty an Affliction – then?
> Tradition ought to know –[60]

Dickinson raises her query in a calmer manner than Plath, without mental agitation. The nineteenth-century poet seems more politely considerate of the flower's grace and feelings; if one crosses the Rubicon to anthropomorphism, one can imagine a tulip taking great offence at 'Tulips', whereas Dickinson's floral audience might find her poem more philosophically and aesthetically contemplative, tactful; less of a head-on assault. But like Plath in attitude, if not in temperament, Dickinson, too, broaches the potential Woe that a Flower may paradoxically inflict, gay as it is: can such Beauty truly make us sad, or ill?

Plath argues that tulips are evil, while Dickinson ends her poem more open-endedly with a final line that offers yet another variant of her frequent valedictory injunction to her reader, just to mull over what she has put forth; to draw some 'inference therefrom'. And that, in a sense, is exactly what Plath has done in her own poem: she has taken Dickinson's quietly perverse accusation, mulled it until it accelerated to a breaking point and consequently increased the poetic volume, the vitriol, a hundredfold. Was Plath consciously in dialogue with Dickinson's prompt a century earlier? I have not found any evidence of this: more likely, Plath's poem is an accidental response. 'Tradition ought to know', Dickinson suggests, if floral Beauty can Afflict us, and the Tradition provides an answer in 'Tulips': yes, it damn well can. Among Dickinson's gifts is prescience: as she tossed this challenge out to the future Tradition of poetry, I imagine she hoped someone would pick up this train of thought, in agreement that we 'ought to know' if flowers are capable of disappointing us, failing us. She could not have known (could she?) that the responder would be Sylvia Plath, who had studied poetry in rural Massachusetts at Smith College, a mere seven miles down the road from Amherst.

Lilacs in the dead land

Parsing the roots of Larkin's and Plath's dour flowers, we must cast an eye back a generation earlier towards the man who shaped modernist poetry. T. S. Eliot, the American-born writer who relocated to Britain in the throes of European cultural collapse brought about by the First World War, became famous for his images of modernity in which a fragmented, corrupted, sterile aesthetic milieu metaphorically 'blossomed' – ironically – out of arid, lifeless soil. His repertoire includes erratic, troubling and depressing flowers: strange but not so bright (as befits his dimly sordid modern tableaux). Instead of 'crowds of flowers', he plants a disparate collection of isolated, fraught specimens: botanical analogues to the alienated people who stumble through his poetry. His flowers play their part in contributing to the sinister mood that resonates throughout his first collection, *Prufrock and Other Observations* (1917). In the surreal, threatening perambulation of 'Rhapsody on a Windy Night', 'through the spaces of the dark / Midnight shakes the memory / As a madman shakes a dead geranium.'[61] Depicting a haunted female presence of some sort (perhaps a streetwalker, or the moon), 'A washed-out smallpox cracks her face, / Her hand twists a paper rose, / That smells of dust and eau de Cologne.'[62] The madman's flowers, or possibly someone else's, reappear: 'The reminiscence comes / Of sunless dry geraniums / And dust in crevices.'[63]

Eliot's flowers are deeply unpretty, dusty and fake, dry and wasted (anticipating the stony, lifeless landscape he would depict five years later in *The Waste Land*). Sunless flowers, by definition, are impossible. Remembering Plath's statement 'I didn't want any flowers,' it is as if Eliot is saying, even more starkly, there simply can't be any flowers. And just as Larkin's wilted church display reminds me that most flower arrangements we encounter are fresh, Eliot makes me appreciate that almost every other flower in the world outside his shadowy, sooty poetry is replete with the sun's power, catching and ecologically recycling its energy, its brightness, for our delight and our sustenance.

As Emily Dickinson's floral sensibilities penetrated and infused her soul, so too do Eliot's – but as his soul is nervous and solipsistic, it follows that the flowers infusing his spirit are consequently squalid. One has to hand it to Eliot: the poetic tradition has depicted many things that have been done to flowers and thought about flowers over the centuries, but a madman shaking a dead geranium – that is a novelty. As nonsensically deranged as it is, still I feel compelled to explain how it fits into this survey of things that people do with flowers in culture. We can try to interpret the troubled character's madness, although Eliot's scenes often elude reasonable explanation. Why would a madman shake a dead geranium, I wonder? Anger at its death? Flaunting the flower's uselessness? Trying to bring it back to life? Or harvest its seeds? I'd call that last guess an unlikely reading, but Eliot's life and art did indeed manage to continue on after and beyond the anguish of his early poetry. New flowers somehow sprout a generation later in his final poems, despite the botanical sterility of his earlier writing.

Eliot didn't create this strange geranium *ex nihilo*: Jules Laforgue, a nineteenth-century French symbolist poet Eliot admired for his own spirit of troubled lassitude, had written, 'Ô géranium diaphanes, guerroyeurs sortilèges, / Sacrilèges monomanes!' (Oh diaphanous geraniums, warrior incantations, sacrilegious mon-omaniac), creating a milieu as eerie as Eliot's geranium scene and even more incomprehensible. In his essay 'The Metaphysical Poets', Eliot quoted that particular passage of Laforgue's, praising his 'obscure words'.[64]

Other prominent literary flowers of madness include Ophelia's from *Hamlet*:

You must sing a-down a-down, and you call him
a-down-a. O, how the wheel becomes it! It is the false
steward, that stole his master's daughter . . . There's
rosemary, that's for remembrance; pray, love, remember:
and there is pansies. That's for thoughts . . . There's fennel
for you, and columbines: there's rue for you; and here's
some for me: we may call it herb-grace o' Sundays:
O, you must wear your rue with a difference. There's
a daisy: I would give you some violets, but they withered
all when my father died.[65]

But Ophelia's is a more explicable and even 'normal' madness, a psychological aberration that everyone else in the play (and audience) understands within the purview of the plot and her character. 'Hadst thou thy wits . . . It could not move thus,' Laertes observes of his sister: 'A document in madness!'[66] Little surprise that when we next hear of Ophelia after her flower-madness, she has drowned.

In Eliot's aesthetic, by contrast, 'a madman shaking a dead geranium' is par for the course in a world of muttering retreats and desolate 'Streets that follow like a tedious argument / Of insidious intent', with yellow smoke that licks the evening's corners while a patient (the poet himself?) lies etherized upon a table. Eliot's nervous, haunted flowers are perfectly of a piece with the aesthetic that pervades his nervous, fractured modern world.

'Portrait of a Lady', another poem in this collection, parodies Henry James's novel: a woman clings to Jamesian Victorian manners in a way that deeply unsettles her modernist gentleman caller, who finds no solace in social conventions.

> Now that the lilacs are in bloom
> She has a bowl of lilacs in her room
> And twists one in her fingers as she talks.
> 'Ah, my friend, you do not know, you do not know
> What life is, you who hold it in your hands';
> (Slowly twisting the lilac stalks)[67]

The flowers are misused. The lady, at least as the young man perceives in his antisocial paranoia, weaponizes them. Her flowers emasculate him as she twists and destroys the stems. (These hollow lilac stems are keenly fitting as a phallic symbol for a man whose sexuality, according to biographers, was itself hollow.) The

gentleman caller smiles and goes on drinking tea for as long as he can stand to, but flees to sit alone in a park the instant he is able. Flowers are part of the outdated world of cultural manners, drawing rooms, conversation and civilization; Eliot's harsh modernist angst rejects all this, so it makes sense that his flowers should be viciously useless. Flowers are a device of romance, a social accessory that may effectuate emotional connection: a simple affirmation that the human spirit can celebrate beauty, grace and pleasure. That's how it is supposed to work – but here, instead, as everything gets turned on its head, the flowers intrude ominously

22 John Millais's *Ophelia*, 1851–2, oil on canvas, features a languorous garland of wildflowers held in the dead character's languorous hand.

87

between a man and a woman in a drawing room. They embody the kind of subconscious irritation that pervades modernism. Twisting the stalk, like shaking a dead geranium, is simply a strange thing to do to a flower, signifying that these flowers seem fundamentally different from what they once were, unable to achieve what they once did.

Eliot's multiple lilacs give a different effect from Yeats's multiple Roses. As the word repeats from the first to the second lines of this passage, it seems oddly awkward, obvious, redundant; and the third 'lilac', accentuated by the distasteful context of its mutilation, becomes one of those words that sounds nonsensical as it is repeated over and over (by a toddler, for instance . . . or a madman). With Yeats, as his poem offered Rose after Rose, we seemed to *have* Rose after Rose. But in 'Portrait of a Lady' there are too many lilacs, just as Plath complained there were too many tulips: both poets overthink and overload their flowers to the point where they become drained of their natural appeal and reconfigured as malevolent; instead of a strange, bright crowd, their flowers comprise an ominous and threatening mob. As the tulips failed to bring calmness, these lilacs fail to promote pleasant social interaction, instead opening an existential rupture. When flowers turn malignant, we are in dire straits.

In 'La Figlia che Piange', Eliot's closing poem from *Prufrock and Other Observations*, the speaker observes a young girl weeping in the wake of romantic collapse: 'Clasp your flowers to you with a pained surprise – / Fling them to the ground and turn / With a fugitive resentment in your eyes.'[68] Again here, flowers are simply not working. They represent exactly the opposite of what they have always meant: bitter loss rather than romantic consummation. Instead of the *pleasant* surprise that flowers should normally facilitate, these flowers provoke a *pained* surprise. Instead of receiving and accepting flowers, this character rejects them, casting them away frantically, desperately, as if they are dangerous. (Her instinct is sound: in Eliot's world, they may well be.)

In Eliot's next collection, 'Whispers of Immortality' (1920) features grotesque flowers of death – 'Daffodil bulbs instead of balls / Stared from the sockets of the eyes!'[69] – anticipating the macabre gardens of *The Waste Land* (1922). Eliot's modernist epic copiously uses images of dry, barren ground to symbolize an intellectually, culturally and spiritually barren society. Unsurprisingly, flowers do not prosper in this soil:

> April is the cruellest month, breeding
> Lilacs out of the dead land, mixing
> Memory and desire, stirring
> Dull roots with spring rain.
> Winter kept us warm, covering
> Earth in forgetful snow, feeding
> A little life with dried tubers.[70]

April is cruel *because* it breeds lilacs out of the dead land: a sensibility that in a few short lines punctures so many traditional convictions and presumptions about the world and its natural cycles. Eliot's opening rewrites and rebuts the opening of Geoffrey Chaucer's fourteenth-century *Canterbury Tales*, in which spring brought hope and excitement as rain nurtured budding new shoots of flowery life:

> Whan that Aprill, with his shoures soote
> The droghte of March hath perced to the roote

And bathed every veyne in swich licour,
Of which vertu engendred is the flour.[71]

A brief etymological digression: Middle English word forms were irregular, mutable. Writers (even the great 'Willm Shakspere' at the dawn of Modern English) put little stock in standardized orthography. So what we know as a *flower* might have been rendered as flur, flure, flowr, flowre, flor, flowur, flore or, in Scotland, flouir, alongside Chaucer's flour. Flour is my favourite, mostly because Chaucer used it, but *flouir* is a close runner-up. What a truly strange, bright crowd of flower seeds the OED sows in the diminutive furrows of its tiny print. One might recite this linguistic inventory, assigning each word (which is similar and related, though not identical) to the inhabitants of an actual vase, flowur by floor, which are likewise similar but not identical to each other. What we now call 'flour' is of course different from what Chaucer meant when he spelled the word that way: our bread-making base is so called because it is 'the "flower" or finest quality of meal . . . whether from wheat or other grain, which is separated by bolting (i.e., sifting)'.[72] I like the resonance of 'flower' used to mean 'finest', and I resolve to increase my use of the word in that sense: 'This paragraph is the flower of your essay!' I will write on a student's paper.

In any case, I return to Eliot's traumatized world: in a post-First World War miasma, with the added personal anguish of being in the throes of a severe nervous breakdown while he drafted *The Waste Land*, it must have seemed better that there should be no flowers, no false hopes that life might improve after a frigid, dead season if flowers would sprout and blossom. The world doesn't deserve floral beauty, but perhaps only tubers (that might conceivably bloom someday, but not now); *dried* tubers, at that: small, cold, buried, forgotten rootstalks. There may be flowers somehow, sometime, in this world as Eliot paints it, but not many, not easily, not soon. This is stunningly nihilistic – has any other poet ever proposed that flowers could not bloom? It is cantankerous, even depraved, but that's where we are in Eliot's world. Growth and regeneration are viewed as suspect, undesirable, inappropriate and ultimately impossible. After Eliot reconfigured flowers as inherently unsatisfying, the mood spread culturally (as so many of his feelings came to infuse the definitive milieu of modernism) to become a widespread presumption about flowers. Plath was channelling this floral scepticism in 'Tulips', and in *Herzog* (1964) Saul Bellow describes late spring as a time 'when the general revival of life troubles many people, the new roses, even in shop windows, reminding them of their own failures, of sterility and death'.[73] Game, set and match, Eliot.

Instead of replenishing the store of beauty and fecundity, flowers in *The Waste Land* betoken ineffability and failure. There are not many flowers in the poem (because it's a waste land, shockingly enough), and what few there are perform dysfunctionally.

'You gave me hyacinths first a year ago;
'They called me the hyacinth girl.'
– Yet when we came back, late, from the Hyacinth garden,
Your arms full, and your hair wet, I could not
Speak, and my eyes failed, I was neither
Living nor dead, and I knew nothing,
Looking into the heart of light, the
   silence.[74]

The hyacinths are overwhelming. In a dead, wasted world, flowers do not help mitigate the gloom even a little bit: instead, they

Syd Edwards del.   Pub. by T.Curtis, S. Geo.Crescent July 1,1806. F.Sansom sculp.

23 It is hard to imagine how such a delightfully ornate flower as *Hyacinthus orientalis* could trigger the kind of existential torpor it does in *The Waste Land*.

remind us tormentingly of some pleasure that seems forever lost. Ineffability – 'I could not speak' – is, for a poet, complete failure, erasure. The thrice-repeated 'hyacinth' here is like the repeated 'lilacs' from 'Portrait of a Lady', and again, unlike the sense of additive floral bounty in Yeats's repeated 'Rose'. It's not that Eliot treats us to more and more hyacinths; rather, we are tortured because we have to hear the word over and over without reaping the satisfaction that, once upon a time, hyacinths could provide. The obsessively repeated flower-words, for most modernists, ironically emphasize how many flowers we do not have and cannot enjoy. For Yeats (who often ran against the grain of mainstream modernism), flowers are good and more flowers are better; for Eliot, flowers are painfully unpleasant and more flowers are worse.

Over the next two decades Eliot recovered, gradually, somewhat, from the profound despair portrayed in *The Waste Land*, his nadir. Britain needed a more comforting aesthetic to help alleviate the agonizing prospect (and then reality) of another war, so Eliot provided *Four Quartets* (1936–43): a series of meditative, calming garden poems commemorating flowery places he had visited. The clematis, lotus, dahlias, roses, sunflowers and hollyhocks in these poems are not quite normal flowers, but they are usually at least tolerable, not horrible, and they are mostly intriguing, rather than repulsive: they resist the most cynical strains

92

of the floral aesthetic from Eliot's early poetry. In *Four Quartets* plants grow as life pushes forwards in its cycles, unlike *The Waste Land*, in which the world seemed comatose. The sad, lonely, tormented, dusty, dead flowers in his tormented, lonely poetry give way to tentatively happier flowers in his happier (or, less miserable) poetry. Eliot's later flowers signify spiritual replenishment, at least aspirationally. A great many roses symbolize what flowers may represent (and have represented in past poetic traditions), philosophically and spiritually.

In the first garden of *Four Quartets*:

> the bird called, in response to
> The unheard music hidden in the shrubbery,
> And the unseen eyebeam crossed, for the roses
> Had the look of flowers that are looked at.
> There they were there as our guests, accepted and
> accepting.[75]

'The look of flowers that are looked at': the tenor is odd, evocative of *Alice's Adventures in Wonderland*, but less neurotic than Eliot's earlier flowers; perhaps just quizzically, rather than frighteningly, surreal. I look at flowers all the time and I wonder, prompted by Eliot's formulation, what exactly might be the look of flowers that are looked at. What do flowers look like when they are *not* looked at? (If a tree falls in the forest, does it make a sound? Is Schrödinger's cat alive or dead? Eliot had trained to be a philosopher before he jumped ship for poetry.)

Flowers provide an animating presence in the landscape of *Four Quartets*, especially in contrast to the parched and fundamentally inanimate terrain of *The Waste Land*.

> Will the sunflower turn to us, will the clematis
> Stray down, bend to us; tendril and spray
> Clutch and cling?[76]

Sunflowers and clematis do, in fact, turn, bend and clutch just as Eliot describes. Still, there is something at least a bit supernatural about Eliot's garden: are these plants haunted? Or spiritually motivated? Perhaps those two states are not so far from each other; again I think of Dante, Eliot's most cherished poetic forebear, whose Empyrean rose is composed of souls, of ghosts: haunted, but in a devoutly calming strain.

Eliot's flowers may seem hypnotized (which is better than 'etherized') in his garden landscapes:

> In a warm haze the sultry light
> Is absorbed, not refracted, by grey stone.
> The dahlias sleep in the empty silence.
> Wait for the early owl.[77]

How do we imagine a sleepy, silent flower? It is there growing in the garden, pretty, blooming, but sedate and numbed: not shouting, like Emily Dickinson's flowers. Eliot's flowers lie still, unthreateningly, but at the cost of the strange, bright vivacity that flowers used to possess in spades. Ghostly, spiritual, supernatural: Eliot's flowers are contemplative, like a mantra, a meditation or a prayer; or a (modernist) poem. They are stylized: not the vital, sublime flowers that once landscaped poems, but instead, symbolically resonant. The sleepy dahlias are not quite the sunless 'dry' geraniums or twisted lilacs from Eliot's earlier poems, but still they are fairly distant from such poetically energized floral euphoria as William Wordsworth's 'then my heart with pleasure fills, / And dances with the daffodils.' Eliot's gardens in *Four Quartets* are cryptic conundrums (as is the entire culture to this not-quite-reformed philosopher), overburdened with the weight of the world.

> What is the late November doing
> With the disturbance of the spring
> And creatures of the summer heat,
> And snowdrops writing under feet
> And hollyhocks that aim too high
> Red into grey and tumble down
> Late roses filled with early snow?[78]

As hard as Eliot works, meditatively and (for a change) sanely, through the process of the long and spiritually alluring poetic sequence that is *Four Quartets*, he cannot suppress images of failed and troubled flowers – overweening hollyhocks, tormented snowdrops. His characterization is decidedly a minority view: snowdrops are not generally considered troubled flowers in the cultural imagination. It is hard to imagine an angst-ridden 'dingle-dangle', its jaunty common name from times past. Galanthophiles (coined by nineteenth-century botanical artist Edward Augustus Bowles to describe aficionados of *Galanthus nivalis*, Carl Linnaeus' term for the genus) admired the demure, immaculate bulb as an emblem of purity and innocence, perhaps because it blooms around 2 February, Candlemas, the festival that celebrates the purification of the Blessed Virgin Mary.[79] The snowdrop/dingle-dangle/*Galanthus* – also known as *perce-neige* in Perpignan and *schneeglöckchen* in Stuttgart – exemplifies the freeplay of flower names: Linnaean, folkloric, regional, beautifully colloquial and so forth. Flowers commonly

defy a fixed nominalism: the names we assign change and multiply. We cannot pin them down, which speaks to their elusive power: some sort of transcendence beyond human epistemology. 'From vases in the hall,' writes Alfred Lord Tennyson, 'Flowers of all heavens, and lovelier than their names, / Grew side by side.'[80] *Lovelier than their names*: to name a flower is to diminish it.

But such rich floricultural intimacy is foreign to Eliot, whose flowers embody existential critiques in what we would now call a deconstructive mode: the flowers undo themselves. If his flowers in *Four Quartets* appear (at first glance) more conventionally appealing than the twisted, ruined specimens from his earliest poetry, they are, finally, not all that much fresher:

> Where is there an end of it, the soundless wailing,
> The silent withering of autumn flowers
> Dropping their petals and remaining motionless . . . ?

> There is no end of it, the voiceless wailing,
> No end to the withering of withered flowers.[81]

The ethos of flowers wafts through *Four Quartets*: heavily worked, abstract, sometimes opaque. Still, readers have found them soothing, albeit elusive. (In this sequence of poems Eliot consciously models his verse on Beethoven's late quartets, which confused contemporary nineteenth-century audiences. The complex beauty of these pieces came to be appreciated only with the unfolding of time.) As florid as Eliot is trying to be in *Four Quartets*, flowers still precipitate at least some ineffability (which is, again, especially ironic for a poet): 'the soundless wailing . . . no end of it, the voiceless wailing' – not music, not poetry, not words, not even sounds.

24 Snowdrops bloom bravely in winter. As stylized in Maurice Pillard Verneuil's Art Nouveau lithograph, they exude infinitely more *esprit* and fortitude than Eliot's 'snowdrops writhing under feet'.

'No end to the withering'– the description is true enough: flowers will always be withering, although a glass-half-full account might instead imagine the eternal freshness of flowers, which is also true.

Le Petit Prince

In Antoine de Saint-Exupéry's *The Little Prince* (1943), one of the world's most-read and most-translated books,[82] the title character leaves his small asteroid to put some distance between himself and a rose with whom he has a love-hate relationship. Unlike all the other literary flowers in this chapter, this one grows in the field of prose rather than poetry, but Saint-Exupéry nurtures such poetic prose (sublime in the original French, but still pretty eloquent in translation) that it earns inclusion here. Smitten with the flower when she first blooms, the prince tends to her diligently, but the rose's demands soon become overtaxing. Saint-Exupéry's fable is an allegory for his own life: he had a comparably difficult relationship with his imperious wife, Consuela, whose posthumous autobiography is titled *The Tale of the Rose*; he was lost for almost a week in the Arabian desert in 1935, generating 'memories of loneliness, hallucination, impending death (and enveloping beauty)'[83] that underlie his book's desert setting; and the prince's departure from asteroid B-612 evokes the author's exile from Nazi-occupied France.

Flowers on this small planet had always been very simple, 'decorated with a single row of petals so that they took up no room at all and got in no one's way. They would appear one morning in the grass, and would fade by nightfall.' But this new one seemed extraordinary, as the prince 'watched the development of an enormous bud', realizing that 'some sort of miraculous apparition would emerge from it', as indeed it does. 'She had no desire to emerge all rumpled, like the poppies. She wished to appear only in the full radiance of her beauty.'[84]

Soon the high-maintenance flower begins 'tormenting him with her rather touchy vanity', demanding constant attention, water on demand, a glass globe to shield her from draughty winds. Coming to resent her manipulations, the prince flees the planet by hitching a ride with a migration of birds. The rose's personification, involving sometimes contentious dialogues with her princely caretaker, is

25 Antoine de Saint-Exupéry's prince tends his flowers on asteroid B-612, a simple task before a demanding rose appears in the garden.

unusual in literature about flowers; Lewis Carroll's floral characters may have inspired this one. The rose's melodramatic self-importance recalls proud, beautiful flowers from classical myths, overcome with their own perfection.

When the prince later recounts the story to the aviator he meets on his travels, he is racked with ambivalence about his relationship with this flower, and his behaviour towards her. One could not expect a flower to be anything other than narcissistic and temperamental, he seems to realize. Flowers are untrustworthy, too appealing and seductive for their own good. One should simply smell and look at them, he advises the aviator: 'You must never listen to flowers.' But soon his judgemental attitude softens, and he accepts his part of the blame for their falling out:

> In those days, I didn't understand anything. I should have judged her according to her actions, not her words. She perfumed my planet and lit up my life. I should never have run away! I ought to have realized the tenderness underlying her silly pretensions. Flowers are so contradictory! But I was too young to know how to love her.[85]

In exile, learning about the universe's foibles and follies, the prince worries about his rose. While she has thorns to protect herself against grazing sheep, still sheep have eaten flowers, thorns and all, undaunted for millions of years. A geographer he meets informs him, to the prince's dismay, that his maps do not include flowers, 'Because flowers are ephemeral'. But what does ephemeral mean, the prince asks? '"It means, 'which is threatened by imminent disappearance'." "Is my flower threatened by imminent disappearance?" "Of course."'[86]

The prince suffers a profound floral disappointment on Earth when he encounters a rose garden:

'Good morning,' he said.

'Good morning,' said the roses.

The little prince gazed at them. All of them looked like his flower.

'Who are you?' he asked, astounded.

'We're roses,' the roses said.

'Ah!' said the little prince.

And he felt very unhappy. His flower had told him she was the only one of her kind in the whole universe. And here were five thousand of them, all just alike, in just one garden![87]

But the prince overcomes this disillusionment. A fox explains that the prince has a unique and valuable relationship with his singular rose, precisely because she has tamed him, and he returns to the garden to inform that strange, bright crowd of flowers:

'You're not at all like my rose. You're nothing at all yet,' he told them. 'No one has tamed you and you haven't tamed anyone' . . .

And the roses were humbled.

'You're lovely but you're empty,' he went on. 'One couldn't die for you. Of course, an ordinary passerby would think my rose looked just like you. But my rose, all on her own, is more important than all of you together, since she's the one I've watered. Since she's the one I put under glass. Since she's the one I sheltered behind a screen. Since she's the one for whom I killed the caterpillars (except the two or three for butterflies). Since she's the one I listened to when she complained, or when she boasted, or even sometimes when she said nothing at all. Since she's my rose.'

The fox confirms the prince's wisdom: 'It's the time you spent on your rose that makes your rose so important.'[88] Preparing to depart Earth, the prince tells the aviator that people on this planet grow five thousand roses in one garden 'yet they don't find what they're looking for . . . And yet what they're looking for could be found in a single rose.'[89]

'One sees clearly only with the heart,' the fox explains in the novella's iconic phrase. *The Little Prince* is about learning to see the world in other ways – qualitative, not quantitative; emotional and subjective, rather than rote and fascistic. In 1943 what the maps that omit ephemeral roses *do* show are borders and battles, conquests and mad ambitions. Being off the map is the safest place to be. And the cultivation of precise, distinct, perhaps arbitrary values – the prince loves his own rose, but all the others are uninteresting – embodies a resistance against totalitarianism, which moulds all people into one person, robotic, easy to manipulate and line up among an array of soldiers in a marching regiment, ready to fire mechanically when ordered. As W. H. Auden, too, celebrated in his poems of this period, eccentricity and idiosyncrasy are not only pleasantly distracting, but they are indeed life-saving: they celebrate characters (and perhaps even inspire those who read about eccentrics) who tune out the propaganda to join the cause and march in battalions. Vast abstractions – whether 5,000 roses or 5,000 citizens with yellow stars sewn on their jackets – are less easy for many people to understand, to connect with and to help, than one single flower, or Jew.

The story's moral is, Adam Gopnik suggests, 'You can't love roses. You can only love a rose.' Saint-Exupéry's quest 'moves away from generic experience towards the eroticism of the particular flower. To be responsible for his rose, the Prince learns, is to see it as it really is, in all its fragility and vanity – indeed, in all its utter commonness! – without loving it less for being so fragile.' On his journey to Earth, the prince meets a series of functionaries – a businessman, an astronomer, a lamplighter, even an impuissant king – who have 'gone blind to the stars': the heavens, the amazement, the mysterious vastness that surrounds them. 'The world conspires to make us blind to its own workings,' Gopnik writes, and 'our real work is to see the world again.'[90]

The prince learns, towards the end, how to make sense of the universe in confusing times: 'The stars are beautiful because of a flower you don't see.'[91] And again: 'The important thing is what can't be seen . . . It is the same as for the flower. If you love a flower that lives on a star, then it's good, at night, to look up at the sky. All the stars are blossoming.'[92] This rose and the adventures she launches are more metaphorical (autobiographically and historically) than many of the other flowers we have encountered. 'You are an extra-terrestrial,' a New York friend informed Saint-Exupéry several years before the book's conception, and in response the aviator admitted, laughing, 'Yes, yes, it is true, I sometimes go for walks among the stars.'[93] Still, this floral parable – like all the imagined sea poppies, amaryllises, daffodils, roses and Roses, Lilacs and lilacs, tulips, geraniums, clematis, lotus, dahlias, and others blooming out to the far horizons of these poetic meadows – is predicated upon the strange, bright phenomenon of a small, beautiful, ephemeral living artefact. Since time immemorial, these flowers have occupied much more of our consciousness than we might logically and reasonably expect. Like the stacks of medical compendia, spiritual treatises and philosophical epistemologies that fill libraries and bookshops, floral musings, too, provide a body of material that helps as much as those other volumes (if not more!) in our humanistic and sense-oriented understanding of the world around us. Although he was a keen and learned student of technology, geography and aviation, Saint-Exupéry's sublime contribution to world literature represents none of those fields, but instead a quirky philosophical meditation on how a distant flower, fussy yet magnificent in impact, motivates our adventures and modulates our hopes and fears in a troubled world.

Fair, and fresh of hewe

Flowers risk debilitation in the modern age: unappreciated, wilted, unusable or exhausted. They are sprawling and brownish, as Larkin sees them; people recoil from their perceived menace, Plath writes. While they captivate us, as Saint-Exupéry describes, they also make us vulnerable to disappointment and confusion; complicated, they require high maintenance. Rather than inspiring us to song, they render us mute, Eliot reports. Devoutly attentive to the tradition of poetry, and concerned about his place in it, Eliot knew exactly what flowers had been, and what they had become. Conscious of all the fecund poetic flowers that came before him, still Eliot's gardens are predominantly feeble and dim. We get what we deserve.

The nice thing about poetic flowers is that if you don't fancy the ones at hand, you can always replace the gloomy volume and select another more to your liking. Perhaps look for an older one, just to be safe – from an age when flowers were immune to human melancholy. In *The Waste Land* Eliot looks back anxiously over his

And Chaucer's Daisy small & sweet.
"Si douce est la Margarete."

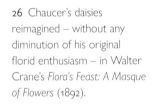

26 Chaucer's daisies reimagined – without any diminution of his original florid enthusiasm – in Walter Crane's *Flora's Feast: A Masque of Flowers* (1892).

shoulder to Chaucer, so let's give him the final flower-words, with his wonderfully overwrought paean to daisies from *The Legend of Good Women* (c. 1386), among the most unselfconscious dithyrambs to a flower ever set down in verse:

> of alle the floures in the mede,
> Than love I most these floures whyte and rede,
> Swiche as men callen daysies in our toun.
> To hem have I so great affeccioun,

As I seyde erst, whan comen is the May,
That in my bed ther daweth me no day
That I nam up, and walking in the mede
To seen this flour agein the sonne sprede,
Whan hit upryseth erly by the morwe;
That blisful sighte softneth al my sorwe,
So glad am I whan that I have presence
Of hit, to doon al maner reverence,
As she, that is of alle floures flour,
Fulfilled of al vertu and honour,
And ever y-lyke fair, and fresh of hewe;
And I love hit, and ever y-lyke newe,
And ever shal, til that myn herte dye;
Al swete I nat, of this I wol nat lye,
Ther loved no wight hotter in his lyve.[94]

'She, that is of alle floures flour': the floweriest flower that ever was. White and red, fair and fresh, virtuous and honorable; a blissful antidote to sorrow: what else needs to be said?

2

FLOWERY ART

Avant tout, je dois avoir des fleurs.
CLAUDE MONET[1]

I feel really frightened when I sit down to paint a flower.
WILLIAM HOLMAN HUNT[2]

The Pulitzer Prize-winning American poet Theodore Roethke spent much of his childhood in his family's commercial nursery, inspiring his highly regarded cycle 'The Greenhouse Poems'. 'Deep in their roots, all flowers keep the light,' he writes in 'The Stony Garden,'[3] foregrounding the *brightness* in my 'strange, bright crowds of flowers' as his insight illuminates both botanically and aesthetically.

Botanically, every plant seeks sunlight for the transformative process of photosynthesis: light energy, absorbed by proteins containing chlorophyll, becomes chemical energy. Stored in carbohydrate molecules like sugars, this energy supports the plant's growth and flowering, and also helps develop root systems, which gather more nutrients and energy. Roethke imagines harnessing light from high up above the earth to store beneath it, deep down in the darkness of soil, evoking something of the magic and mystery of flowers. Their ecosystem, omnipresent, draws energy from not only light but rain, wind, climate, geological erosion enabling soil formation, and the contiguous cycles of life – especially the lives of birds, bees, bugs and other proximate creatures – that augment flowers' energies as organisms in their habitat reproduce, die, decompose and become fertilizer. Biologically, this system is predicated upon light: *Fiat lux.*

And aesthetically: thinking of flowers as biological systems driven by light provides a luminous entrée into my gallery of artistic flowers – representations that, like their living, blooming counterparts, also 'keep the light'. We must turn on the lights to see the art in the first place (unless it is sited outside). Spectatorship begins as we perceive the colours (and of course light is made up of colours) that are probably the first- and most-noticed aspect of actual flowers: the daffodil's boundlessly rich yellow, the lantana's orange and pink, the azalea's magenta, the violet's violet. Inspired by light, these colours also reproduce light as they come together on a canvas to depict sunflowers, water lilies, lilacs or plumeria situated in vases, field and garden vistas, flower markets or other cultural forms – jewellery, furniture, wallpaper, couture – that integrate floral hues. All these representations of flowers flourish by means of human artifice – canvas and paint, sculpture, embroidery, glass blowing and so on – instead of pollen, seed, rhizome or bulb. And these crafted images, along with photographic, film or digital representations, also 'keep the light'. Like actual flowers, art flowers could not exist without light; they, too, capture and preserve this effulgent energy as they shine generation after generation. Sometimes, though, an artwork's light and colour dissipates over time: Vincent van Gogh – frustrated that the newly fabricated synthetic pigments he and his contemporaries used were less stable than traditional paints that had been hand-ground from dyes and minerals – complained to his brother, Theo: 'Les tableaux se fanent comme les fleurs' (The paintings fade like flowers).[4]

There is nothing one could paint, not even the sun itself (too incomprehensible and indistinct, too bright) that would do a better job than flowers of showing light and embodying light: depicting the beauty that light enables, and demonstrating how light is transformed into life. We can think of the sunlight that produces real flowers as analogous to the artist's light – the authentic light in her studio or in the sky and the mimetic light she fabricates by mixing paint on her palette to 'arrange' hues and shapes (as a florist arranges actual flowers) on her canvas. As we look at artistic constructions of light that mirror botanical constructions of light, note that we ourselves, as viewers, are implicated in a figurative version of heliotropism: leaning towards the light. We grow (intellectually, imaginatively, emotionally) as we perceive, transform and store these flowery cultural artefacts that are created by light.

Ancient images

Flowers have not been artistically depicted for as long as animals, which are believed to be the earliest representational subject.[5] Recently discovered seals painted by Neanderthals in Malaga's Nerja Caves are 43,000 years old,[6] and pigs and buffalo drawn on Indonesian cave walls are about the same age,[7] pre-dating what had previously been considered the earliest art, the horses, stags, bison and felines, along with (possibly) the odd human being, created 17,000 years ago by Palaeolithic artists in southern France's Lascaux cave.[8]

But flower art has caught up with – and, I would argue, surpassed – animal art in its fecundity. The Tomb of Perneb (c. 2381–2323 BCE)

27 Ancient floral decoration from the Tomb of Perneb, 2381–2323 BCE.

from the necropolis of Saqqara includes one of the earliest-known human depictions of flowers, a relief painting of bowls filled with blue lotuses from Perneb's mortuary feast.[9] Egyptian art from the fifteenth century BCE began to feature floral representations (again, mainly lotuses) more commonly in paintings, ceramics, jewellery and amulets. Flowers were not just a subject but also a medium: Tutankhamun's embalming cache (c. 1325 BCE) contained a necklace made of linen interspersed with cut blossoms – symbolizing rebirth – from sunflowers, cornflowers, poppies and blue lotuses.[10]

Once flowers started flourishing in art, they bloomed everywhere: Mediterranean mosaics, medieval codices, Tang dynasty landscape paintings, Mayan murals, Aztec temples, Renaissance tapestries, and on and on. They were in the foreground and background, on the frames as well as the canvas; they were stylized, or adapted into emblems, wallpaper designs and architectural motifs. Flowers were depicted growing, or cut and arranged in a still-life; sometimes in precise botanical detail, sometimes abstract.

'Flowers have been very lucky in the world of art,' write curators Paul Hulton and Lawrence Smith. 'On the whole those who have painted and drawn them have enjoyed them, whatever their object in depicting them.' Not William Holman Hunt, judging by my epigraph. I have been unable to dig up any further details about his botanical anxiety (and his paintings are indeed notably less flowery than the Pre-Raphaelite norm). But few artists evince this sort of apprehension: much more commonly, they follow Auguste Rodin's harmonious sentiment that the artist is 'the confidant of nature' and plants 'talk to him like friends . . . The flowers commune with him by the gracious swaying of their stalks, by the singing tones of their petals – each blossom amidst the grass is a friendly word addressed to him by nature.'[11] (Remember Lewis Carroll's Tiger-lily, happy to talk to anyone worth talking to.) Flowers have 'mostly escaped the attentions of artists who wished only to express

28 Floral floor mosaic in Masada's Byzantine church, 5th century CE.

themselves'.[12] I like the idea that floral beauty self-selects for non-egotistical admirers. I will pluck and arrange a few small blossoms from this vast floral corpus to explore what happens as flowers become art.

Renaissance flowers: Dürer and Brueghel

In sixteenth-century pictorial traditions, floral depictions trumpeted scientific progress. Albrecht Dürer's paintings exemplify such naturalist method. *Tuft of Cowslips* highlights the plant's organic forms – leaves, stems, blossoms – as well as nuances of colour which make this image seem consummately alive in ways that earlier flowers didn't. Other German artists immediately began to imitate him, leading to a tradition of precise nature studies. Such images, reflecting disciplinary advances in description and classification, helped viewers identify plants and learn about newly discovered species.[13] He is known to have drawn or painted at least a dozen botanical studies, including peonies, a martagon (or 'Turk's cap') lily, some common bugloss, columbine, greater celandine (which he would have called *Schöllkraut*), and two different studies of irises. But the crisp botanical detail of Dürer's flowers, their scientific functionality, does not impede their austere Teutonic splendour.

In the early seventeenth century flowers became prominent in the still-life genre. Jan Brueghel the Elder, with sixteen such paintings, was nicknamed 'Flower' Brueghel. His *Big Bouquet in a Wooden Vessel*, one of the art world's pre-eminent still-lifes, reflects not a real bouquet 'but rather an encyclopaedic overview of rare species. In the highly meticulous, virtuoso reproduction of 130 different flowers, art and scientific interest unite.'[14] The painting almost resembles a museum case, befitting a period that produced some of the first

29 Albrecht Dürer,
Tuft of Cowslips, 1526,
gouache on vellum.

112

illustrated natural-history catalogues and encyclopaedias.[15] The smaller flowers near the top – tulips, snowdrops, periwinkles – could not possibly have stems long enough to reach down into the bucket so that they would stay hydrated. But this is less a literal flower arrangement than it is an archive, a bricolage. 'In this picture I have accomplished all of which I am capable,' Brueghel writes in a letter. 'I do not believe that so many rare and varied flowers have ever been painted, and with such diligence.'[16]

Paintings like this make viewers feel as if they are 'entering a psychedelic version of a florist's shop,' writes art critic Alastair Sooke:

> spot-lit and radiant, a profusion of intensely coloured blooms and sinuous, tangled stems, massed closely together like freakishly fabulous specimens cultivated by a supernaturally gifted grower . . . Despite their breathtaking illusionism, detailing with bejewelled precision individual blooms, as well as insects including silkworms, butterflies and sundry other critters, they do not reflect reality . . . A typical Dutch flower painting presents a panoply of rare petals that could never actually bloom together at the same time. In other words, it is a construct, a botanical impossibility, an exercise in sublime artifice pieced together from earlier studies.[17]

Such unrealistic still-life tableaux were considered improvements upon actual flowers, featuring effects that Nature could not equal.

Collecting flowers, in tandem with painting flowers, had become a passion in the Netherlands during Brueghel's lifetime. The most

30 Jan Brueghel the Elder, *Big Bouquet in a Wooden Vessel*, 1606–7, oil on canvas.

prized art featured especially unusual (strange, bright) blooms, many imported from the Balkans, Asia and the New World.[18] They were not usually painted from real specimens, which were inaccessible or too expensive. Instead, artists used cheat-sheets: *tulpenboeken*, for example, catalogues for buyers of these valuable flowers and bulbs, contained images that became models for floral still-lifes (see illus. 54). Brueghel and his contemporaries composed their canvases by a technique not so different from what we would today call Photoshopping.

Dutch flower-painting testified to contemporary senses of wealth ('tulipmania' imbued flowers with an explicit and exaggerated market value), control and imperial power. Artists from this age of global discovery and conquest construe flowers as cosmopolitan souvenirs or proof of travel; as a claim to newly colonized territories; as possessions, as inventory, as commodity, as mastery (encyclopaedic, intellectual, scientific); and as agricultural prowess that advanced self-flattering Edenic typologies. Not to put too fine a point on it, these are very loaded flowers. Like animals in zoos and menageries, and also like such other commodifications of nature as ivory carvings, tea and silk, flowers serve as exotic beauty/booty that casts the imperial enterprise as graceful, aesthetic, luxurious. (And today? On some level, I'd say, flowers cannot escape this legacy. To a considerable extent, flowers are mainly for rich people; they accessorize prosperity.)

The longer one studies *Big Bouquet*, the more one discovers. It is difficult at first to discern the individual specimens in this overwhelming crowd, but eventually singular details emerge: a dragonfly, just by the centre of the bucket; a few strawberries near the bottom, and also some rosemary, induce me to (figuratively) sniff the painting for its olfactory notes. I see several irises (the painting is

sometimes known as *Bouquet with Irises*); lilies and tulips; a few daffodils; lots of carnations; a stalk of hyacinth. Ranunculus? A wild
rose near the top? And a larger white rose, facing backwards, in the
centre. A few laggard specimens sprawl on the table; could Brueghel
not fit them into the bucket? Were they not flowery enough? Did
they wilt, or just fall off? (Vanitas: flowers are transitory.) Finally,
after I think I have seen all the strange, bright specimens that are
'keeping the light', I notice the darkness, the striking, deep empti-
ness of Brueghel's background: beyond the bouquet, where there
are no flowers, there is nothing.

Flowery fabrics: Palampores

Flowers in decor – crafts and useful objects that circulate mainly
outside museums – often get marginalized in the canon of high
art. Eighteenth-century Indian palampores (from the Hindi *palang-
posh*, bedcover) are florally voluptuous: rich and complex, delightful
and fashionable, these flowers hold their own alongside all the
other strange, bright crowds. The vibrant, detailed cloths under-
went an elaborate manufacturing process: the ancient *kalamkari*
technique involved steeping the fabric first in bleach and cow dung,
then buffalo milk; washing it dozens of times to eliminate the
odour; hand drawing with a tamarind twig and also block printing;
dyeing, sun-drying and starching. Made in the open air near a river,
a palampore took months to complete. The painters, lower-caste
families creating fabrics for wealthy patrons, worked together,
each responsible for a different part of the project.[19]

Like Emily Dickinson's little Arctic flower 'wandering down
the latitudes', palampores, too, enact far-flung floral migrations.
The textiles travelled around the world to please European and

American customers; the East India Company's palampore trade became one of their most lucrative product lines. And culturally, too, the flowers depicted on these cloths were diasporic: local reinterpretations, somewhat fantastical, of such unfamiliar non-native flowers as geraniums and chrysanthemums – arranged around a serpentine tree-of-life at centre, which *was* an Indian motif – adapted from sample pattern books that European merchants sent to the palampore factories. The stylized flowers seem evocative of William Morris's famous patterns and he did indeed admire the Indian textiles. Criticizing fabric production in his own time, he writes approvingly of 'that character which you so easily recognize in Indian palampores' that retain their appeal for so many generations: 'we are always attracted towards them, and the chief reason is, we feel at once that there is something about the designs natural to the craft.'[20] It seems likely that palampores influenced the patterns, styles and colours of Morris's own fabric designs. Popular as wall hangings, bed and table coverings, curtains and pelmets, palampores were made mostly for European export (especially to the Netherlands and Britain), but also sometimes for intra-Asian sale: the example shown was made on India's Coromandel coast and marketed to Sri Lanka's European communities.[21] Like Brueghel's *Big Bouquet in a Wooden Vessel* and many other visual celebrations of flowers, this Indian genre reflects the sensibility that more is better: I counted more than one hundred individual flowers on the border of this palampore before I gave up, and there seem to be at least as many more blossoms in the interior.

31 Indian painted cotton palampore, early 18th century.

Flowers with text: Botanical illustrations, Chinese fans

Botanical illustrations appear early in the tradition of floral art, though there is disagreement over whether they should be considered as art or as science. The images may be dismissed as 'merely copying', though that subjective distinction could disqualify almost any work of art. *Art* and *science* do not seem mutually exclusive to me. I will simply opine that botanical drawings can be extremely beautiful, thoughtful, captivating, resonant and flowery, suggesting (to my mind) that they are indeed, impeccably, flower art; and, obviously, they serve scientific purposes as well. They are commonly reproduced as decorative items in homes and offices, on tea towels and placemats, suggesting that their appeal – their composition, their aesthetics, their historical resonance, and their depiction of flowers as both simple natural beauty and object of scientific knowledge – endures as strongly today as it did in original iterations. Most flowers that we encounter, whether real or in cultural representations, are seen and enjoyed holistically. With its text and graphics, its contextualizing terminology and diagrams, botanical drawing reminds us that there is more to a flower than meets the eye: underlying aspects that scientists from an earlier time 'discovered' and recorded, in a discourse that still today spotlights a flower's hidden complexities.

In addition to depicting vividly detailed images of flowers and flower parts, botanical illustrations often include text with names and information about the specimen and its life cycle. (See illus. 7, 23, 33 and 54 for examples of drawings augmented with text; though some, like illus. 32, have none.) In times when artists lacked direct access to certain flowers, such reference works served as copybooks for their own renderings. The golden age of botanical drawing was

32 The first artist to graphically capture the process of metamorphosis, Maria Sibylla Merian drew a banana flower and plant, along with the insects it nurtured, for her 1705 book *Metamorphosis Insectorum Surinamensium.*

Monadelphia Polyandria

Bombax ceiba, of Linnæus.

Seemul.

1750 to 1850, though the practice goes back at least as far as the first century CE, when the Greek botanist Pedanius Dioscorides created a 'herbal', as such works are known. *De materia medica*, which identified and illustrated plant species for medicinal purposes, was copied many times over the following centuries.[22]

Eighteenth-century botanical discoveries, advances in printing techniques, and patronage for books and collections of botanical illustrations produced masterworks by such artists as Maria Sibylla Merian. Considered the world's first ecologist, because she depicted insects' life cycles against the background of their host plants, Merian drew flowers which blossomed with a brash, vibrant exuberance that seems ahead of its time. Franz Bauer, who worked at Kew's Royal Botanic Gardens for half a century and served as 'Botanick Painter to his Majesty', studied new-flowering plants as they were acquired and specialized in painting orchids; his brother, Ferdinand, travelled on botanical explorations to Greece and Australia and depicted the flowers he encountered. Anne Pratt, a Victorian artist, helped popularize botany by writing and illustrating more than twenty books. Marianne North travelled the world painting flowers – more than nine hundred species from seventeen countries – which are now displayed in a gallery at Kew that bears her name. Naturalist, artist and philosopher Ernst Haeckel drew flowers and other life forms with a mesmerizing complexity that engaged viewers in the mysteries of the natural world.

Chinese flower-fan drawings do not provide the same function as botanical illustrations, but they do have a significant point of relation, which is the common inclusion of some sort of text that augments or contextualizes the image. Chen Hengke's modern fan drawing *Narcissus and Orchid*, for example, recalling similar compositions of fragrant flowers by the eighteenth-century painters Wu

33 Cotton tree flowers, c. 1800. The British engaged local artists (whose names are often, as here, unrecorded) to depict the flora in their imperial territories. The Seemal tree blooms with bright orange flowers and when its fruits split open, silky fronds of cotton waft to the ground, which are collected and used to fill pillows.

123

Changshi and Li Futang, and the sixteenth-century painter Chen Chun, includes a calligraphic inscription informing that it 'is inspired by the Xiao and Xiang Rivers. The fragrance is wafted by the River Luo.'[23]

In Chinese flower-fan calligraphy the writing is at least as important an element as the drawing. Calligraphic fans have been made since at least the Ming and Qing dynasties, reaching back to the fourteenth century. Eighteenth-century Europeans would have seen such fans in museums and private collections, so the combination of flowers and text in botanical illustrations may well have been influenced by those Asian artworks. The text on European botanical drawings was fairly laconic – usually just names of the flowers, both common and scientific, and labelling of various botanical details – although some textual commentaries (especially from French botanists) expand upon sparse scientific discourse to offer more florid narratives: In Étienne Denisse's *Flore d'Amérique* (1846), for example, his illustration of cotton tree flowers – native to India (see illus. 33), but also found in such American tropical climates as the Caribbean islands, where he painted – carries this text: 'After the giant baobab tree comes this one; with its trunk one can make big canoes or dugouts in one piece, for sailing on the sea. Its cotton is good for making mattresses and wadding; its bark cures chest inflammation, and its root causes vomiting.'[24]

Chinese calligraphy, as the *Narcissus and Orchid* fan shows (illus. 34), tends to be more subjective and poetic than the language accompanying European botanical illustrations. If the fans are less scientifically explanatory than European botanical texts, they are still, albeit more impressionistically, ecologically descriptive. They might describe where the flowers were found (a detail that botanical drawing, too, could include), as in the simple inscription on Hu

34 Chen Hengke, *Narcissus and Orchid*, 1920, folding fan mounted as an album leaf.

Yuan's nineteenth-century fan *Herbaceous Peony*: 'The resplendent beauty of Fengtai.'[25] The fan might also express the artist's sensation as sparked by the flora. A 1941 fan, *Lychees*, by Ding Fuzhi, depicting both flowers and fruit, includes the calligraphic inscription: 'This delicious and rare fruit grows in warm places. A traveller shipped a basket to me. After eating the fruit I felt happy and in a mood to paint. The day I finished this picture was one of unending pleasure.'[26] Often there is an homage to an earlier artist, emphasizing the centuries-long tradition of such combinations of art and text. 'Once I saw a handscroll by Chen Laolian depicting a branch of apricots,' reads the calligraphy on Wu Xizai's nineteenth-century fan *Apricot*. 'His inscription mentions that it is in the style of a Yuan master. I have imitated it. Dedicated to Zihong.'[27] Botanical illustrators, too – though less explicit about citing their influences – follow keenly in the footsteps of earlier artists, botanists and explorers; their genre depends on received tradition as much as the art of Chinese fans does.

There is a remarkable consistency in the style and composition of Chinese floral images over time: a distinctive delicacy, simplicity, understatement, as if the flowers need little elaborate or heavy-handed intervention by a human artist. Unlike the sense that European botanical drawings give, of laborious, slow, careful composition, the fan images usually seem quickly sketched in ink and watercolour, not out of carelessness or inattention but rather to convey a sense that these flowers' aesthetic beauty is obvious, natural and easily represented. The simplicity of an Asian flower drawing often evokes, for me, the simplicity of a flower's beauty, perhaps more immediately and more convincingly than a highly artificed image.

Photographic flowers: Bayard and Atget

Twentieth-century flower photography presents eclectic, creative compositions in such touchstones as Imogen Cunningham's dramatic 'portraits' of morning glories, flowering cacti and calla lilies; Man Ray's vivid and weirdly lit close-ups of sunflowers, passion flowers, hibiscus and also calla lilies; erotic floral tableaux by Nobuyoshi Araki, where botanical furrows and protuberances have suggestive undertones; and the work of Robert Mapplethorpe, whose flowers radiate a stark physical sensuality.

Their nineteenth-century forebears photographed flowers in ways that may seem more documentarian than artistic. Like botanical illustration, early flower photography has been commonly considered technological rather than creative, relegated to the tradition of science rather than art – but twentieth-century flower-art photographers owe those first generations a debt that exceeds merely scientific experimentation and innovation.

Early flower photography richly embodies creative and imaginative potency. It would be both a silly and impossible task to depict a flower in a way that was not somehow aesthetically charged. How could flower photographs not be artistic when the subjects are inherently so full of form and drama, life and colour? The colour, of course, could not be captured in those first photographs, but it was an absent referent: photographer and viewer both knew flowers were profusely colourful, and likely they imagined those colours in their minds' eyes when they saw black-and-white images.

As pioneers in a new medium, nineteenth-century photographers presented flowers in ways that painters couldn't. If the loss of colour forsakes a significant store of inherent beauty, photographers made up for it through the penetrating, almost supernatural, discourse of light. Their photographs allow viewers to see 'inside' and 'through' the flowers, glimpsing their essences in entrancing and aesthetically compelling ways.

I highlight two French photographers, Hippolyte Bayard and Eugène Atget. If later artists like Cunningham and Mapplethorpe depicted flowers' moods and characters with extraordinary resonance, so too did Bayard, in his own way. He discovered the power that inhered not in the flower's image, or adaptation, or symbolism, but in the flower itself. He saw (and conveyed) beauty, magic and other perceptual revelations that propelled forwards the genre of flower art.

Bayard's camera-less direct positive process involved darkening a paper coated with salt water and silver nitrate in the sun, then smearing potassium iodide on it and exposing it, fixing the image with ammonia. For these 'photograms' or 'photogenic drawings', Bayard arranged various objects, frequently flowers, on this treated (light-sensitive) paper and then exposed it to light. Each flower's opacity blocks the light in relation to its density, creating a silhouette-like outline on the paper, but not a monochromatically dark one: shades of light appear proportionate to the lightness of the flowery subject. Thick leaves and stems block out more light, and thus appear lighter in the (negative) image that remains, than delicately diaphanous petals, which appear a bit darker, paradoxically, because they allow some light through.

Bayard's composition (illus. 35) recalls Emily Dickinson's herbarium (compiled at almost the same time): his flowers present a similar kind of display, with a comparable sense of botanical variety and plenitude. His images captivated audiences as novel representations of the flowers they had seen often before in

35 Arrangement of flowers by Hippolyte Bayard (c. 1839–43), salted paper print, negative.

gardens and vases, paintings and fabrics. These specimens, which resemble real (pressed) flowers, live forever, and they do so – as in Roethke's dictum – by keeping the light. The light that originally nurtured these flowers, coupled with the light that Bayard channelled for his reproduction, hits us with direct force as we look at this arrangement. Each flower retains its own size, form and design, but all the colours have become uniform, generalized as simply, purely, light. Stems, leaves, bracts and calyx diffuse the same nuanced light (in varying intensity) as petals and blossoms. The flowers in this powerful new trope explode like freeze-framed fireworks.

Detached from any kind of familiar human or natural context – a garden or meadow, a vase, a botanical diagram – Bayard's flowers float in space, their unusual and eerie light making them seem to hover in a dreamy tableau. If flowers have generally been used in the service of beauty, courtship, wealth, cultural metaphor and design, Bayard's disembodied forms seem to defy all that. As nineteenth-century viewers looked at these images, they must have been defamiliarized by the medium. Whether as artist or scientist (or both), Bayard achieves a strikingly idiosyncratic achievement in affect and aesthetic. Not a tussie-mussie or a still-life, these flowers in splayed, random array are liberated from any pre-existing tradition (as they initiate a new one). The only governing principle seems to be to get as many blooms as possible, a lush profusion, onto the light-paper without making too overwhelming a display. 'Arrangement' has always been a key aspect of presenting flowers, but here the visual novelty of the medium and its requirements takes precedence over the arranging. It disrupts (and even deconstructs, *avant* Jacques Derrida) the long-established forms and patterns of flowers.

Twentieth-century photographers would return to Bayard's early camera-less technique to create 'retro' images: László Moholy-Nagy, Berenice Abbott, Imogen Cunningham, Man Ray and Christian Schad all experimented with this process (which Ray called 'rayographs' and Schad called 'Schadographs', following photographers' self-promoting tradition that commenced with Louis Daguerre's daguerreotypes).[28]

A half-century after Bayard another French photographer, Eugène Atget, began a career-long enterprise to capture the city of Paris, notably focusing on its ubiquitous flowers. As with Bayard, one might question whether Atget regarded himself as a full-fledged artist or as a supporter of artists – a supplier of resources. In the 1890s a shingle outside his 5th arrondissement studio read 'Documents pour artistes': he provided textile designers, wallpaper designers and painters with sourced images that they would use for their own creations. But his work strongly influenced and inspired later practitioners. The eminent American nature photographer Ansel Adams dismissed any implication that his French antecedent was a mere handmaid to artists when he called Atget's prints 'direct and emotionally clean records of a rare and subtle perception, [which] represent perhaps the earliest expression of true photographic art'.[29]

Atget's image of a cluster of lilies against an out-of-focus background that features dozens more (illus. 36) highlights both the appeal of a large mass of flowers and the more precise appreciation of a few seen up close. As in Bayard's monochromatic images, the flourish of colour is lost here, perhaps the flower's most important sensory aspect, we might think – though such later photographers as Mapplethorpe and Helmut Newton, too, often opted to produce flower images in black and white, highlighting

a formalist aesthetic, at a time when they obviously could have
created coloured photographs if they had wanted to (and indeed
they sometimes did). In monochromatic floral images,[30] we may
regret the loss of multicoloured allure, but we may not immediately
notice a compensatory power. In the absence of natural colour, the
viewer is all the more attuned to composition and form, which
Agtet 'focuses' on both metaphorically and literally in this new
medium. The perspective on his lilies, simultaneously focused and
unfocused in appearance, makes them seem spatially off balance

– a surreal 'arrangement', unsettled and unsettling. It may seem as if the foreground flowers are growing towards the viewer, reaching out, inviting us to lean in and meet them halfway. Atget shows us clear flowers and blurry flowers, challenging his readers to appreciate a multiplicity of perceptual and spatial points of engagement with these lilies. He invites us to stop and smell the flowers . . . and then, perhaps, to perambulate further (perceptually – imaginatively) across the frame to see more of them close-up, where we might again (figuratively) pause to enjoy them.

Glass flowers: Chihuly and the Blaschkas

Atget and his contemporary photographers used glass (plates, lenses) and light to depict flowers, but actual glass flowers are another example of how the vitreous medium figures in artistic traditions. Glass sculptor Dale Chihuly oversees a famous and prodigious franchise that utilizes teams of subcontracted artisans to produce hundreds of floral artworks, enlivening gardens and conservatories, office buildings, hotels and museums worldwide.

His flowers show the influence of Louis Comfort Tiffany and Venetian Murano glass: Chihily's training included a Tiffany Foundation fellowship and an apprenticeship at Venice's Venini Fabrica. The extensive number of installations and other merchandise that his Seattle studio produces – for both museum exhibitions and commercial galleries – prejudices some in the contemporary art world to regard his work as decor rather than high art, because there is simply too much of it. He has alienated many in the art world and beyond who accuse him of outsourcing his art to a production-line factory, exploiting his studio staff and not crediting the team of workers who contribute significantly to his creations.

37 Glass flowers in a glass house: Dale Chihuly's 2005 Kew Garden exhibition.

Yet however we adjudicate their aesthetic pedigree, Chihuly's flowers dazzle, colourful and ebullient, in their profuse and delicate unreality, attracting large crowds of human audiences eager to experience the buzz of his installations, just as real flowers attract the buzz of bees. His glass flowers 'keep the light', in Roethke's words, stunningly. More than once I have overheard spectators at Chihuly exhibitions remark that his sculptures are as beautiful as stained-glass windows – the ancient genre widely considered the most exquisite glass art in our culture – in terms of how intricately they interact with sunlight to achieve a glorious symbiosis with the world around and above them. People sit and watch Chihuly's art, as they watch windows in medieval cathedrals, to see the sunlight dance, shining and fading as it filters through the coloured glass. My favourite venue for seeing Chihuly's work is in botanical gardens: numerous travelling exhibitions blossom every season in conservatories around the world, and permanent installations may be seen at Crystal Bridges gardens in Bentonville, Arkansas; Frederik Meijer Gardens in Grand Rapids, Michigan; the DeCordova Museum Sculpture Park in Lincoln, Massachusetts; and Hakone, Japan's Glass Forest – where his glass blooms amid the real flowers, amplifying the beauty of nature and art in tandem. Chihuly's flowery artworks seem especially delicate outdoors – and yet, like actual flowers, they survive and flourish perfectly well.

In contrast to decorative artefacts like Chihuly's, the medium of glass is also felicitous to 'naturalistic flowers', a term which means 'that the artist *looked at* and *analysed* that flower before working, or while working', curators Paul Hulton and Lawrence Smith write, and 'that they were seeing the flower more "really" rendered than before.' This might convey 'more accurate detail of structure', or 'the sense of the plant's being alive'.[31] Decorative flowers, on the other hand, are merely pretty, they suggest, in what seems like another science vs art contretemps.

In any case, the Harvard Museum of Natural History's world-famous glass-flower collection epitomizes the naturalistic tradition. Leopold and Rudolf Blaschka, nineteenth-century German glass artisans (father and son), practised their family craft – the lineage of which dates back to the fifteenth century. Harvard's Botanical Museum founder, George Lincoln Goodale, wanted lifelike representations of flowers for teaching botany and rejected the crude models available at the time. The Blaschkas' main business had been fabricating costume jewellery, chandelier attachments and

38 *Rhododendron maximum*: visitors commonly praise Leopold and Rudolf Blaschka's glass flowers, found in Harvard's Museum of Natural History, as being prettier than the real thing.

other luxury goods, but some marine specimens and flowers they had made just for themselves caught Goodale's attention. He commissioned them to create a 4,300-piece collection over half a century (1887–1936), featuring 847 species with remarkably accurate anatomical sections and enlarged flower parts.

Their process, flameworking, was an old technique in which rods of glass were bent with pliers, made malleable after having

been heated over a small burner[32] (supplying the *light* that these flowers *keep*). 'Flowers are perishable,' Goodale explained at the museum's 1890 dedication. 'When dried they are distorted, when placed in alcohol they are robbed of their color.' Drawings, while 'spirited and truthful', were flat. Wax or papier-mâché flowers, sometimes used in funeral wreaths, were 'exaggerated and grotesque'.[33] In addition to more accurately representing the real thing, glass flowers are also liberated from seasonal cycles and ephemeral life-spans: since they are always in bloom, 'tropical and temperate species may be studied year-round'.[34] While Harvard's specimens are eternal, still they

39 Pane of 15th-century stained glass in the chancel of St Peter's Church, Cowfold, West Sussex.

have their own material precariousness: the first shipment, roughly handled by customs officials, arrived in pieces. But even so, Goodale could see how fine the work was.[35]

Both Chihuly's and the Blaschkas' flowers resplendently keep the light: the translucent medium of glass celebrates the interactivity of colour, form and light. And as realistic and educational as Harvard's specimens are designed to be, there is nothing remotely unlovely about them: 'naturalistic' and 'decorative' flowers are not mutually exclusive, if such a distinction even exists.

There's nothing new under the sun: glass flowers have been around for centuries. They feature prominently in medieval stained glass: in foregrounds and backgrounds, borders and individualized depictions. Like many in this medium, these simple and geometrically precise flowers mirror the larger geometries of the window's glass and lead ribbing. The forms and colours, however pleasing on their own terms, are incomparably enchanted by the light when it shines through to illuminate the flowers both aesthetically and, in a sense, botanically, showing again how flowers 'keep the light' in multiple senses.

40 Egyptian glass plaque (100 BCE–100 CE).

Glass flowers flourished even many centuries before these medieval representations. Flowered glass plaques made in Egypt during the Ptolemaic and Roman periods served as interior decorations. The small plaque depicting nelumbo lotus flowers was created by fusing mosaic canes, coloured strips, and chips of blue-green glass, then polishing it smooth. While it is one of the oldest images discussed in this book, its style and aesthetic are surprisingly contemporary, timeless: these flowers would not seem out of place in a beaux-arts ceramic tile or a Marimekko fabric design. The sharp colours, the vibrant forms, the jouissance of these brightly dancing lotuses all suggest a cultural universality that makes sense in light of the fact that, as Gertrude Stein (almost) said, a flower is a flower is a flower is a flower.

Symbolist flowers: Redon

Odilon Redon's early twentieth-century still-life arrangements are less precise and 'naturalistic' than Brueghel's. Symbolism, the movement in which he was a leading figure, depicted alternative experiences beyond the rational logic of naturalism and impressionism, which for Redon means infusing flowers with heightened luminosity and sensuous form. Having worked almost exclusively in black and white for two decades – his famous earlier 'noirs' were dark, foreboding, spectral charcoal drawings – Redon changed tack and engaged with colour late in his career, a development that culminated in flower paintings that feature sparkling colourful patches against a misty field.

Brueghel's heaping bucketful of flowers, exhaustive and overwhelming, contrasts with Redon's quieter still-life. Brueghel conveys the weight of flowers, their abundance, their suprafloral semiotic import and their imperial pedigree, all of which befitted his moment in the tradition and his relationship to Dutch society. And so, too, is Redon age-appropriate in his determination to lighten his flowers, to strip them of their cultural burdens. A build-up in the thickness of form, detail and ornamentation that had increased for centuries in European art begins to abate in the modern age as artists pare away the excess. 'Less is more,' said the German architect Ludwig Mies van der Rohe, at the same moment in time as Redon was painting.

Redon re-enflowers his flowers, returning them closer to what they actually are. They do not domineer or preen, or celebrate their culture's hegemony; they are intended simply to delight, characteristic of the resurgence of decorative arts and crafts in the late nineteenth and early twentieth centuries. Flowers of Europe's

41 Odilon Redon, *Flowers in a Vase*, c. 1910, oil on canvas.

138

imperial aesthetic were prone to extravagance, and profusely embellished. The art of flowers seemed to demand, voraciously, more flowers, and then still more, until the artefact overbrimmed. Artists of Redon's era were prone to present, instead, *enough* flowers: not too many.

If the flowers arranged in Brueghel's paintings seemed contrived – unwieldy, impossible – Redon's seem more natural and honest. The logic of their arrangement and presentation is guided solely by the flowers themselves: the colours, the shapes. Longer-stemmed flowers appear higher; species and forms are chosen to go with each other, just as any painting seeks a compositional balance. If Brueghel's flowers were difficult to take in (because there are so many, all clamouring for our attention) until we examined his canvas meticulously, Redon's canvases require no such challenge: we may see everything at first glance. And then certainly we may still, as we do with Brueghel's art, keep looking at the painting, moving our eyes around the arrangement at our own pace, dwelling on the clusters of daisies or chrysanthemums as our fancy inclines. I think a viewer who spends a spell of time looking at Redon's flowers doesn't necessarily discover more previously unnoticed details, but rather may enjoy her first impression of the flowers, and then the same again, and once more, as long as she regards the image.

Redon's *Vase of Flowers* (see illus. 2), at the head of my introduction, strikes me as a prototypical image, a clear and simple starting point, wonderfully obvious at the same time as it is luxuriantly graceful. Two more of his paintings, *Flowers in a Vase* and *Wildflowers*, differ in some details but exhibit the same fingerprint (flower-print?). I wonder why still-lifes tend to have such dull, formulaic titles. So as not to steal the flowers' thunder? Because . . . what else could they be called?

42 Odilon Redon, *Wildflowers*, c. 1905, pastel on paper.

The backgrounds are artfully, but not distractingly, speckled with light and colour. They are as strikingly light as Brueghel's background is dark. The effect, I think, is that while Brueghel's flowers seem to be full of bright light, it is a light restricted to the flowers themselves, whereas Redon's blossoms seem to spread some portion of their light and colour onto the rest of the canvas (and implicitly, beyond). If both painters' flowers 'keep the light', Brueghel's keep it for themselves while Redon's keep it for all, come who may.

The large, curvy vases that Redon collected – colourful, formally striking – feature understated tones which complement, but do not compete with, the flowers' colours. Symbolist aesthetics explain why they seem to be poised on barely suggested tables, as if they are hovering. (Compare this floating appearance with the solidity of the big wooden vessel that anchors Brueghel's still-life.) But it is the flowers themselves, and nothing else, that dazzle and please. Their colours, wild and wonderful, are not random. In *Flowers in a Vase*, we detect groupings of different (but similar) shades of red, mostly at the bottom and moving into the centre; a counterpoised array of blues at top right also reaches towards the centre, and a path of whites and light yellows moves through and alongside the blues and reds. Symbolists featured such vivid colours as an expressive element, independent of form – prominent colours, rather than line or shading, typify the depiction of form.

The flowers are identifiable, or almost identifiable, as carnations (or possibly zinnias?), daisies and blue cornflowers, the last of which thankfully manifest no hint of fascism: indeed, one could scarcely imagine a more apolitical and purely, proudly, decorative grouping. Added to this is a bit of greenery from the leaves at the bottom. Leaves rarely get their due in considerations of flowers, an oversight that I regret perpetuating myself; they are more prominent in Japanese flower arrangements. Flower-masters 'always associate the leaves, if there be any, with the flower,' writes Kakuzō Okakura, 'for the object is to present the whole beauty of plant life,' while in Western arrangements, 'we are apt to see only the flower stems, heads as it were, without body, stuck promiscuously into a vase.'[36]

Redon's *Wildflowers*, similarly, features thematic colour groupings – here, orange, yellow and blue (more cornflowers), with, again, a frame of leafy greenery – and a display of forms and shapes that could certainly be compositionally anatomized, as one does with a painting, but could also be regarded, with little sacrifice of artistic insight, as simply a group of flowers: from a florist's bouquet perhaps, or also quite possibly, freshly picked (perhaps even by an amateur!) in a garden or a field. Both paintings show the flowers 'arranged', but not fussily or formally: more as if they were simply put into the vase, with perhaps a quick consideration of heights and masses. One senses that there is not a great deal of intervention or studied arrangement here, not much symbolic fodder, no drama, no moral allegory. It is mostly, resplendently, flowers – simple, fresh, beautiful, full stop. Redon makes it look easy to paint flowers, and easy to enjoy them. The art here – though of course it is Redon's art – seems almost as if it is the flowers themselves: he lets them convey their own beauty.

Minimalism/maximalism: Van der Leck and O'Keeffe

The flowers in Bart van der Leck's *Lilies* are slight, sketchy almost to the point of evanescence, but I would argue that they are nevertheless (against the odds) full-fledged flowers, and even that they are pretty. The colours, shapes and visual organization evoke Piet

Mondrian's De Stijl aesthetic, where representationality gives way to – or *evolves into*, as a more sympathetic viewer might put it – mere elemental colours and basic geometric forms. 'De Stijl' means, simply, 'the style'; van der Leck, alongside Mondrian and Theo van Doesburg, was among its founders in 1917, though he subsequently rejected the movement. His work, however, retained the familiar abstraction (intended to suggest universality) of simplified compositions featuring a limited range of basic shapes and colours.

Lilies might strike some as a diminution of flowers, which embody so much more nuance in real life than the artist's simple arrangement of dash outlines and polygons conveys. Reflecting on all the resplendent curves and contours, the rich shades and dynamism, that artists like Claude Monet and Vincent van Gogh celebrate so sumptuously, we might almost wonder if van der Leck has quite finished his painting; perhaps it is just a draft.

But precisely since we *do* know what flowers and flower paintings look like, bringing with us detailed familiarity with the still-life (of which museumgoers will have seen many in other rooms on the way to this one), van der Leck need not do all that foundational work himself: he doesn't have to reinvent the wheel. Perhaps it is the viewer's task – and not such a difficult one – to fill in the dots here. We are invited to help 'paint' this picture ourselves, fleshing out the detail and becoming actively aware of how resonant flowers are, even in this strangely skimpy depiction, and how well we can recognize their prolific beauty even with only the faintest prompt. 'Good continuation', a term from Gestalt psychology's principles of perceptual organization, describes how people may intuit a wholeness and unity in an image even when pieces are missing: in our minds we continue and complete what is not explicitly evident, but suggested.

Floral minimalism: Bart van der Leck's *Lilies*, 1922, oil on canvas.

Van der Leck's minimalism suggests a pared-down, less-is-more iteration of *Big Bouquet in a Wooden Vessel*. Brueghel's and van der Leck's paintings are in some sense opposites, but opposites are two sides of the same coin, making it possible to appreciate similarities in these two paintings that at first seemed so different.

Or perhaps *Lilies* connotes the exhaustion of flowers, and van der Leck is simply bored of painting the same old angiospermae that others have been painting for centuries, so this is his way of telling us that the genre is dissipating. Proposing both affirmative and subversive statements about the visual beauty of flowers and the still-life tradition, this painting triggers its audience to decide on the spot where we take this: how we extrapolate van der Leck's aesthetic, or solve his riddle. We may pursue either a defensive or deconstructive analysis of flowers, and art-flowers; van der Leck has set the stage for a good, rousing argument.

While I can see how this painting might disappoint some viewers – promising something as wonderful as lilies and then only barely sustaining that undertaking – I am more inclined to see it as testimony to the enduring strength of flowers. These aren't conventional blooms, nor are they in any way photorealistic, or aesthetically traditional. But it isn't that hard to see the lilies, despite the strange, bright aesthetic, and to imagine that van der Leck is just trying to do something new with flowers, to make his own mark. With just primary colours, simple, straightforward lines and forms, and clean visual elements – a reaction against what De Stijl artists perceived as the florid deluge of Art Deco and the excessive detail of a neo-Baroque resurgence – van der Leck is trying to be of his time, and to depict flowers that are, similarly, of his time.

As luxuriant as Georgia O'Keeffe's paintings are – an antithesis to van der Leck's slight forms – they too can be construed as minimalistic in that they depict simply and fully flowers: nothing extraneous, nothing contextual. Everything else has been stripped away. In this regard, O'Keeffe, who spent most of her life painting unusual and spectacular flowers, was a kindred spirit to Emily Dickinson, whose own minimalism – short lines and compact images that convey the literary equivalent of full-frame flowers – helps illuminate O'Keeffe's. Both immersed themselves in flowers, and both seemed to see in flowers, and then to convey in their creations, a cosmos of vibrant, life-affirming beauty that emanated therefrom with a force that made everything else superfluous. They revered flowers as others in society value wealth, fame or power. Probably the best-known twentieth-century flower artist, O'Keeffe painted poppies, irises, calla lilies, canna, heliconia, plumeria, petunias, sweet peas, morning glories, roses, larkspur, Jack-in-the-pulpit, cactus flowers and jimson weed, among many others – a vast catalogue suggesting that a maximalist assessment of her canon probably beats out a clever minimalist interpretation.

O'Keeffe's flowers fill her canvas so completely that there is barely any room left for anything else. (Dickinson's poems are similarly loaded with flowers to the exclusion of other things, though she can usually squeeze in a Bee.) These blossoms are so striking because of their sumptuously smooth and compelling forms, their astounding, rich colours, their forcefully precise composition, and the sense they give (that O'Keeffe gives them? That they and O'Keeffe together convey, just as Dickinson worked in tandem with her flowers?) that they are all-powerful and transcendent. They are in your face, and you are happy to have them there.

There is nothing more resplendent in this world, O'Keeffe's paintings shout in the same exuberant timbre as Dickinson's poems: nothing more worth looking at or thinking about. In the hands of these women, a flower is a metaphor for beauty, brilliance, sensory and spiritual perfection, and it is at the same time a literal embodiment of those attributes. Their flowers retain their natural botanical properties, and along with this they are loaded with poetic/painterly devices, ideas and dramatic properties that make our quotidian thoughts falter when we confront them, our breath a bit knocked out of us, as we acknowledge: yes, this is sublime. It's not that art or

44 Georgia O'Keeffe,
Hibiscus with Plumeria, 1939,
oil on canvas.

literature is a competition, but if it were, all the worthy entrants, the
epics and tragedies, the portraits and histories, lyric and abstraction,
spiritual devotion, ironic deconstruction . . . all those tropes, while
worthy in their own ways and effective in their own circumstances,
finally pale before the eloquence of a simple flower that catches our
eye from Dickinson's and O'Keeffe's strange, bright crowds.

148

Hibiscus with Plumeria exemplifies O'Keeffe's vision of the enormity of flowers (enormous not just in terms of how much of the canvas they occupy, but how much of the world they occupy, and how much of our better selves, our higher thoughts and actions, they inspire). They do not completely fit on the canvas: in their magnificence, they exceed the frame's boundary. The art is so close-up – so intimate, inviting of very close inspection of the petals and colours – that other parts like leaves and stems are omitted. There are just a few small bits of sky and clouds, acknowledging the rest of the world in the most succinct way possible, but virtually all that concerns the artist is the flower. The degree of importance that O'Keeffe, like Dickinson, invests in flowers is inspirational to the viewer, the reader, of such flowers. They are all and everything.

In my introduction, discussing the sexual dynamics of botany, I observed that floral eros was usually only minimally or subliminally apparent to human eyes (though bees and their buddies think of nothing else). O'Keeffe's paintings, however, are famously regarded as being among the most explicitly sexualized representations of flowers. The shapes, especially the curves and enfoldings of O'Keeffe's flowers, seem to suggest female genitalia: vagina, vulva, labia and/or clitoris. Sometimes, too, viewers see phallic symbols along with the yonic ones. Her art resounds with a pervasive aura of sensuality – floral sensuality, but also strongly connoting a cognate human sensuality. Painters create moods through their canvases' colours and forms, symbols and allusions – moods of violence, or angst, or fear, or imaginative fantasy. Many of O'Keeffe's paintings, especially her floral paintings, evoke the mood of sexuality and erotic dynamism.

She herself denied that this was her intent, and some art critics support her in resisting such a totalizing analysis, calling it reductionist and essentializing, which is to say that we may be inclined to see vaginas in her flowers simply because she is a woman and therefore what else could she be painting? (Imagine if every skyscraper erected by a male architect was assumed to be a phallic symbol!) Sexual readings of O'Keeffe's paintings proliferated following the lead of Alfred Stieglitz – her husband, colleague and promoter – in interpreting and publicizing her work. Stieglitz and his circle used 'themes of sexuality in their art as a declaration of being avant-garde,' Randall Griffin writes.

> Stieglitz read virtually all of Freud's books, as well as Havelock Ellis's six-volume *Studies in the Psychology of Sex*, which argues that art is driven by sexual energy. Thus, for Stieglitz, sex was a liberating source of creativity. O'Keeffe may or may not have thought of Freud when she painted her flowers, but the psychologist's writings were a cultural touchstone at the time, with his ideas widely known in a simplified fashion.[37]

In rebuttal, O'Keeffe stated quite clearly: 'When people read erotic symbols into my paintings, they're really talking about their own affairs.'[38] And again: 'you hung all your own associations with flowers on my flower and you write about my flower as if I think and see what you think and see of the flower – and I don't.'[39] Still, even if O'Keeffe did not intend for her artwork to arouse and celebrate erotic imagery, many viewers enjoy this sensual passion that resounds in her painting, and ultimately an artist cannot control what people see once her art is out in the world. 'Since the early 1920s the vast oil works have been dogged by erotic interpretations,' writes Hannah Ellis-Petersen, 'and, despite O'Keeffe's six decades of vigorous denial that her paintings were in any way sexual, it remains a commonly held assumption to this day.'[40]

So if O'Keeffe persistently denied this, let us agree to disagree and enjoy all the more whatever it is about her art that gives pleasure. In her brash, original manner, she captivated audiences with the power and astonishing beauty inherent in her strange, bright crowds of flowers. Certainly people already realized how amazing flowers were, but O'Keeffe made that point even clearer, as Dickinson had done a few generations earlier. While we thought we already appreciated flowers as keenly as possible, O'Keeffe and Dickinson, in the immortal words of *This Is Spinal Tap*, turn the dial up to 11.

Contemporary curiosities: Collishaw, Carrington

Floral images tend to remain stable from one age to another, one style to another. It may seem surprising that such a universal trope should feature more repetition than innovation, but as the wise old saying goes: if it ain't broke, don't fix it.

The most recent movements and media, though – Post-impressionism, Cubism, Fauvism, Modernism and Postmodernism, photography, film and digital/new media – have effectuated more variations in the past century than in the millennium before that. A few have indeed tried to fix what ain't broke with some strikingly radical aesthetics. Contemporary artists put the *strange* into 'strange, bright crowds of flowers', idiosyncratically reconceptualizing the simple blooms that so many other crowds of artists have engaged with straightforwardly, and that have served so many so well for so long. These artists – iconoclasts? – seek originality in a subject that most other artists and audiences have seemed happy for centuries to see basically the same old thing in.

A series of photographs and videos by Mat Collishaw called 'Burning Flowers' depicts exactly what its title promises. The images are equivocal: beautiful and troubling, sacred and profane. Collishaw says he is interested in the idea of sacrifice, and also novelty: 'I wanted a sequence where the flower . . . retained some of its biological *strangeness*, something that is not apparent when looking at a flower in real-time' (emphasis added). He sees flowers as 'metaphors for a

45 Mat Collishaw sets the art world on fire with *Effigy*, 2014.

certain moral decay and sickness in our relationship to the world', reminiscent of Charles Baudelaire's *Les Fleurs du mal*.[41] Unsurprisingly, Collishaw was one of the Young British Artists, a coterie known for gratuitously shocking imagery. Defacing flowers is indeed shocking and, to my mind, indecent. Are there any other reasons to do it? What malice does he bear towards flowers, I wonder: do they threaten him because they exhibit too much beauty? Are they too easy to admire?

Collishaw 'began creating photographs of enchanting but tainted flowers in 2002, and this has become a repeated motif in his work,' his website explains. The burning flower 'is both given life and destroyed by the surrounding flickering flames'.[42] He notes that 'Most flowers have a very high water content and just refuse to burn! I tried pretty much every flower I could get my hands on' – which is why he had to resort, finally, to digital incineration.[43] Perhaps his difficulty torching flowers might have been a sign of some sort: adapting a Christopher Fry title,[44] the flower's not for burning! (Do these flaming flowers 'keep the light'? I don't know – perhaps somehow, perversely?)

Virginia Woolf described metaphorical flower conflagration in *Mrs Dalloway*: Clarissa, surveying the florist's bounty, recalls 'the moment between six and seven when every flower – roses, carnations, irises, lilac – glows; white, violet, red, deep orange; every flower seems to burn by itself, softly, purely in the misty beds.'[45] I wonder how Woolf would have felt about Collishaw's literalizing her figurative flower fire; I cannot imagine she would have seen, in his blaze, anything like the pure, soft, misty glow her prose describes.

Ann Carrington, too, creates flowers *sui generis*: hers are perhaps as odd as Collishaw's, but they don't seem as intentionally troubling, or incendiary. She transforms silverware into vases overflowing with flowers. (Why not just sculpt . . . flowers? Again, it has been done; today's flower-artists crave the shock of the new.) 'Through the careful arrangement of these familiar objects, welded and soldered together, Carrington has created a piece that resembles a bouquet of flowers such as roses, hydrangeas and proteas,' Alexandra Jones writes, noting that she is inspired by the memento mori symbolism common in sixteenth- and seventeenth-century Dutch still-lifes.[46]

Memento mori – 'remember that you will die' – is a trope in vanitas paintings: a genre that aims to emphasize life's transience. Skulls, rotting fruit or an hourglass are interspersed with flowers to connote a quickly impending loss of beauty. Omar Khayyam anticipated this mood in his twelfth-century *Rubaiyat*: 'The Flower that once has blown for ever dies.'[47] Vanitas means empty or worthless – 'Vanity of vanities, saith the Preacher, vanity of vanities; all is vanity' (Ecclesiastes 1:2) – and vanitas flower arrangements depict a fearful, morbid sense of what people risk by taking too much delight in such frivolities, which embody merely momentary prettiness, instead of attending to more eternal concerns. The theme was popular in Chinese aesthetics, too, around the same time as it flourished in European art. Shen Zhou featured falling flowers prolifically in his painting, poetry and calligraphy to lament the passage of time and ephemeral mortality. In a scroll from 1505 he writes:

> I fell ill for an entire month. When I finally arose from bed I rushed outside only to find that the blossoms had been swept clean of the trees, bits of red and white filling the ground. I missed their opening and only saw their

falling. This filled me with such sadness. Encountering objects, I created verses. I titled the ten quatrains *Falling Blossoms*.[48]

Carrington explains her modern twist on this enduring motif:

I've always been attracted to the tradition of memento mori, art that reminds us of the passing of time . . . In looking at those pictures of half-consumed food and fading flowers, I realized that one of the only things that could have survived to today was the silverware, and I thought, Wouldn't it be fun to try to make something out of that?[49]

While cutlery seems like an eccentric medium, a strange link between art and nature, Carrington demonstrates that soup spoons can indeed make excellent peonies; berry spoons become hydrangea; and teaspoons are just right for rose petals.[50] In contrast to Philip Larkin's sad sprawling flowers from 'Church Going', Carrington's sturdy metal flowers will never droop or sprawl (though they may tarnish, but that is reparable). 'They're quite difficult to make,' she says. Each arrangement takes three months from silverware-sorting to composition to completion; she makes each individual flower separately until she has a sufficient stash of them to weld into a bouquet: 'Each flower requires a different kind of spoon, and each metal requires a different heating technique.' Good: recreating flowers *should* be difficult. 'To be honest, making them is not a pleasurable process,' she admits. 'It's just a bit perverse to sculpt flowers, because you're competing with nature. Plus, it's rather filthy,' and also dangerous: once, while she was welding a lily, an errant drop of molten metal fell into her

46 Ann Carrington's 2016 'Weeping Willow', from her series *Bouquets and Butterflies*, represents a fork in the road for artistic flowers.

boot and burned her heel.[51] (Her torch, once again, illuminates Roethke's axiom that 'all flowers keep the light.')

Public art: Koons, Catalano, Choi

If Collishaw's florapyromania is strangely destructive, and Carrington's flatware flowers are strangely unexpected, Jeff Koons's 10-metre-tall (34 ft) *Bouquet of Tulips* is strangely gigantic and strangely metallic – more jarringly so than Carrington's metal still-life, whose sensitive artistic transformation lulls viewers into imagining the cutlery as softer, flowery. Koons's colossal sculpture also seems strangely geometric – not in a flower-geometry kind of way, with symmetrical petal patterns or Fibonacci-sequenced

spirals, but in a more brusque, mechanical mode: reductive, cylindrical, consummately unflowery. Are they even really tulips, or is
it a colossal 'bouquet' of lollies, or balloons, or marshmallows, or
brightly coloured buffalo-mozzarella balls, or smuggled heroin
bricks?

And the hand. I find this element of the sculpture even stranger
than strange: offputting, scary, surreally discomfiting. But I learn
even from things I dislike, and this hand prompts me to think

47 Jeff Koons's grossly
exaggerated *Bouquet of Tulips*
(rendering, 2016); human
figure included for scale.

more about all the 'normal' hands that hold 'normal' flowers elsewhere in art. Hands, I have come to notice, form an interesting bridge between flowers and culture. Often, although not here, they function as an organic link between human life and botanical life. The hands are temporary holders: the flowers have come from a field, or a florist, into the hand and must be relatively quickly transferred to another, whose attached person will then place them in a vase (unless the person is Mat Collishaw, in which case they may be torched). The hands – again, not in Koons's case – are often poised with a studied careful grip, at once tight (so the flowers do not fall and scatter) and gentle (so as not to crush the stems). One feels slightly awkward holding a bouquet of cut flowers for more than a minute: they want to be settled elsewhere.

To belabour the obvious: hands don't give flowers, people do. The missing person in Koons's grotesque tableau is a significant, even an existential, failing, especially if Koons means to evoke the consummately human gesture of giving flowers as a gesture of sympathy and support to a person, or a community, that is in pain. These tulips (that don't even vaguely resemble tulips) offered from a hand (that doesn't evoke a person) are an attenuation, perhaps even a postmodern *blague*.

Koons encountered an unenthusiastic reception when he tried to donate *Bouquet of Tulips* to the city of Paris in 2016. Its citizens denounced the installation's design as botched flowers. A year after the horrifying massacre at the Bataclan theatre, and across the city, Koons offered this gift to the French to honour their courage and to soothe their trauma. But many felt the sculpture was a misfit in terms of its spirit. The attack struck at the city's cultural soul: its nightlife, music, food and sport; its very essence. Blood was running in the streets, and at least for a time the attack robbed Paris of its innocence, its jouissance. The sculpture, on the other hand, seemed twee: bright and large, emotionally inappropriate to the massacre. Paris squares had been filled with oceans of actual bouquets that people left in the days and weeks after the attack – those seemed sincere and comforting, while Koons's seemed like a ditzy parody. The pallid disembodied hand, some suggested, was an especially tone-deaf miscalculation: a severed body part unlikely to comfort victims of terrorism.

Koons probably intended to echo another large sculpture with a prominently large hand – a more satisfying and appropriate hand (that was actually attached to an arm and a person, as hands should be), which France gave to the USA in the nineteenth century. Interestingly, before Frédéric Auguste Bartholdi's Statue of Liberty was complete, the stand-alone 'Arm of Liberty', as it was called, journeyed to Philadelphia and New York, where the piece – at 12.8 metres (42 ft) tall, similar in scale to Koons's sculpture – highlighted a campaign to raise funds for the statue's pedestal, which was not included in the gift. If that hand was temporarily disembodied, it was destined to be eventually attached to a whole human figure: in fact, the more one donated, the sooner that might happen. Koons's gift, too, was incomplete: while he donated the design, he did not cover the costs of fabrication and installation, which ran to €3 million. *Le Monde* called his offer a 'cadeau empoisonné', more of a curse than a blessing.[52] And, unlike Bartholdi, Koons had no plans to supply a body for this free-standing hand.

Original plans to install Koons's sculpture opposite the Eiffel Tower and between the Musée de l'art moderne and the Palais de Tokyo sparked a fierce pushback on the grounds that the site was too prominent (and had no relation to the terror attacks), and that the work itself was unworthy. A group of artists called his work

banal, a 'symbol of "industrial", assembly-line art',[53] deeming it 'symbolically inappropriate, undemocratic, and architecturally, patrimonially, artistically, financially, and technically "shocking"'.[54] The controversy abated somewhat when a less conspicuous site, near the Petit Palais, was substituted, but when the installation was finally completed in 2019 reactions were even more vituperative than at its inception. After the unveiling, philosopher Yves Michaud described it as 'eleven colored anuses mounted on stems'.[55] Its irrelevance as a memorial to the terror attacks was confirmed when no survivors spoke at the ceremony and no victims were memorialized there. Or perhaps they were, albeit insipidly: there are eleven flowers instead of a dozen, Koons explained, because the missing tulip is meant to represent the victims.

While Koons's absurd scale was a significant flaw for many Paris citizens (*tellement américain!*), immensity is not inherently proscribed in flower art. Consider another large metal flower, Eduardo Catalano's 23-metre-tall (75 ft) *Floralis Genérica* in Buenos Aires, with a fascinating botanical feature: a mechanical system (when it is operable, which is not all the time) opens the flower's petals in the morning and closes them at sunset, to the delight of crowds that gather to watch what has become a civic icon. It also has a wind gauge that automatically closes the flower when wind speeds reach more than 40 km/h, or if a storm is approaching. Catalano meant the title to be a tribute to all flowers, though he has said that he was inspired specifically by watching a hibiscus closing at evening.

We could try to identify aesthetic criteria to explain why people enjoy and appreciate Catalano's giant metal flower so much more than Koons's bouquet, digging into the sculptures' siting, form, materials, colour, historical and cultural context. Or we could just use this comparison to conclude that sometimes a large metal

48 *Floralis Genérica*, Eduardo Catalano's 2002 stainless steel sculpture in Buenos Aires.

art-flower fits, and sometimes it doesn't; sometimes the art works, and sometimes it fails. The mechanical reiteration of nyctinasty (when a flower 'goes to sleep' by closing its petals) is innovative: people enjoy human culture acknowledging nature's marvels. I had never thought about why tulips, crocuses, magnolias, daisies, poppies and most legumes, among other species, open and close at daybreak and nightfall, until seeing Catalano's sculpture prompted me to look it up. I discovered that scientists have not definitively determined why it happens. Charles Darwin thought it might be to reduce their risk of freezing at night; others hypothesize that nyctinastic flowers might be saving their energy and their odour for the daytime, when pollination usually happens, or they might be keeping their pollen dry from dew to make it easier for insects to gather.[56] Geoffrey Chaucer offers his own hypothesis in *The Legend of Good Women* (rendered here in modern English):

> And when it is eve, I swiftly hie,
> As soon as ever sun sinks in the west,
> To see this flower, how she does sink to rest,
> For fear of night, she so hates the darkness!
> Her face is wholly open to the brightness
> Of the sun, for there it does unclose.[57]

Another large and kinetic modern flower installation is Choi Jeong Hwa's *Breathing Flower*, a 7.3-metre-wide (24 ft) red lotus; he has also made companion pieces in white, green, pink, black, gold and yellow. Like the Argentinian sculpture, this too moves: a motorized fan at the base lifts inflatable fabric petals up and down, much more vigorously than the diurnal opening and closing of Catalano's large flower but, like his, an imitation of the flower's natural

movement, its respiration, its life force. *Breathing Flower* also moves in the sense that its various iterations have been exhibited around the world – Taipei, San Francisco, Boston, Perth, Sydney, Guangzhou, London, Beijing, Paris, Honolulu, Venice and Seoul – displaying a mobility that rivals Emily Dickinson's world-travelling Arctic flower.

If this polyester contraption seems un-flowerlike, I would cite the artist's own explanation about the non-binary fluidity of natural and artificial objects. A park or garden, too, is 'manicured and landscaped by people, it didn't just happen in the wild,' he said, 'and flowers like this, inflatable, or even plastic flowers, in a way might even be better than natural world because they

49 Choi Jeong Hwa's 2012 *Breathing Flower* adorns the plaza outside San Francisco's Asian Art Museum.

never die.' (Harvard's glass flowers evoke the same sentiment for some aficionados.) 'The nature and man-made objects are not two different things but they are one.'[58] Choi's commitment to outdoor public art makes him a good spokesman for real flowers, which may themselves be regarded as public art, especially if nature and culture, as he suggests, are intertwined.

Most public spaces already feature ample displays of real flowers: why do we need more flower sculptures, and what communal message do these large civic installations disseminate? They are notably, almost ostentatiously, large and expensive; if they are effective, they are keenly eye-catching. They remind both intentional viewers and accidental passers-by that their government has chosen to dedicate resources to a public work that is perhaps not as manifestly vital as a transit route or a sewer system, but nevertheless adds value to the community. People notice this art, and notice other people noticing it. Public art was once meant to honour a society's heroes: explorers, officers on horseback, victory arches. The new phenomenon of public flower art – and it is indeed a trend: see Wrocław's *Dandelions*, Minneapolis's *Blossoms of Hope*, Lyon's *Flower Tree*, Baton Rouge's *One Plant, Many Flowers*, and Mashhad's *Paper Flower*, among many others – suggests a more humanistic ideology. Less nationalistic than public art of the past, and more ecologically attuned, these artworks encourage the citizenry to enjoy the simple ubiquitous beauties of nature: stop and smell the flowers (not the metal or polyester versions, of course, but the real ones that these extravagantly evoke). Public art affects large crowds of people, including those who may not regularly visit museums. It has a strong 'wow factor': if it catches on, as *Floralis Genérica* did in Buenos Aires, its popularity goes viral, and if it flops, like Koons's bouquet, then the mockers will spread their thoughts far and wide. This art's outsized visual power is matched by a comparably large force of cultural circulation.

One final thought about grand artistic scale. When Georgia O'Keeffe began painting she wrote, 'In the twenties, huge buildings seemed to be going up overnight in New York.' If she painted flowers at life-size, 'no one would look at them because I was unknown. So I thought I'll make them big like the huge buildings going up. People will be startled – they'll have to look at them – and they did.'[59] She intended her flowers to embody a immensity that could hold its own amid the increasingly large world of her time. She also explained that her flowers are large for a reason that seems so obvious as to need no explanation: so people can see them better, and appreciate their detail under her magnification. Once, she explained, she wanted to paint a specific flower that 'was perfectly beautiful. It was exquisite, but it was so small you really could not appreciate it for itself. So then and there I decided to paint that flower in all its beauty. If I could paint that flower in a huge scale, then you could not ignore its beauty.'[60]

50 Back away from the tulips, you grabby capitalist imp! A 1937 Federal Art Project public information poster.

3

FLOWER SELLERS

Flowers . . . are always fit presents . . . because they are a proud assertion that a ray of beauty outvalues all the utilities of the world. These gay natures contrast with the somewhat stern countenance of ordinary nature; they are like music heard out of a work-house.

RALPH WALDO EMERSON[1]

Behind each stem is (everyone agrees) absolutely the worst, shittiest, most fantastic business in the entire goddamn world.

THE ECONOMIST[2]

Is there something morally dubious about the flower trade, which transforms wild expressions of botanical splendour into fiercely marketed, convenient, homogenous product lines? Do we sublimate the hypocrisy of our consumer fetish for flowers that may violate their authentic essence? Our flowers of choice – peonies and liatris, calla lilies and carnations, larkspur and freesia, roses and tulips – could not be (absent our commodification) easily acquired en masse. Their life force and bioprosperity are firmly grounded in specific habitats, or at least they were until the industrial-age mania to domesticate and monetize the living world. If the flower trade supposedly celebrates natural beauty, then why do its minions hoodwink nature, subverting its cycles and distorting its equilibrium, by growing flowers in places and times they were not meant to be grown, in quantities that exceed normal botanical yields, bred with properties that do not naturally occur, commercially dispersed in far-flung places they were never meant to be seen? It would seem as if the guild of florists voted to repeal Barry Commoner's third law of ecology: 'Nature knows best.'

Recall, for instance, the credo of Emily Dickinson ('If you would like to borrow . . .'): perhaps flowers should be enjoyed on loan from nature, not bought and sold. Rather than bringing them into our world we could go to visit them in theirs, where they live and grow. In the 1930s New Deal artists were put to work designing posters with slogans and morals designed to lift the USA out of the slough of economic depression and towards a more prosperous and equitable society. One such broadside shows two children in a park: a small boy wants to pick some tulips for himself (he has already severed one stem and reaches for a second), while a girl tries to dissuade him with a 'hands off' gesture.

She might have tried to neutralize her rapacious little friend by recalling Rabindranath Tagore's maxim – 'By plucking her petals you do not gather the beauty of the flower'[3] – or Edna St. Vincent Millay's poetry: 'I will touch a hundred flowers / And not pick one.'[4] Francis Thompson, too, tells us to leave blooms alone: 'Thou canst not stir a flower / Without troubling of a star.'[5] What we now call the butterfly effect – the idea that a small change somewhere can create a larger impact in some distant part of the universe – reso-nates in Thompson's poetic expression that all of nature is connected. 'You become very happy when you get a flower,' writes Turkish nov-elist Mehmet Murat ildan. 'But what about the poor flower? How does it feel? It doesn't feel anything because it is dead, it has been killed for your unethical happiness!'[6] And in Mary Tyler Peabody

Mann's *The Flower People* (1838), one flower in a bright crowd of violets tells her human visitor, Mary, how much she looks forward to the coming gay summer months – 'I hope I shall live to see the Roses' – and enjoins her: 'Do not pluck me, little girl. I will tell you more about myself if you will not pluck me.'[7] Mary appreciates the violet's integrity and the flower, safely unplucked, teaches her science, geography and moral knowledge (with a Transcendentalist flavour). Remembering Lewis Carroll's Tiger-lily, who is happy to talk whenever she encounters anyone worth talking to, Mann's violet, too, deems young Mary a worthy interlocutor to carry a message back to her human community: 'thoughtless people often do a great deal of mischief' to flowers.[8]

Whether or not the poster's creators are explicitly channelling this tradition of floral rights, its message is one that Tagore, Millay, Mann and Thompson would all endorse: 'Enjoy, don't destroy.' It is not hard to see in this scene an allegory for conflicting world views: every-man-for-himself capitalist-imperialist domination versus leftist-feminist greatest-good-for-the-greatest-number communitarianism. The New Deal's Works Progress Administration (WPA) created parks and gardens, playgrounds and public art, intended to encourage sharing experiences and things, including flowers, that should be accessible to all. Extractive industrial harvesting of nature was the work of robber barons whose wealth engendered dire economic imbalances; the WPA meant to recast nature as a place for everyone's enjoyment rather than a resource for profiteers.

Some things should not be for sale in an ethical society: pledges and words of honour, justice, bodily organs, trafficked human beings, ecosystemic cleanliness and sustainability. Do flowers belong in this rarefied company? Are they too delicate and pure, too ecologically important, to taint with the filthy lucre of human commerce?

Some disturbing things happen behind the scenes in floristry: should flower sellers be better than this? Isn't there some Zen of flowers that should moderate the commercial infrastructure?

But idealism be damned: flowers are too valuable to escape our clutches, comprising a $75–100 billion worldwide business.[9] A small sector bypasses the ornamental/decorative mainstream, commercializing flowers for potpourri, lip balm, candles, soaps and bath salts. Parfumiers create fragrances with oils extracted from roses, violets, lavender, jasmine, narcissus and frangipani.

Flowers are occasionally sold as edibles: hibiscus petals to steep in tea, nasturtiums for trendy salads, violets in iced drinks. 'Most flowers have a mild vegetal flavor,' says Ezra Woods, a parfumier who likes to cook with pea tendrils, rosemary flowers, nasturtium and marigolds. 'Sometimes they're a little spicy, like arugula. I love nothing more than flowers. There's something magical about being able to eat something so beautiful,' Woods says. 'I find when I make edible-flower food that it has this crazy energy to it.'[10] Orchid tempura is an Asian delicacy, and Thai dishes are often plated with fresh orchid blossoms, although when I eat the flowery garnish every so often – always hoping I might enjoy it because I am such a devout floraphile – I find that it just tastes pretty much like . . . flowers.

(Orchids were Charles Darwin's favourite flowers. His next book after *On the Origin of Species* was *On the Various Contrivances by which British and Foreign Orchids are Fertilised by Insects, and on the Good Effects of Intercrossing* (1862), a demonstration of natural selection examining the co-evolution of orchids and their insect pollinators. Darwin wondered about one orchid, *Angraecum sesquipedale*, a Madagascar specimen with an abnormally deep nectary, 'Good Heavens what insect can suck it?' He hypothesized that there must exist a moth with a similarly elongated proboscis, at least 25 centimetres (10 in.), to pollinate it. Such a creature was found 25 years after Darwin's death: a subspecies of the giant Congo moth, named *Xanthopan morganii praedicta* to acknowledge that Darwin had predicted its existence. Darwin's hypothesis was finally confirmed in 1992 when observers recorded that moth feeding on his strange, bright orchids and transferring their pollen to other flowers.[11])

A popular mid-nineteenth-century commodification, possibly an antecedent of modern-day essential oils, was Dr Fontaine's Balm of Thousand Flowers. 'For the Toilet, the Nursery, for Bathing, and

51 Dr Fontaine's 1840s Balm of Thousand Flowers promises to abate many and sundry ailments.

many Medicinal Purposes', recommended by 'almost every Physician and Nurse in Boston, New York, Philadelphia, and other cities', this balm 'is the greatest luxury a fashionable Lady or Gentleman could wish, for the improvement of health, for comfort and personal embellishment'. Priced at $1 per bottle, it 'eradicates every defect of the Complexion', promotes hair growth, and 'is a most useful article for Shaving'. It also serves as 'a Dentrifice for cleansing the teeth' and it eliminates freckles and ulcers.

The 'doctor' declined to reveal precisely what kinds of flowers comprise his miracle treatment. The label's border features a floral flurry, but these seem like random nineteenth-century clip-art. Dr Fontaine's other popular patent medicines included Catarrh Snuff, Nipple Salve, Cutaneous Balsam, Worm Powder (actually *anti*-worm powder), Syrups and Elixirs, Reviving Bitters, Vegetable Bilious Powders and Female Medicines. Dr Fontaine may have been a maestro in the tradition of American quackery, but still I would enthusiastically try his Flower Balm myself – '*highly perfumed by its own ingredients*' – if I could lay hands on a jar that had survived the ravages of time and rationalism.

But miraculous concoctions of yore, like today's camomile teas and lavender soap, are niche commodities, minimally impacting the flower industry. Some pharmaceutical/therapeutic markets for flowers still exist, especially in traditional Chinese medicine: during the coronavirus pandemic in 2020 China's government distributed 'plague-repellent capsules' called 'lianhua qingwen jiaonang', made of forsythia and honeysuckle.[12] Even in perfumery, surprisingly, flowers are a relatively minor ingredient, overshadowed by grasses, spices, fruit, roots, resins and balsams, leaves, gums and animal secretions, like musk and ambergris, in addition to synthetic ingredients like alcohol, petrochemicals and coal tars. The business model for flower sales is fundamentally geared towards the obvious product lines: blooms for bouquets, boutonnières, vases, holidays, funerals, weddings and other grand occasions.

'In spite of some basic survival uses, such as edible or medicinal flowers,' a 2017 Israeli psychological study concludes, 'most flowering plants grown in the flower industry in modern times are not used for any purpose other than visual pleasure and emotional satisfaction.'[13] Give flowers to thank a host, to apologize to your romantic partner, to celebrate your niece's recital. ('Give flowers' is a more generous, less consumeristic expression of what florists really want customers to do, which is *buy* flowers.) Flowers will cheer up a sick friend, brighten a busy office, let your mother know how much you appreciate everything she did for you. Mother's Day is 'the Super Bowl for florists', who start planning next year's campaign as soon as the previous concludes.[14]

Notice how many cut flowers you come across in hospitals, hotel lobbies, restaurants, fancy restrooms, Hindu pooja thalis, synagogues, churches, Buddhist monasteries and other spiritual shrines, banquets, cemeteries, parade floats, holiday wreaths, corsages, dinner parties, ceremonial and festive garlands, and you will begin to appreciate the scope of the industry that supplies this product. For a decadent delight, give (buy) yourself flowers: you deserve it! If it seems narcissistic lean into it, and pick up a bouquet of narcissus. Six reasons to buy yourself flowers, according to the Internet: improving your mood, refreshing your senses, revamping your decor, enchanting guests, sparking creativity and strengthening confidence.[15]

Floral commerce

'Breeders pour big money into building a better flower,' writes the horticulturalist Amy Stewart in *Flower Confidential*: 'one that lasts longer in the vase, one that doesn't drop petals or shed pollen, one that meets the peculiar demands of autumn brides or supermarket shoppers.'[16] Since most flowers sold in North America are from Central and South America, and most European flowers are grown in Africa, one of the most important breeding ideals is 'suitability as freight'.

The cut-flower trade is a 'struggle between what is natural and unspoiled and what is mass produced and commercial. We like being able to buy a summer flower in February – in fact, we've built a holiday around it – but we also distrust fakery.' The industry boasts 'new breeding techniques, advanced greenhouse technology, and global transportation systems,' Stewart writes, 'but modern flowers have lost something, too. They're tamer, better behaved, less fickle, and less seasonal. Many have lost their scent, and I wonder if they are also losing their identity, their power, or their passion.'[17]

Flowers have flourished in global commerce for better and for worse. Better: more people can have more flowers, more easily and more affordably. If flowers are good, more flowers are great, right? Although there is a limit: *The Economist* reports that at 'the pinnacle of New York society, the city's wealthiest, whose Upper East Side penthouses can be spied from the Met's roof, might spend $10,000 a week' on flowers,[18] which is just gross, conspicuous consumption. No one person could possibly deserve such expansive floral bounty. More than a century ago the Japanese writer Kakuzō Okakura disdainfully regarded 'the wanton waste of flowers among Western communities' (compared with Asian arrangements that were more spare and minimalist):

> The number of flowers cut daily to adorn the ballrooms and banquet-tables of Europe and America, to be thrown away on the morrow, must be something enormous; if strung together they might garland a continent . . . In the West the display of flowers seems to be a part of the pageantry of wealth, the fancy of a moment. Whither do they all go, these flowers, when the revelry is over? Nothing is more pitiful than to see a faded flower remorselessly flung upon a dung heap.[19]

Worse: capitalism alienates the industry's workers, the ground-level growers and sellers, and sublimates such unpleasant externalities as its considerable carbon footprint. People and societies suffer in the name of ephemeral beauty. And perhaps we appreciate flowers less because they are ubiquitously accessible year-round; when I was a child, watermelon and asparagus seemed more appealing than they do now, more of a treat, because they were not available out of season; when they finally arrived in stores, people were pretty excited. The sack of oranges my grandmother brought when she came to visit from Miami tasted of her love and seemed like a trick we had played on winter.

People have been importing flowers for a very long time. When Sargon of Akkad invaded Anatolia, around 2350 BCE, he brought home roses. Floral arrangements were common in ancient Egyptian funerals and Roman celebrations. A 2,000-year-old funerary garland found at Egypt's Hawara burial site contains chrysanthemum flowers, twigs of sweet marjoram and hibiscus petals. During

Overleaf:
52 A Dutch flower farm: this large-scale overview of floral produce is very different from how people normally experience the pleasure of tulips.

53 *Cosiddetta Flora*, an image of the goddess from a 1st-century Roman fresco near Pompeii.

Floralia, the spring festival honouring Flora, the Roman goddess of flowers and fertility, women wore floral wreaths (precursors of May Day garlands) in their hair, and Roman brides wore crowns of verbena. For another festival, Rosalia, Romans decorated burial sites with roses. Little is known about how the flowers were provided for these rituals, but there must have been some kind of business infrastructure for growing, harvesting, transporting and distributing the celebratory flowers.

The Dutch launched the modern flower trade (and remain dominant players today), abetted by the commercial networks that developed with their empire. Turkish and Persian bulbs imported along Central Asia's Silk Road kindled the infamous seventeenth-century tulipmania (*tulpenmanie*). Luxuriant albums (*tulpenboeken*) featured varieties and hybrids with such strange, bright grandiose names as Semper Augustus, The Great Plumed One, and General of Generals of Gouda.[20] 'A severe trial of that nation's stability and ethics',[21] capitalist fetishization set off supply-and-demand bidding that drove prices to astronomical levels: wealthy customers 'handed out much money for a rare plant in order to boast to their friends that they own it'.[22] The economic vicissitudes of the tulip bubble's collapse in the 1630s generated a case study still taught in business schools four centuries on. In retrospect, the Dutch experience suggests a karmic recoil for those who value flowers – unwisely, greedily – as a means to wealth and power rather than simply appreciating them for what they are. Dante would have called it *contrapasso*: what goes around comes around; or, to put it florally, we reap what we sow.

In modern history, floristry was generally propelled by the rise of capitalism, and more specifically by customs, such as Queen Victoria's passion for flowers. She liked giving her friends small bouquets, which became a fashionable practice: today we would call her an influencer. Tussie-mussies, as they were called, were arranged to convey a 'language of flowers' or 'floriography': mimosas symbolized chastity, honeysuckles signified devotion, sweet peas meant departure and so on. Lady Mary Wortley Montagu is credited with having invented the language of flowers in a 1718 letter that explained to her friend the meanings of the flowers she

54 Four prized tulips recorded in watercolour from Jacob Marrel's 1630s–40s *Tulpenboek*: 'Boter man' (Butter-man),' Joncker' (Nobleman), 'Grote geplumaceerde' (Greatly Plumed) and 'Voorwint' (With-the-wind).

enclosed.[23] As floriographic texts blossomed profusely over the next two centuries, though, there was little agreement about exactly what a particular flower meant. The 'translations' of symbolic flowers were mostly arbitrary and inconsistent – with occasional exceptions, such as the forget-me-not[24] – and varied enormously from one interpretive guidebook to another. 'The notion that young Victorian lovers courted one another through the careful arrangement of floral bouquets is a fantasy of our retrospective construction of Victorian quaintness,'[25] writes Robert Hemmings.

'Bring Flowers,' evangelizes a 1836 article in *American Ladies' Magazine*: 'We scarcely think how much of pleasure and instruction

55 Kate Greenaway's *Language of Flowers* (1884) informs that a flytrap means deceit, a foxglove means insincerity, a French marigold means jealousy and a frog ophrys (also known as bee orchid) means disgust.

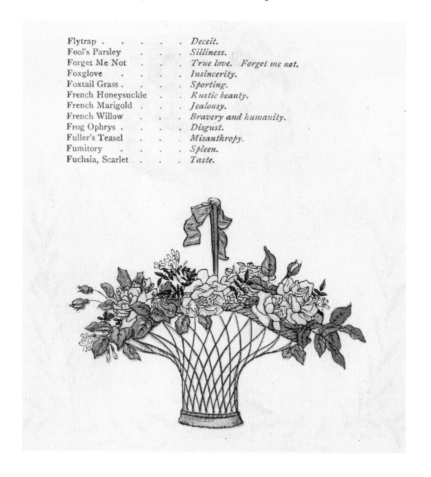

Flytrap	.	.	.	.	*Deceit.*
Fool's Parsley	.	.	.	*Silliness.*
Forget Me Not	.	.	.	*True love. Forget me not.*
Foxglove	.	.	.	*Insincerity.*
Foxtail Grass	.	.	.	*Sporting.*
French Honeysuckle	.	.	*Rustic beauty.*
French Marigold	.	.	*Jealousy.*
French Willow	.	.	*Bravery and humanity.*
Frog Ophrys	.	.	.	*Disgust.*
Fuller's Teasel	.	.	*Misanthropy.*
Fumitory	.	.	.	*Spleen.*
Fuchsia, Scarlet	.	.	*Taste.*

we may and do derive from flowers.' If the sentiment now seems commonplace, the writer's tone suggests a conviction that she is just at that moment in history discovering and disseminating this insight. 'True, flowers are but of little visible use,' she writes, confronting a puritanical frugality that consumers may still feel today, perhaps subconsciously: *What a waste of money for something that is here today, gone tomorrow.*

> But this very reason gives them, in our eyes, a peculiar charm. We connect them with the idea of purity, and delicacy, which would be lost, if we should associate them with the coarse and common processes by which roots, seeds, and fruits are converted into food for the sustenance of animal nature.[26]

Touché! Down with utilitarianism: flowers are good because flowers are good. In Ralph Waldo Emerson's 1844 essay 'Gifts', he too differentiates between pedestrian versus sublime manifestations of nature. A flower's 'gay nature' contains a 'ray of beauty [that] outvalues all the utilities of the world,' he writes, in 'contrast with the somewhat stern countenance of ordinary nature', echoing what *American Ladies' Magazine* calls 'the coarse and common processes' of sustenance. Whether intentionally or inadvertently, such writings bolster the branding of flowers, elevating them (above plain old woods and fields with their trees, grasses and crops) in the cultural imagination at the same time as the business of floristry is taking off.

With the enormous number of American Civil War deaths, capped by President Abraham Lincoln's, flowers became popular at memorial ceremonies, and heightened consumer appeal drove

56 Fanny Downing's 'Memorial Flowers' (1867) testifies to the prevalence of funereal flowers after the U.S. Civil War's massive death toll.

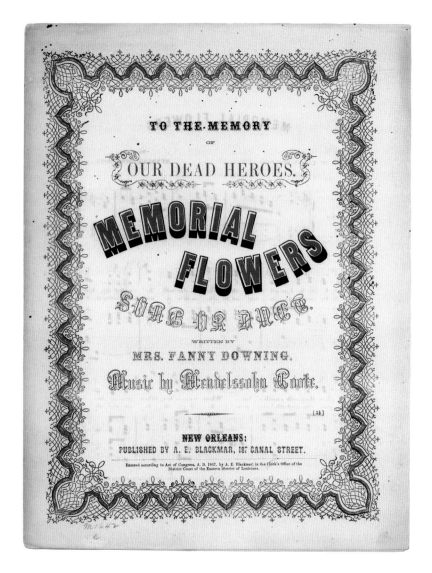

commercial value. Funeral flowers helped mourners express, physically, a metaphysical grief, tempering their trauma, even if only in small measure, by integrating something pure and beautiful into the ritual of loss. Fanny Downing illustrates the sentiment in her song 'Memorial Flowers': 'Each nameless nook and scattered spot, Where sleeps a Southern soldier true, I mark with the Forget-me-not, In Heaven's own blue.'[27]

In the mid- to late nineteenth century, flower shops, often including the greenhouses where inventory was grown, sprouted up across Europe and the USA. The twentieth-century invention of Mother's Day as a secularized American Mothering Sunday provided a hook for flower sales – a 1917 'Say It With Flowers' campaign is one of the most successful and enduring advertising jingles ever – inspiring floral marketing for many other holidays and occasions as well.

Within the last few generations, flower commerce has shifted from speciality stores to supermarkets and from local growers to international industrial-scale suppliers. 'In 1970 Americans shopped at local florists, who were supplied by wholesale markets, which bought from American farms. Now Americans buy 80 percent of their flowers from abroad, with about 66 cents of every dollar spent in supermarkets or online.'[28] Mass global agribusiness means larger consumption of resources and a higher carbon toll, but also more employment and economic benefit for some of the world's poorest citizens from less developed countries.

Flowers come to market via breeders, brokers, traders, truckers, stockers. The near-disappearance of conventional florists in this supply chain, supplanted by armies of corporate logisticians, attenuates a customer's personal connection to this commerce. As with other obsolete occupations like milkmen, telephone switchboard operators, lift attendants and (soon) postal workers, there is a social diminution consequent upon the

57 Dear old mum! At bottom, the advertisement offers 'A beautiful sixteen-page booklet on the etiquette, use and care of flowers, sent free on request,' in case mother might be mystified by her monkshood.

disappearance of the human go-between. Consumers engaged more richly with milk, flowers and lifts when we interacted with people whose jobs involved these commodities and services. Remember how respectfully we once regarded mail, delivered by people in smart livery, whose faces we recognized, walking industriously through our neighbourhoods, compared to the vacuous electronic blather that now spews from our devices?[29] Are depersonalized flowers destined for a similar fate?

Few modern-day florists resemble Virginia Woolf's Miss Pym, who was so full of botanical passion, sense, wisdom and appreciation that she seemed as if she had transformed herself into one more bloom in her shop: 'button-faced Miss Pym, whose hands were always bright red, as if they had been stood in cold water with the flowers'. Today's consumers generally acquire their flowers (self-selected, without input from a professional) from a designated section of the supermarket, often abutting the produce, where they are reasonably priced and highly dependable in their uniformity, bunch after bunch, week after week; or from a website connected to some wholesale infrastructure which (less dependably) delivers overpriced flowers that minimally resemble the advertised product in terms of species, arrangement, plentitude or freshness. The merchandise will be swaddled, or more accurately smothered, in a large sheet of cellophane wrap, a crinkly and unwieldy, non-recyclable, rubbish-bin-filling, toxically (carbon disulphide) fabricated, chemical-smelling contraption, impermeable to air, bacteria and water, isolating the flowers from every scintilla of nature: an unpromising semiotic signifier of what these commodified blossoms are (and what they are not). Flowers are now one more item to pick up on a shopping list alongside toilet paper and teabags, or to click-and-buy efficiently (thoughtlessly) via e-commerce. The industrial standardization of this commodity prioritizes efficiency and scale over quality and serendipitous delight. Indeed, customers complain in website reviews that delivery service flowers are often not all that fresh, splendid or worth the price:

> The flowers that were delivered to my wife on Valentine's day were totally embarrassing. I paid over $100 and couldn't believe what I seen. Droopy roses – already dead – lightly filled with filler flowers. It was a total scam. Second rate flowers at a premium price.

> Ordered the bouquet of the month for my mam's birthday . . . never seen worse flowers in my life. Considering the photo on the website shows lovely flowers, they are nothing like the photo!!!! complete waste of £30. I wouldn't give them to my dog let alone my mam!

> Their website photos are misleading to say the least. I'm honestly not sure how they get away with such blatant misrepresentation. Absolute waste of money. Never, never, never order from them again! I feel absolutely cheated.[30]

Recipients of mass-market floral mediocrity clearly seem disappointed with the product's value, and yet we do not see a resurgence of dedicated florists, except occasionally in the gentrification niche – and such businesses often open and close in short order. An industry survey finds that the number of flower shops in the USA declined by 40 per cent from 2005 to 2019,[31] and, like bookshops and record stores, they are unlikely to return in any significant number.

The personal touch that used to be a fundamental aspect of the florist trade stands out especially starkly in (as they now seem) nostalgic old-fashioned representations. Belle époque artist Victor-Gabriel Gilbert painted dozens of late nineteenth- and early twentieth-century scenes depicting the gravitas of the Paris flower business. His art illustrates the professional, methodical attention that vendors added to the value of their cut flowers. The women in his tableaux are serious workers, undistracted by the frippery of flowers (though of course their customers are free to indulge in as 'fripperous' a delight as they desire). They are there primarily to ensure that each bouquet's quality and aesthetics are first rate. From their heaps of flowers they will assemble, mix and recommend. Pruning out imperfections, they ensure that the buyer receives the best possible product. Their stiff, businesslike mien reminds us that there's more to the flower trade than just flowers.

Today, a boilerplate movie scene will show an unprepared man grabbing a bunch of random roadside or garden flowers at the last moment when he is about to meet someone to whom, he realizes belatedly, he should be handing a bouquet. The flowers always look as bedraggled as the unprepared flower-giver. Note that this isn't necessarily accurate. One could quite easily assemble a completely beautiful, fresh, personal bouquet of flowers from one's own garden or a verdant field: one doesn't *have* to purchase them. But Gilbert's art suggests that you'd be best advised to do business with the sort of tradespeople he paints. The proprietary command and expertise over a product that grows (or at least, *could* grow) wild is an intentional commercial strategy to convince people to pay for what they might find for free; this proposition has undergirded the flower business since its inception.

58 Victor-Gabriel Gilbert (1847–1933), *A Flower Seller on Les Grands Boulevardes, Paris*, oil on panel.

While Gilbert's paintings depict a great many flowers, they don't seem as outrageously sumptuous as one might imagine such a depiction to be. They are still being fixed and fussed over; the seller has a few in her hand. There are still decisions to be made, compositions in process: these raw materials are not quite ready for public consumption.

Compare this with today: only one retail florist in my city still has freestanding buckets I can scrutinize and select stem by stem. After I've made my selection and brought a wild armful of flowers to the cashier, we have the same conversation every time. Florist: 'Would you like me to arrange these for you?' (or sometimes, 'Shall I clean these up for you?') Me: 'I thought they *were* arranged: this is just how I like them.' Her: cold, polite stare with side-eye. Me, apologetically: 'I guess I'm a bit of an iconoclast' (sometimes, 'anarchist').

59 Victor-Gabriel Gilbert,
A Parisian Flower Market, 1881,
oil on canvas.

Perhaps, just once, I should let her 'arrange' them and see what she can do. Would they be significantly better than what I have done myself? I usually shuffle them around a bit as I place them in the vase, according to no particular aesthetic principle (though of course I am aware that flower-arranging precepts exist, and they are even taught in classes), but just my own intuitive composition. If my stems had been professionally arranged, I might feel compelled to leave them exactly as they were, which would mean missing out on the most enjoyable part of buying flowers: touching and fondling them, fiddling and primping, as I prepare them for display on my table. My own style seems more natural, and hers, judging by the bouquets I watch her prepare for more compliant customers, somewhat formal and ceremonious, but I'm sure both of us are playing out our own cultural presumptions of how flower displays should look and how the transaction should be conducted. As much as I prefer patronizing florists (at three times the cost, but I think you usually get what you pay for), I like that supermarket cashiers don't hassle me about arranging (rearranging) what I have selected, but remain impassively non-judgemental. They are happy to let me take care of the flowers on my own (as they trust me also to deal with my toothpaste and pickles in whatever fashion I think best).

But if I could transport back in time to patronize Gilbert's *vendeuses de fleurs*, I feel sure I would lack the temerity to propose arranging the flowers myself. I would humbly take the bouquet precisely as mademoiselle had prepared it for me with no resistance, *pas un mot*.

In *The Lower Market, Paris*, Gilbert's busy scene depicts multiple merchants at a *marché aux fleurs*: male and female, selling potted as well as cut flowers, along with carters and buyers and browsers amid various other onlookers and those passing through. We notice how attentive these workers seem towards their flowers, appreciating the delicate value of their elegant wares, and the flowers seem to respond in turn, displaying the vibrant, colourful exuberance that these vendors have drawn out through their attention.

Even accounting for the incomparable elan any market scene will have simply because it is in Paris, Gilbert's rendition exemplifies what a magnificent urban flower market might have aspired to be back in the nineteenth century, or even today. (A few hardy survivors, still as resplendent as Gilbert's, include Rome's Campo dei Fiori, Cape Town's Adderley Street Flower Market, New Delhi's Phool Mandi, London's Columbia Road, and of course Paris's Marché aux fleurs on the Ile de la Cité, where flowers have been bought and sold since 1808.) Gilbert's markets are places of business and social intercourse where people dress up with as much finery as the flowers, augmenting their own colourfully worked loveliness by procuring gerberas and irises. (The iris is generally considered the model for the stylized fleur-de-lis that King Louis VII adopted as the national emblem in the twelfth century, even though lis means 'lily'.)

Gilbert captured the flower trade as a central element of the work of the city, its commerce, its rhythms, its characters – just as Virginia Woolf did in Mrs Dalloway. Flower vendors were part of urban life in ways that have vanished: the few that remain are no longer really regular stores, but retro boutiques or pop-ups. They are disappearing like so many other precise businesses that provisioned one small but vital part of our material lives: buttons and ribbons, cheese, cameras, hats. Although it was not all that long ago, still, it is hard to remember what it was like when each of these products had its own dedicated specialist.

Not all Paris flower sellers were as admirable as Gilbert's. Henri de Toulouse-Lautrec's drawing is painfully stinted: the unloveliest

flower seller I have come across (not in terms of her physical appearance but her mien, her mood). She is a stern, pallid woman in pale clothes whose force of personality may be strong but who seems nonetheless battered down, not at all cheered by the flowers she carries. A few slender, grudging stems in her basket are only mildly more colourful (or, slightly less colourless) than the rest of the composition. It is a study in disappointment, a reminder that even flowers have their limits. We can only guess why she is so defeated. Perhaps her sadness is compounded by the irony of being around flowers all day but still not tapping into their spirit. Usually, each (the flower stock, the vendor) burnishes the other; here, it seems, each degrades the other. This is one of those paintings that gets bleaker and darker the longer I look at it; chalk it up

60 Victor-Gabriel Gilbert, *The Lower Market, Paris*, 1881, oil on canvas.

61 Morose: Henri de
Toulouse-Lautrec,
The Flower Seller, 1894,
oil and chalk on paper.

to Toulouse-Lautrec's fin *de siècle* cynicism. Her pose, her attitude, her line of sight, all seem . . . off: foreboding. If you wanted some flowers and came across this woman with this basket, would you dare approach her? Neither would I.

192

My recoil from Toulouse-Lautrec's seller makes me think about what we expect from our vendors, and what role they play in our flower-buying habits. When I purchase flowers, it is safe to say that I am probably happy: I have successfully conquered (before entering the store) any puritanical qualms about decadent expenditures, and I am about to have in my hands, ready to carry back, to my own home or a friend's, what Emerson called 'a ray of beauty . . . like music out of a workhouse'. My salesperson, whether at my flower shop or even in the supermarket, always seems to share in my happiness at least gamely: glad to be able to furnish me with something I am clearly so pleased to have. If I am buying local flowers at a farmer's market, I find myself overwhelmed with the bliss that the sellers share with me (usually the whole family is in attendance), combining their enthusiastically detailed accounts of growing these flowers with their gratitude that I have come out early on a Saturday morning to complete the circle of commerce. They seem confident that I will display their flowers with the requisite appreciation. We like when our flowers come with a dose of unfettered joy and human connection, but perhaps this conceivably faux happiness (in what is, after all, finally just a commercial transaction) is somehow analogous to the faux life that inheres in these flowers, cut, dying, ecologically dubious. Possibly all the other flower sellers are faking their pleasantry, and it is Toulouse-Lautrec's figure who actually shows us the reality behind the curtain, the tedium of vending flowers day in, day out.

But let us dispel that unpleasant hypothesis with a happier picture, a less sardonic vision of the flower seller. The young woman in Léon-François Comerre's *The Flower Seller* is as contagiously happy as anyone could want her to be. She conveys no resentment about class oppression; no Marxist alienation from the

62 Léon-François Comerre (1850–1916), *The Flower Seller*, oil on canvas.

fruits (flowers) of her labour; no concerns about toxic pesticides that don't yet exist. She and her basket of roses are at one with the world. Comerre unabashedly painted beauty: beautiful women,

beautiful flowers, *sans* the misanthropic bit-
terness Toulouse-Lautrec foregrounds. The
bonnet, the beauty spot, the dimpled chin,
the lush red lips, the guileless friendly smile,
the easy, natural eye contact (unlike Toulouse-
Lautrec's flower seller, stubbornly refusing a
human glance), the heavily ribboned bodice,
incroyable . . . How utterly ridiculous, what a
blatant fantasy-fulfilment. I'll take a dozen
stems, *votre panier entier, s'il vous plaît.*

Flower girls

Nineteenth-century 'flower girls' sold their
product out of baskets on busy city streets
and squares. Victorian social researcher Henry
Mayhew presents poignant first-person
accounts as he describes the business in

THE WALLFLOWER GIRL.
[*From a Daguerreotype by* BEARD.]

London Labour and the London Poor (1861). Sunday is the busiest day
for flower-selling, he writes (wallflowers, lavender, moss roses and
china roses are the best-sellers), for the hundreds of girls and
young women who sell 1 million bunches per year. Lavender is
'sold principally to ladies in the suburbs, who purchase it to deposit
in drawers and wardrobes; the odour communicated to linen from
lavender being, perhaps, more agreeable and more communica-
ble than that from any other flower.'[32] A garrulous costermonger
tells Mayhew her story:

63 One of Henry Mayhew's
flower girls, from his 1861
*London Labour and the London
Poor*, a wood engraving
by H. G. Hine (after a
dauguerreotype by Beard).

> I sell flowers, sir; we live almost on flowers when they are
> to be got. I sell, and so does my sister, all kinds, but it's

195

very little use offering any that's not sweet. I think it's
the sweetness as sells them. I sell primroses, when they're
in, and violets, and wall-flowers, and stocks, and roses
of different sorts, and pinks, and carnations, and mixed
flowers, and lilies of the valley, and green lavender, and
mignonette (but that I do very seldom), and violets again
at this time of the year, for we get them both in spring and
winter. The best sale of all is, I think, moss-roses, young
moss-roses. We do best of all on them. Primroses are good,
for people say: 'Well, here's spring again to a certainty.'

She buys her flowers at Covent Garden, paying a shilling for a
dozen bunches of whatever is in bloom, and then 'out of every
two bunches I can make three, at 1d. a piece.'

We make the bunches up ourselves. We get the rush to tie
them with for nothing. We put their own leaves round
these violets. The paper for a dozen costs a penny;
sometimes only a halfpenny. The two of us doesn't
make less than 6d. a day, unless it's very ill luck. But
religion teaches us that God will support us, and if
we make less we say nothing . . . I always keep 1s.
stock-money, if I can. If it's bad weather, so bad that
we can't sell flowers at all, and so if we've had to spend
our stock-money for a bit of bread, [the landlady] lends
us 1s., if she has one, or she borrows one of a neighbour,
if she hasn't . . . We live on bread and tea, and sometimes
a fresh herring of a night. Sometimes we don't eat a bit
all day when we're out; sometimes we take a bit of bread
with us, or buy a bit . . . I think our living costs us 2s.

a week for the two of us; the rest goes in rent. That's all we make.[33]

They live in 'lodginghouses, the stench and squalor of which are in remarkable contrast to the beauty and fragrance of the flowers they sometimes have to carry thither with them unsold', Mayhew writes, highlighting the ironic underside of Victorian London's flower business. The rich get richer (happier, more elaborately florified) as a consequence of the flower trade Mayhew describes, but the sublimity of primroses and violets does little to improve the lives of those who sell them.

'Flower girl' is one of those malleable, imprecise female identities in patriarchal culture that hovers between innocence and disgrace (like 'actress', 'flapper', 'pregnant', 'working girl', 'paramour'). These impoverished 'girls' – both women and children – sold flowers and sometimes also sold themselves, Mayhew explains:

> Of flowergirls there are two classes. Some girls, and they are certainly the smaller class of the two, avail themselves of the sale of flowers in the streets for immoral purposes, or rather, they seek to eke out the small gains of their trade by such practices. Their ages are from fourteen to nineteen or twenty, and sometimes they remain out offering their flowers until late at night. The other class of flowergirls is composed of girls who,

64 'Flowers, penny a bunch', from Andrew Tuer's 1885 *Old London Street Cries and the Cries of Today*.

"*Flowers, penny a bunch.*"

65 A flower seller from Gustave Doré's 1872 *London: A Pilgrimage.*

wholly or partially, depend upon the sale of flowers for their own support or as an assistance for their parents. They are generally very persevering, more especially the younger children, who will run along barefooted, with their, 'Please, gentleman, do buy my flowers. Poor little girl!' or 'Please kind lady, buy my violets. O, do! please! Poor little girl! Do buy a bunch, please, kind lady!'[34]

In Paris, too, flower girls faced sexual victimization: 'Many prostitutes of the lower orders, in order to protect themselves from the activities of the police, pretend to have a trade,' writes Octave Uzanne in his 1912 book *The Modern Parisienne*:

This is particularly the case with girls under age. Some of them are as young as fifteen, some even younger. The disgraceful evil of the small flower-girl is everywhere; you see them passing by the terraces of cafés and stopping opposite those whom with their precocious perspicacity they judge to be susceptible to their attractions.[35]

Somewhat more enlightened today, we now realize that the 'disgraceful evil' inheres not in the victimized girls but rather in the appalling men who exploit them. Uzanne's description of these men as 'susceptible to their attractions' is a variant of today's victim-blaming: 'she was asking for it.'

198

In paintings like Augustus Edwin Mulready's *Little Flower Sellers*, are the girls simply poor or are they victims of trafficking? Still today, as in the nineteenth-century flower markets/flesh markets, unscrupulous men may seek out disempowered women and girls willing to submit out of economic necessity to situations that (in the aggressor's self-serving rationalization) benefit both parties.

How do we read the photographic narrative of *Beggar Girl*, in which an old man, the wealthy Victorian industrialist Robert Thompson Crawshay, ogles a flinching flower girl? He seems predatory, powerful; she seems afraid, vulnerable. Plucking and selling flowers disturbingly suggests plucking and buying the little girls who carry them: it's almost as if they are inviting sexual advances, Mr Crawshay might well imagine.[36]

66 Augustus Edwin Mulready, *Little Flower Sellers*, 1887, watercolour.

In George Bernard Shaw's *Pygmalion* (1913), Eliza Doolittle was a flower girl – not a prostitute (she insists upon her virtue: 'I'm a good girl I am!'), but still that possibility lurks in her character as the patriarchy appraises her. Eliza's father, for example, tries to procure from Henry Higgins whatever he can get for her. Shaw's stage direction is reminiscent of the flower girls Mayhew documented a half-century earlier:

She is not at all an attractive person. She is perhaps eighteen, perhaps twenty, hardly older. She wears a little

sailor hat of black straw that has long been exposed to
the dust and soot of London and has seldom if ever been
brushed. Her hair needs washing rather badly: its mousy
colour can hardly be natural. She wears a shoddy black coat
that reaches nearly to her knees and is shaped to her waist.
She has a brown skirt with a coarse apron. Her boots are
much the worse for wear. She is no doubt as clean as she
can afford to be; but compared to the ladies she is very dirty.
Her features are no worse than theirs; but their condition
leaves something to be desired; and she needs the services
of a dentist.[37]

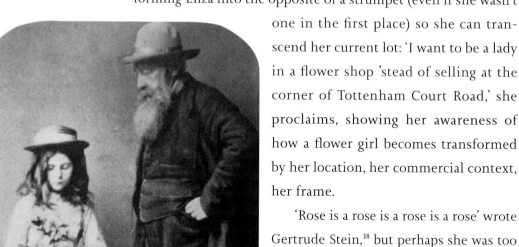

67 The millionaire industrialist
Robert Thompson Crawshay is
both photographer and subject
in *Beggar Girl*, 1877.

At the opening, Eliza's station seems identical to that of poor
Victorian flower girls, but Shaw shows Higgins diligently transforming Eliza into the opposite of a strumpet (even if she wasn't
one in the first place) so she can tran-
scend her current lot: 'I want to be a lady
in a flower shop 'stead of selling at the
corner of Tottenham Court Road,' she
proclaims, showing her awareness of
how a flower girl becomes transformed
by her location, her commercial context,
her frame.

'Rose is a rose is a rose is a rose' wrote
Gertrude Stein,[38] but perhaps she was too
idealistically egalitarian: some flowers are
more equal than others. As it is transposed
from its natural habitat to a cultural desti-
nation in the bustling marketplace, a mere
flower's straightforward properties are

keenly inflected by a more polyvalent sheaf of cultural and socio-
economic semiotics. A flower manifests the decorum of a bespoke
establishment, as Shaw's protagonist fantasizes about elevating her
station and becoming 'a lady' who sells flowers to other ladies.
Flowers sold on street corners, though, are insufficiently decorous
to redeem the flower girls who move among not just the streetwalk-
ers (with whom they might be conflated) but also street urchins
and other street wanderers; street organists; street dogs; street fight-
ers; street robbers; street bookies; and a variety of other street
dealers and street traders, street musicians and street singers, all of
whom jostle together at the bottom rung of the social hierarchy
that is the class system. Eliza perceives a market economy that
deploys a snob factor, meaning that flowers sold on the streets are
inherently worth less than the same flowers that her betters would
trade in a posh shop.

Still today, women in the flower business are vulnerable to
exploitative assumptions about their sexual availability, assumptions which may become actual enactments of exploitation. Around
some of Kenya's largest floriculture compounds, ethnographer
Megan Lowthers writes, women travel to bars in nearby communities to 'exchange sex for employment at flower farms', or 'engage in
transactional sex with flower farm managers' to supplement their
incomes with part-time sex work; when their temporary farm job
contracts end, the prostitution may become full-time. Such experiences, Lowthers writes, are typical for women in seasonal and
migratory labour pools. An outreach worker who supports women
in Kenyan floriculture reports,

> In most of the flower farms, 70 percent or more are women.
> They also don't hire elderly women, they target young

women. The flower farms are a gold rush. They come with very high expectations; it's town life, a job. There are very few men who are there, they get attracted to them [young women]. Some of them [the women] are forced to sleep with them [men] to retain that job.[39]

Lowthers tells a story about a worker who seems almost as if she could have been a sister to Mayhew's flower sellers in Victorian London. Rose, a 38-year-old single mother, had migrated to Kenya's Lake Naivasha area, where most floriculture was centred, in the 1990s in search of employment to help support her young daughter. A female relative introduced her to a farm manager:

who offered her employment in exchange for sex. This was the first time Rose slept with a manager to secure employment at a flower farm; however, she estimated that over a period of fifteen years she slept with ten managers and supervisors for employment or promotion at three different flower farms in Naivasha. Because of her low salary, fluctuating between 4,000–4,500 Kenya shillings (approximately 40–45 U.S. dollars) per month, depending on the farm, Rose supplemented her income with transactional sex and part-time sex work while working at all three flower farms. She now does sex work full time because she feels the working conditions are more favorable in sex work than at the flower farms: 'You end up sometimes [exchanging sex for a job] because you're hustling. And at every level there's a manager, a supervisor, and they all want you. You want a better job . . . I worked in three

farms and slept with maybe ten managers. Few used
a condom. I got the better positions. Throughout that
time I used to do sex work, mostly on the weekends.
. . . Now I feel like I don't want to work anymore at
the farms, I just do the other job [sex work].'[40]

Branding flowers

The business of flowers today is largely conducted by multinational
aggregators that have swallowed up smaller distributors and individual florists. These industries seamlessly facilitate an anniversary
bouquet delivery ordered by a daughter in Detroit for her parents
in Pomona: flowers within hours. Florists' Telegraph Delivery (now
just FTD) was founded in 1910 and in its prime was the world's most
profitable flower company; Berlin's Fleurop, founded in 1908, and
Interflora, formed in the UK in 1920, are now subsidiaries. (Its
market dominance has triggered several antitrust lawsuits by the
U.S. Department of Justice.) Telegraph Delivery Service, which
became Teleflora, launched in the U.S. in 1934 and accumulated its
own vast roster of subcontractors. Another large-scale competitor, 1-800-Flowers, arose in an age when orders came by telephone
rather than telegraph. If you type flowers.com into your browser's
address bar, assuming there must be such a business, you will find
that indeed there is, though it seems to be the same operation
as 1-800-Flowers, adding an Internet name to go along with its
telephone name.

Amazon has laid the groundwork to disrupt the industry in
the era of e-tailing, promoting a bland, anonymous-sounding
storefront, 'Benchmark Bouquets', to fulfil their orders. If they
wanted to evoke the tradition of floristry, I can think of many

better benchmarks than Benchmark: Covent Gardens, or perhaps Gilbert's Marché de Paris, or Tulipmania, or even Corolla. How about strangebrightcrowdsofflowers.com? Benchmark bouquets have facile names, frequently alliterative: 'Blissful Blossoms', 'Big Blooms', 'Flowering Fields'. The insipid jargon of marketing and commodification generates such products as 'Kabloom Sapphire' and (a misbegotten mash-up of Édith Piaf?) 'Life Is Good Red'. Unfortunately, life seems not to be as good as Amazon promises: 'Bouquet on the page was beautiful,' a typically tepid review informs, 'bought as a birthday bouquet because the colors were perfect for mom. Disappointed with the bleh bouquet that was delivered.'[41]

As flower selling became big business, corporate lobbyists and promoters arose to protect this oligopoly's interests, staunchly warding off market threats. In *The Florist's Daughter*, Patricia Hampl's memoir of growing up in a mid-twentieth-century family that ran a flower business, she writes that her parents 'did not take kindly to the dreary "memorials preferred" directive, tacked at the end of small-minded death notices.'

'In lieu of flowers!' my father would exclaim as he read the paper at the breakfast table.

He appealed to my brother and me, asking us to consider our funeral wishes. 'Wouldn't you rather have a beautiful display of flowers?' he asked, looking for confirmation of the right values of the world. We nodded loyally over our oatmeal – definitely, we'd take the flowers over the check for cancer research.

'I mean, cancer research, sure,' he would say magnanimously, willing to meet medical science halfway, 'but you have to have flowers.' Love and flowers, death and flowers.

> But flowers, flowers, always flowers, the insignia of death,
> the hope of resurrection.[42]

The Society of American Florists ('Your growth is our business,' their motto proclaims) takes pride in their pushback against the trend Hampl's father bemoans: 'The 1950s saw "in lieu of flowers" become a nationwide problem,' their corporate history explains, and 'SAF's Florist Information Committee won a national public relations award for its efforts to deal with the problem.'[43]

The idea that anything could serve 'in lieu of flowers' posed an existential threat. Long-standing flower-giving traditions could be disrupted in a moment: challenging their centrality at funerals could be the thin edge of the wedge for floral commerce at large. Might other gifts or gestures be found to be more useful than flowers? Are flowers too ephemeral? Too decadent? 'Ni fleurs ni couronnes' (no flowers or wreaths) is a comparable sentiment for French funerals, a plea for a simple ceremony, rejecting the old-fashioned French tradition of heaping blankets of flowers over coffins before burial.

More than a half-century after SAF first confronted this consumer revolt, the battle is still being fought. A floral syndicate website, inlieuofflowers.info, presents a many-pronged refutation of the idea that anything could possibly substitute for flowers. 'Families deserve the right of complete freedom of expression at time of death,' writes a funeral director. 'People are not cut from the same spiritual or emotional mold. Therefore, they should be free to express themselves in the manner which best conveys their emotions. Any expression which is the result of dictate ceases to be an act of the heart.'[44] The webpage advises:

The death of a family member or close friend is one
of life's most painful episodes. Those in mourning need
support and most of us are anxious to find some way
to comfort them. One of the most appropriate and
appreciated ways to express sympathy and compassion,
as well as respect for the deceased, is by sending flowers.

Occasionally, the obituary announcement includes
the phrase 'In lieu of flowers, contributions may be made
to . . .' Often times, this terminology is used to encourage
charitable gifts but not necessarily to discourage other
expressions. Most families sincerely appreciate all personal
expressions and may later regret having too few flowers
at the funeral. It is important that each giver make their
own choice and many people are choosing to send a floral
remembrance to the service or family home as well as a
donation to the charity indicated. While a monetary
donation is a worthy tribute, there is really no substitute
for beautiful flowers at a sympathy service. They comfort
the living as they commemorate the lives of the deceased.[45]

Anti-anti-flower arguments are offered. An 'in lieu of' request
could cause embarrassment if some ignore it and send flowers,
to the chagrin of those who heeded the request and didn't. People
may resent being told how to express their sympathy: they like
to decide for themselves whether to send flowers, make a donation, send a card or extend a helping hand. There is room for both
flowers and charity, this website counsels, and it is important to
place each in its proper perspective.

The florists cite a (SAF-funded) research study entitled 'The Role
of Flowers and Plants in the Bereavement Process': investigators

surveyed funeral directors, grief therapists and mourners 'to understand the value and role of flowers and plants in the funeral service
and bereavement process' and 'to determine who sends flowers,
when flowers are sent, why flowers are sent'. Funeral directors said
they did not like arranging funerals without flowers because the
setting was cold. Therapists believe receiving flowers assists the
grieving process: 'Eighty-two percent of the bereaved agreed "sending flowers is a way I show someone I care." The giving of flowers
symbolizes the love, care, and concern for the survivors.'[46]

In addition to contesting 'in lieu of', SAF's advocacy includes a
slew of campaigns to rebut what they call 'harmful floral publicity'.
SAF approaches companies that disparage flowers, because they are
trying to persuade consumers to buy their own merchandise or
services instead, 'and asks them to reconsider their approach . . . to
promote products on their own merits'.[47] In 2017 they launched
such campaigns against Coach leather goods ('Forget Flowers: Give
Mom something that's just her style'); Ancestry.com ('Forget the
flowers, connect Mom to her roots'); Jiffy Lube ('This Mother's Day
Forgo the Flowers: Get her an oil change that will last her thousands
of miles!!'); Frontier Airlines ('Send yourself instead of flowers');
Nebraska Crossing Outlets ('Looking for a gift that lasts longer
than flowers?'); and Sonny's BBQ Restaurants ('Skip the roses, get her
BBQ'). 'Success comes when the advertiser ceases running that particular promotion or at least takes note not to go that route in the
future,' says SAF's mole-whacker.

They defend the importance of flowers on other fronts, quoting
research studies that show how flowers improve emotional health
('The presence of flowers triggers happy emotions, heightens feelings of life satisfaction and affects social behavior in a positive
manner far beyond what is normally believed'); alleviate anxiety

Fitch del et lith.   Reeve & Nichols imp.

68 and 69 What could possibly serve 'in lieu of' *Rondeletia amoena*, a hardy spring-flowering evergreen with generous fragrant clusters?

('People who lived with flowers in their homes for just a few days reported a significant decrease in their levels of stress and improvements in their moods'); and boost well-being for the elderly ('A six-month behavioral study by Rutgers on the health effects of flowers on senior citizens demonstrates that flowers ease depression, inspire social networking and refresh memory as we age'). The effects they believe flowers generate for older people seem intuitively reasonable:

> Seniors who received flowers re-engaged with members of their communities and enlarged their social contacts to include more neighbors, religious support and even medical personnel. 'Instinct tells us that flowers lift our spirits, but, their effects on seniors are especially profound, if not surprising,' said lead researcher Jeannette Haviland-Jones. Specifically, 81 percent of seniors who participated in the study reported a reduction in depression following the receipt of flowers. Forty percent of seniors reported broadening their social contacts beyond their normal social circle of family and close friends. And, 72 percent of the seniors who received flowers scored very high on memory tests in comparison with seniors who did not receive flowers.[48]

Do flowers need such fraught vigilance and advocacy? Are academic studies necessary to prove that people who have flowers feel more contented than those who do not? It's interesting to ponder how flowers ever accrued the appeal that they did back in the day without a lobbying agency. Or perhaps we might consider Chaucer, Dickinson and the Wordsworths as associates of just such a promotional bureau, *avant la lettre*. And why am I mocking these ferocious floral propaganda campaigns? Aren't they promoting reverence for ranunculus and rondeletia quite similar to what I myself extol as I ramble through my own strange, bright crowds of flowers?

Is it fair to deride flower corporations for doing the same thing within their own discourse that I am doing in mine? Probably not. Apologies. Buy more flowers! 'Common sense tells us that flowers make us happy,' writes Dr Haviland-Jones. Fair enough: we have a meeting of the minds.

Global and local flowers

Flowers, so fundamentally local and place-bound, have become paradoxically a commodity of globalism. Indeed, that paradox likely accentuates the allure of bouquets that feature far-flung flowers – the harder something is to acquire, the more we desire it (hence, imperialism). The carbon footprint of getting, say, a Kenyan flower to a Dutch buyer seems enormous. But because Kenya has so much more natural sunlight, it may actually be more sustainable to take advantage of that resource: 'Flowers flown from Africa can use less energy overall than those produced in Europe because they're not grown in heated greenhouses.'[49] And European imports create half a million Kenyan jobs, so the flower trade spreads economic benefit around the world.

Amid Brexit upheaval in the UK and Europe, flowers turn out to be one of the more susceptible goods whose commerce promises to be significantly disrupted by new regulations and trade agree-ments. The British (like everyone else) have come to expect cheap, easy access to flowers of the world, and Leave voters likely hadn't realized they were endangering this. 'Brexit Could Leave Wedding Bouquets Stuck at the Border' reads a news headline that tells the whole story in a phrase. One billion dollars annually of flowers destined for the UK (that is, about 80 per cent of the total UK flower market) move through Amsterdam's central flower markets, where, before Brexit, they were transported seamlessly on having already cleared customs. As the UK and the Netherlands become separate markets, time-consuming checks and sanitary inspections will take place at the border, and duty-free goods may find tariffs imposed.[50] The disruption is especially dire for flowers because their shelf-life is so limited: their value is their freshness. If UK businesses quit Amsterdam's trading market, with its extensively choreographed system of auctions, transport and distribution, they will be disadvantaged by lack of access to that centralized hub. The EU has extensive flower-business trade agreements with Kenya, but the UK would have to negotiate its own.

One English wholesaler, Dennis Edwards, who counts Prince Charles among his clientele, worries 'that we will have aggravation getting our stuff in'.

From where he stands – in the midst of roses of every conceivable tint – Brexit amounts to a historical step backward. 'I'm old enough to remember how it was before,' he says, meaning when British customs would inspect shipments arriving at the English port of Dover from the Dutch shipping hub at Rotterdam. 'We'd be waiting for a consignment of orchids from Singapore and they'd find one insect and condemn the whole lot,' he says. He would find himself uttering expensive words to his customers: 'Sorry we've let you down.' He frets that Brexit could make these words commonplace again. 'If someone's doing a hotel at 5 in the morning and the flowers don't get there until 8, it just messes everything up,' he says. 'The Dutch still want to serve us, and we still want to buy their product. But nobody knows what will happen. We're all just in the dark.'[51]

And we know from our school science lessons that flowers cannot grow in the dark.

Like everything in nature, flowers are biochemically complex. Naturally occurring hydrocarbons – myrcene from lilies, eugenol from carnations, eucalyptol from chrysanthemums – are extracted for flavourings, oils and naturopathic medical applications. But many dangerous chemicals are added in large-scale horticulture: crops tend to be overdosed because (as Dennis Edwards observed above) an entire flower shipment can be refused entry to a country if inspectors find even a single pest. Some of these organophosphate pesticides are known carcinogens. Neurotoxic pesticides (neonicotinoids) kill bees, profoundly endangering ecosystems, and even DDT is still in use: 'It is estimated that one-fifth of the chemicals used in the floriculture industry in developing countries are banned or untested in the US.'[52] Floriculture is exempt from regulations on pesticide residues since flowers are not edible crops, so they contain significantly more synthetic compounds than are allowed on foods. (Maybe that's why I find my orchid garnish in Thai restaurants unpalatable!) A bouquet of flowers sometimes induces headaches from chemical residues. Overexposure to pesticide and fungicide toxicity can afflict anyone in the flower chain, including purchasers, but is most dangerous for growers, who are susceptible to genetic damage, dermatitis, cataracts, stillbirth and birth defects, and cancer.[53]

In Cayambe, Ecuador, an indigenous woman who worked sixteen years preparing soils for rose beds says her farm used highly toxic 'red-label' chemicals '*siempre*', always. 'I developed spinal problems, bad circulation, pain,' says María Imbaquingo. 'I have red rashes and open wounds that won't go away.' Doctors 'told me not to go back to work', but that was not an option with children to support on $160 per month. Her colleague César Estacio, a former grower who now heads a support organization for Ecuadorian workers, has had persistent throat problems. 'It's upside down,' he said. 'The people have become the plants. They're the ones getting sprayed.'[54]

Fortunately there is resistance. Worker- and ecologically focused activism takes place under the leadership of such international organizations as Fairtrade, ProFlowers, VeriFlora, Florverde and Fair Flowers Fair Plants. Flower sellers prominently advertise seals of approval from these agencies to address customers' concerns about their flowers' ethical and environmental backstories. I worry about 'greenwashing', the practice of merely paying lip service to ethical standards or making cosmetic tweaks without really pursuing fundamental change. But I hope the flower-buying public cares enough to monitor reform and demand transparent compliance.

Activist agencies work to eliminate child labour, forced labour and sweatshops; guarantee safe working conditions; and support larger projects to improve social conditions for workers' communities. As these industries tend to employ (and exploit) more women than men, watchdog groups pay special attention to women's rights issues. Unions and collective bargaining are promoted, along with protocols for inspections, audits and complaints.

These groups try to mitigate the industry's impact upon climate change via efficient processes that minimize such energy-intensive inputs as fertilizers and pesticides, encouraging greener alternatives. Growers are asked to reforest native species. Best water-management practices minimize the exploitation of this resource; waste water must be tested to ensure safety.[55]

Perhaps we prefer not to dwell upon far-reaching ethical issues when we're picking up our alstroemerias: can't we just focus on the flowers and let our gaze stop there? And it's never just one thing: if we start down the path of interrogating our flowers, we quickly get caught up in the extensive web of conservation (Barry Commoner's first law of ecology: 'Everything is connected to everything else') and then we have to think about our food, and our commute, and our recycling, and our consumption, and and and and . . . do we always need to worry about everything? Isn't the point of buying flowers precisely to 'stop and smell the flowers', tuning out the fraught world beyond?

(Apropos of nothing – or, perhaps, everything – let me put in a quick commendation for alstroemerias, also known as Peruvian lilies, which tend to be the least expensive and most reliable super-market flowers you can find. For about four dollars, pounds or euros, eight heady stems will overflow a large vase; three or four bouquets will make your house look like a flower shop. Bright and eye-catching, they do not look at all 'cheap', and they last longer than most other flowers, up to two weeks. Roses, resting on their laurels as the quintessentially delectable specimen, are feeble by comparison: they rarely stay perky beyond the weekend.)

The closer one looks, the more disturbing the ecological picture becomes. Most flowers are imported, on average, from more than 4,800 kilometres (3,000 mi.) away: a 35-tonne flower plane leaves Colombia every three hours. Flower farming is so intensive that Kenya's Lake Naivasha (its third largest lake), which provides water for fifty nearby flower farms, is rapidly drying out, and the remaining water is heavily polluted because of chemical runoff.

There are four responses: do without flowers – go and look at them where they grow instead of harvesting them ('Enjoy, don't destroy'), and learn to savour them, as William and Dorothy Wordsworth did, by just remembering them or writing a poem; grow your own flowers – without chemicals, please; patronize ethical suppliers like Florverde and Fairtrade; or buy local flowers. Option five, I suppose, would be some mix of these four responses.

In *The 50 Mile Bouquet* Debra Prinzing promotes 'slow flowers', a sustainable flower movement. 'How did something as natural and ephemeral as a flower spawn a global industry?' she asks. 'And what, if anything, had we lost along the way?' Her book seeks 'a new way of enjoying unfussy, chemical-free, natural flowers' that 'take us back to our grandmothers' gardens, and to the flower farms that used to surround every large city, offering sweet peas in spring and dahlias in late summer and cherry blossoms in February'.[56]

The appeal of the 'slow food' campaign resonates in the world of flowers, as Prinzing explains:

> We are drawn to the people – growers and designers –
> who are actively participating in the local, seasonal and
> sustainable movement . . . Just as a diner asks the chef
> 'is this a wild-catch or farmed salmon?' we are beginning
> to witness flower consumers wanting to know 'where was
> this flower grown – and how?' and 'who grew it?' Customers
> appreciate the option of going green, such as sourcing only
> locally-grown flowers for a wedding bouquet or special
> occasion.[57]

Prinzing profiles a field-to-vase florist, Jennie Love, from Philadelphia, who says:

> What 'sustainably grown' means to me is this in a nutshell:
> being careful not to take more from the land and the
> community than I am putting back into them. In my
> daily farming practices, I am using cover crops, compost,
> all-natural fertilizers, good watering practices, limited
> tilling of the land, lots of native plants so the local insect
> population has food sources, nurturing old antique/
> heirloom flowers that might not necessarily be money
> makers but are going to disappear from our world if
> growers like me don't keep using them, and generally
> being very thoughtful about how everything I do in
> the field is going to impact not just that field but the
> forest that surrounds the field, the underwater streams
> that run from the field to the rivers, and the flora and
> fauna in that field and elsewhere in 5–10 years. And I
> never use synthetic chemicals to fight bugs or weeds.
>
> I work hard at engaging and educating my immediate
> community – literally my neighbors . . . I try to always
> be transparent about what I am doing . . . I have a rule:
> My flowers never go further than 75 miles from where
> they grew. I want my flowers and my business to enrich
> the lives of those who live around me in as many ways as
> possible.[58]

Another way to improve sustainability in the flower trade is by
recycling flowers: just as social agencies distribute leftover and
unsold foods that remain edible, people have started gathering

216

used flowers after weddings and banquets, along with castoffs that didn't make it into florists' sold products, for repurposing at senior centres, homeless shelters and other places where residents may not usually receive many bouquets. Kaifa Anderson-Hall's non-profit group Plants and Blooms Reimagined recovers flowers for horticultural therapy, 'bringing nature to people who are margin-alized, isolated and in need of support' so that expensive flowers, 'arranged and displayed for a few hours before being discarded', can be more widely appreciated. Anderson-Hall tells her suppli-ers they can 'offer their clients the added bonus of feeling good about what happens to the flowers once an event is over'.[59] She reports that older people who spend time arranging blooms have developed greater dexterity and hand strength, and that home-less people have found her workshops to be emotionally calming distractions from their difficult situations.

A vital mission for locally oriented flower commerce is help-ing to save bees by growing and selling plants that are best suited to enhance apian prosperity. Beekeeper Lori Weidenhammer calls it 'gardening for our lives. We need to undo the damage we have done to make the world inhospitable for the very bees that make our planet livable.'[60] Bee-positive horticulture sets aside some land as a bee habitat. Like other organic growers, flower farmers should select plants conducive to biodiversity, rather than invasive. The most valuable flowers for bees have a rich reward-to-plant-mass ratio – that is, a high volume of nectar and pollen for the amount of space taken up by the plant. They bloom continuously over a long period and feature an alluring bee-attracting scent and strik-ing visual design; healthy weed-growth in the field is also good for enhancing biodiversity and protecting the soil, and they should be grown far from car-exhaust particulates and herbicides.[61]

70 Excessively exotic: heliconia.

What kinds of things grow in your garden, and in the gardens next door, and in nearby parks and fields? If they seem less spectacular than exotic specimens like heliconia or protea, they are also less trafficked, less contrived. They belong in your community, and people who receive these cut flowers may consciously appreciate this, or they may be informed, as you present them with local bouquets, of their proximate terroir: a teachable moment. Heliconia is a breathtaking botanical composition of colour and form: odd, dramatic, bizarre, outrageous. 'Lobster claws' is its common name; sometimes also 'toucan beak'. But do I need it in my flower arrangements in Atlanta? Do I deserve it? How does it get from where it grows to where I live? If I saw a flower like this once every few years in an arboretum's tropical room, or perhaps came across one (just once! – remember, 'once-in-a-lifetime' used to be pretty high praise) in a garden, or even in the wild in Cuba or Brazil, Costa Rica or Venezuela ... wouldn't that be a better experience, with a more potent claim on my memory and my senses, and wouldn't it instil a more accurate representation of the flower and its relation to my world, than if I buy a stem week after week to set off as a funky accent against lilies and hydrangea?

If this tropical flower has anything remotely resembling feelings, sensations, awareness, symbiotic connection to its environment – and how can it not?! – does it enjoy a twelve-hour trip in the belly of a jet cargo to get to Houston or Frankfurt, where it moves through cavernous warehouses to end up in a small vase completely isolated from any element of its natural ecosystem?

I don't think this heliconia is happy to be commodified. Its pollinators, mostly hummingbirds, must wonder where their flowers have run off to. (The rufous-breasted hermit also uses the heliconia for nesting: how cool a bird crib is that? Bats, too, and beetles, must be disappointed when they discover their residences have been removed to become ornaments in someone else's residence.)

Nor should *we* be happy about what has happened here. It is a disruption, a manipulation: a sign of our power, our reach, our control over the world, our development of incredibly (and dangerously) elaborate commercial infrastructures. It is a manifestation of our hubris: we *can* have heliconia in our flower arrangements, but *should* we, in the Anthropocene? The entire planet is under extreme stress, facing uncertain but scary instabilities across the board. We have already begun to see exponentially increasing incidences of melting, burning, flooding, famine and climate-based conflict. We are losing fish, coral and bees, among untold thousands of other living species, because of our unbridled and inconsiderate expressions of our power over nature, and our ecological short-sightedness: our failure to exercise sage and safe stewardship. Given our culpability in impending ecological collapse, it is at least ironic, if not perverse and downright hypocritical, to buy flowers harvested from around the world. They may, in the short term, palliate (or sublimate) our Anthropocenic anxieties – 'the world must still be healthy, thriving, if it produces such beauty' – at the same time they accelerate ecosystemic implosion. Archaeologists in a distant future who find heliconia fossils in a Vancouver garbage dump will struggle to understand the inhabitants of a culture that seemed to have so much information about the world around them and yet didn't put two and two together.

Protea, a hardy African flower (given that name by Linnaeus because it had so many different forms) symbolizes change and hope in its local culture. What a portentous 'inference therefrom' we may draw in terms of the *changes* that *I hope* we will enact to save our flowers along with all our fellow plants and animals, and indeed our planet. Enjoy the protea in the photo here, but forego this flower for your own vase in favour of some columbine (if you live in Colorado) or cowslips (if you live in Crewe). Pretorians and Port Elizabethans, feel free to procure all the protea you want (within reason). The king protea, South Africa's national flower, will feel right at home in your arrangements.

Habituated to expect far-flung, heavily commodified, hyper-perfect, out-of-season floriculture as the norm, we may be pleasantly surprised to see how satisfying a plain old local bouquet strikes us. The taste of radishes and rocket (arugula) sold this morning by folks who grew them in the next town over, dirt still on their jeans from kneeling in the furrows to harvest the veggies before they set up at your farmers' market, has a freshness (actual? imagined? both?) and honesty that is a world away from mass-market, plastic-packaged produce. Flowers, too, nurtured in the same locale that nurtures us, have significant appeal and value. You can get them, alongside the radishes, at growers'

71 *Protea cynaroides*, native to South Africa.

markets stocked by nearby agricultural collectives, and also from a few enlightened florists. Some chains like Whole Foods coordinate sales of 'locally sourced' flowers – those grown within a seven-hour truck drive of the store, according to their guidelines; 'micro-local' flowers grow within a two-hour radius.[62] And some local growers even take to the Internet, challenging megasellers on their own cyberturf: California Organic Flowers, for example, describes itself as the anti-FTD. 'Flowers bring the joy and beauty of nature into your home. If there is a sad story of chemical sprays and exploited workers behind your flowers, the joy of the flowers is diminished.'[63]

You cannot buy whatever you want whenever you want it if you're committed to locally grown flowers. But better than that, you can look forward to when a flower will become available. For me, that means amaryllis and snowdrops early in the winter, quince in March, dogwood in April and May, calla lilies and Queen Anne's lace in June, then snapdragons and hydrangea as the summer wears on (though climate change has been pushing hydrangea earlier, to late spring), amaranth and bluebeard as autumn approaches, mums and broom corn for Halloween. Spending the entire year anticipating amaranth makes it pretty exciting when it finally turns up at market.

Artisanal growers dispense advice we don't get from supermarkets, which helps us better appreciate the properties of these flowers so that they start to seem more like actual natural beings rather than decorations. For maximum vase life, cut peonies 'in bud': gently squeeze the bud, which should be squishy like a marshmallow. Stored flat in a cooler or refrigerator, peonies can be saved at this stage for a month; re-cut them and put them in a vase when you're ready and they will burst open. Put fresh flowers in warm water for a few hours when you first bring them home to 'harden'

72 Every flower in its time: Robert Furber's print *Twelve Months of Flowers* (1730) depicts each month's harvest. March offers such blossoms as hyacinth, anemone, iris, Jerusalem cowslip, 'lesser black hellebore' and 'Palto Auriflame Tulip'.

them, as the warmer water moves up the stems more quickly. Try all the folk-wisdom suggestions for extending flowers' freshness – toss a copper coin in the vase, or a few drops of lemonade, or aspirin, or vinegar, or vodka – which usually work as well as those little cellophane packets of 'flower food' containing citric acid, sugar and bleach. Daffodils have hollow stems containing a sap-like substance that gives the stems their turgidity; when that liquid seeps out, it shortens the freshness of other flowers in the vase, so they are best kept segregated. Harvest lilacs when most of the florets are open: they will not open any further when they are cut. Shave the cut stem like a pencil to expose the underbark, which absorbs water better.[64]

Acquire flowers from friends: barter a bunch of your own for some of theirs, or shovel their winter pavement in exchange for a couple of baskets full of their summer blooms. Years ago my friend LeeAnne came to a party with an overflowing armful of her front garden's deep blue irises, long-stemmed, crazy colourful, imperfectly perfect, and it is among the few actual bouquets of flowers (despite the hundreds that have cycled in and out of my house since then) that I remember vividly, gratefully, specifically. Things that grow in your city, in your neighbourhood, may seem less glamorous but they are more authentic; they feel more like yours, and more at home when they are in your home, than exotic imported flowers do. Like local honey, local vegetables, local bread, they seem better because they are fresher, and because your body and mind intuitively appreciate that they are part of your ecosystem.

1 Royal Widow Auricula.
2 Dwarf white starry Hyacinth.
3 White Roseamon Narcess.
4 High Admiral Anemone.
5 Rhayen Narcess.
6 White passe flower.
7 White grape flower.
8 The lesser black Hellebore.
9 Danae Auricula.

10 White flowering Almond.
11 Dwarf blew starry Hyacinth.
12 American flowering Maple.
13 Goldfinch Polyanthos.
14 Larger blew starry Hyacinth.
15 Virginian flowering Maple.
16 Narcess of Naples.
17 Best Claremon Tulip.
18 The checker'd Futillaria.

MARCH

19 Large leav'd Norway Maple.
20 Double pulchra Hyacinth.
21 Queen of France Narcess.
22 Pateo duri flame Tulip.
23 Blew Oriental Hyacinth.
24 Single bloody Wall.
25 Admiral blew Anemone.
26 Bell Baptice Anemone.

27 Monument Anemone.
28 Red flowering Larch tree.
29 Blew passe flower.
30 Rose Jonker Anemone.
31 White flowering Larch tree.
32 Purple strip'd Anemone.
33 The Velvet Iris.
34 Jerusalem Cowslip.

Design'd by P.r Casteels.

From the Collection of Rob.t Furber Gardiner at Kensington. 1730.

Engrav'd by H. Fletcher.

4

FLOWERS, GENDER, SEXUALITY, RACE AND CLASS

I love another man, and it makes me feel like a pretty flower.

RAPUM KAMBILI[1]

Sigmund Freud offers an anecdote (personal, before becoming more dispassionately psychoanalytical) about gender and flowers in *The Interpretation of Dreams*:

The cyclamen is the favourite flower of my wife. I reproach myself for so seldom thinking to bring her flowers, as she wishes. In connection with the theme 'bringing flowers', I am reminded of a story which I recently told in a circle of friends to prove my assertion that forgetting is very often the purpose of the unconscious, and that in any case it warrants a conclusion as to the secret disposition of the person who forgets. A young woman who is accustomed to receive a bunch of flowers from her husband on her birthday, misses this token of affection on a festive occasion of this sort, and thereupon bursts into tears. The husband comes up, and is unable to account for her tears until she tells him, 'To-day is my birthday.' He strikes his forehead and cries, 'Why, I had completely

forgotten it,' and wants to go out to get her some
flowers. But she is not to be consoled, for she sees
in the forgetfulness of her husband a proof that
she does not play the same part in his thoughts
as formerly.[2]

Do not forget flowers for your wife, Herr Doctor advises in no
uncertain terms; she will be perturbed. (Is Freudian therapy really
necessary to achieve such an obvious insight? This narrative sounds
almost as if it could have been an advertisement for FTD, although
that flower company would not be founded until a few years after
Freud wrote this.)

Women are widely considered more fitting flower fanciers than
men. In a subordinate role, men may facilitate floral experiences by
buying bouquets to woo women; to apologize for something; to
commemorate a promotion, an anniversary or Mother's Day; or just
because. Remembering flowers may be manly, or a manly concession to womanliness, but actually enjoying the flowers is seen as
women's work.

When Freud writes 'I reproach myself for so seldom thinking
to bring her flowers, as she wishes,' does his self-reproach seem sincere? Do we imagine that he learns from his uxorious deficiency as
expressed here, and then makes (and keeps) a resolution to buy
Martha a cyclamen bouquet every Friday? I hear an unspoken but
implicit disparagement in his observation about flowers and gender,
which, if I am not overreading the master of overreading, floats a
passive-aggressive accusation that women spend a great deal of
time (possibly *too much* time, too obsessively?) waiting for men to
bring them flowers, forgetting that we have more worldly things to
do. A plangent eighteenth-century word (resurrected in T. S. Eliot's

poetry[3]) captures Freud's tone here: 'velleity' means 'the fact or quality of merely willing, wishing, or desiring, without any effort or advance towards action or realization'.[4]

Women's passion for flowers, Freud implies as he proffers velleities about being a more dependable flower-giver, is a pleasant-but-silly manifestation of their nature. All things equal, you would do well to bring flowers as expected to women who are dear to you, but sometimes you will forget – and 'forgetting is very often the purpose of the unconscious' that 'warrants a conclusion as to the secret disposition of the person who forgets' – suggesting that the flowers were never all that consequential in the first place. They may have seemed important to her, but in the normal (male!) psyche, their necessity is overblown.

Flowers, masculinity, sexuality

In the early nineteenth century, the first 'florists' were ladies' maids whose skills developed as fashion accessorizing, 'making up bouquets and sprays of flowers for ladies to wear'.[5] Flowers became keenly identified with women's realms as they began to blossom in apparel and design, and to decorate homes, parties and weddings. When Queen Victoria began avidly exchanging bouquets, flowers became irrefutably associated with women's culture.

Gender-specific floral customs accentuate stereotypical perceptions that women, like flowers, are soft, pretty and delicate; and men, on the whole, are not. Women present themselves in flowery styles: wearing flower-print dresses and scarves, using floral scents and soaps, choosing make-up and fashion hues that evoke a florist's palette (while men are largely restricted to grey and dark blue outfits), wearing rings and brooches, hats and sandals that feature flower patterns. Bouquets and vases of flowers are rarely found in such presumptively male venues as construction sites, sports arenas or police stations (all of which may, of course, accommodate people of any gender), and flower imagery rarely decorates golf clubs, electric saws or craft beer growlers.

The seeming incompatibility of conventional heterosexual masculinity and flowers spotlights precisely what is deficient in the codes and habits of conventional heterosexual masculinity: the beauty and pleasure we decline to embrace. What are we afraid of? Are straight men such soulless creatures? In the inadvisable event that a woman persists in her determination to give a man flowers, still, the Internet can at least mitigate the 'problem' by helping to preserve gendered proprieties despite her floral faux pas. A webpage, 'Tips for buying Masculine Flowers', lists 'a few things you might want to keep in mind when selecting flowers or plants for men: Men tend to prefer stronger shapes and bolder colors. Stay away from pastels. Tropical inspired flowers and plants are good choices for guys.' Potted flowers and other plants are safer than cut flowers, experts advise. Perhaps the work of growing (as virile farmers do) seems masculine enough to overcome the unfortunate daintiness of flowers.

In these masculine corners of Internet commerce, arrangements feature flowers specially chosen to be more popular, or at least less repugnant, to fathers, husbands and boyfriends, including a few species deemed to be somewhat gender-fluid: birds of paradise, red roses, green gladioli, protea, aspidistra, flax and kalanchoe (a succulent with strong, firm leaves and tightly packed, almost mechanically precise inflorescence: not at all flimsy or prissy).[6] FTD's 'Manly Flowers' category promotes arrangements 'with bold colors and strong shapes that any man would love': peace lilies, Peruvian

227

lilies, gardenia and white dendrobium orchids might be sufficiently non-feminine, they advise.

Flowers branded as projecting vigorous fortitude will pass muster. 'If you need last minute birthday gifts for a husband or a sentimental Father's Day present, masculine floral arrangements are the way to go. Find buds in earthy hues to complement his rugged aesthetic or crisp cuts for a sleeker, minimalistic style.'[7] Specifying 'a *sentimental* Father's Day present' implies that flowers would not be a *normal* gift like a hammer or a tie; perhaps dad is in his dotage. 'Earthy hues' are better than pink, violet, mauve, magenta and all the other delightful colours that women are allowed to enjoy (and don't even think about variegated flowers, which are insanely effeminate). Dull, dark crowds of flowers, it seems, are men's destiny.

Teleflora's 'Flowers for him' masculinizes its product line by arranging blooms in containers shaped like cars: a Chevy Camaro, a Ford Mustang or a simple pickup (and vintage cars at that: a 1948 Ford pickup, a '65 Mustang, a '67 Camaro, from back in the days when men were men).[8] The vase, apparently, is part of the problem of overfeminized flowers: possibly the idea of flowers emerging from a cylindrical cavity is too shockingly evocative of biological femininity (about which, much more below).

Floraqueen (shouldn't there be a bespoke Floraking division?) claims to have consulted their male customers who 'have told us that for them bouquets must be bold with strong shapes and colours, such as red, orange and yellow. They emphasised how they were much less keen on flowers made up of pastel colours and overly frilly arrangements.'[9] Certainly it is true in fashion and design that some colours, forms and styles figure as more traditionally masculine or feminine. But the more one looks at the rules

228

and suggestions for male-appropriate bouquets, the more it seems that the vast majority of flowers' basic properties (pastel, frilly, delicate, sweet-smelling, enchanting, sublime) render them appropriate only for women. Bold red chrysanthemums, Floraqueen advises, would be a safe choice for Frank or Bob. In an online article entitled 'Flowers That Will Actually Add Masculinity to Your Home', the word 'actually' connotes a subliminal dismissiveness that recalls Freud, implying that flowers are an unfortunate, if necessary, concession to the frivolity of feminine domesticity. Snapdragons might be acceptable, this article suggests, as they are 'said to resemble the mythical fire-breathing beast (sounds pretty manly, right?)'. But 'avoid pretty pink snapdragons and combine the red and yellow varieties for a more manly arrangement.' Other ideas:

> Hops is the wonder flower responsible for flavouring beer, and for that reason alone it deserves a place on our list of dude-friendly flowers . . . The Heliconia's brilliant red and yellow flower (flanked by large green leaves) is actually related to the banana, and you don't get much more masculine than that! . . . Leave delicate perfumed petals to the ladies and embrace the waxy sturdiness of Anthurium flowers.[10]

What is wrong with men? Why can't we enjoy the simple pleasures of strange, bright crowds of flowers in their glorious full range? Why do we have to wall ourselves off and make sure that if we *do* engage with flowers, we will tolerate only a small subset of carefully delineated waxy, sturdy, non-threatening, not-too-flowery specimens that read completely macho? Are we afraid people will think that we are femme, or queer?

Floral anxious masculinity is, indeed, a quagmire reserved for straight cismen. Everyone else can do whatever they want with flowers without fear of being called out for violating fixed gender identities. In fact, one might hazard, the more flowers women and queer folk dote on, the better for straight men, because it leaves fewer to risk encountering themselves. Flowers may be invoked in the service of both old-fashioned and newly enlightened attitudes towards sexuality. Homophobic florists sometimes refuse to design floral settings for same-sex weddings, which I find shameful. They will often invoke religious freedom, or even artistic licence, to justify their intolerance of gay human rights.

But if flowers may abet conformist heterosexual apprehensions and prejudices, they may also flourish for others who defy such bigotry. Hip-hop star Tyler, the Creator announced his bisexuality on his 2017 album *Flower Boy*, using a garden shed to represent the closet where he had been hiding his authentic sexuality (*guardin'* his feelings, he raps, a nice homophonic twist on 'garden'). Coming out of that shed, he introduces his queer identity with flower metaphors: don't kill a flower before it blooms, he sings, explaining how he blooms and he grows.[11] Nigerian writer Rapum Kambili's queer art anthology 'We Are Flowers' begins, 'Let the flowers bloom!' and a photo caption reads: 'I love another man, and it makes me feel like a pretty flower.'[12] Jonathan Van Ness, from television's 'Queer Eye' ensemble, starts his 2019 memoir *Over the Top*: 'You know those plants that are always trying to find the light? Maybe they were planted in a location that didn't necessarily facilitate growth, but inexplicably they make a circuitous route to not only survive but bloom into a beautiful plant. That was me – my whole life.'[13]

Oscar Wilde famously wore his green carnation, an 'unnatural' colour for a flower, to mock the prejudice that love between men was unnatural. Wilde's flower was a code, a queer badge recognized by those in the know. Violets, similarly, symbolize lesbian community, plucked from Sappho's poem 'I have not had one word from her':

> If you forget me, think
> of our gifts to Aphrodite
> and all the loveliness that we shared
>
> all the violet tiaras,
> braided rosebuds, dill and
> crocus twined around your young neck.[14]

Édouard Bourdet's 1927 Broadway play *The Captive* featured a same-sex romance in which one woman sends the other violet posies as a subtly queer gesture, though apparently not subtle enough. Police raided and closed the show on grounds of obscenity. Subsequently, in protest against this censorship, giving violets became popular in New York's lesbian community.[15]

Robert Mapplethorpe is another gay man who did what he wanted with flowers. His photographs of large phallic stems and other flagrantly erotic floral forms (including the birds of paradise that florists recommend for their male customers, and Jack-in-the-pulpit, which will *not* appear on any lists of safe straight flowers) give Georgia O'Keeffe a run for her money. 'Whether it's a cock or a flower, I'm looking at it in the same way,' Mapplethorpe explained, 'in my own way, with my own eyes.'[16] Indeed, he photographed many of the same species that O'Keeffe painted, in similarly large, sleek, close-up portraits, and it's interesting to notice how her visions of those flowers exude such striking strains of

73 Jack-in-the-pulpit is a favourite flower for artists interested in sexy forms. The flower's hood (the 'pulpit'), technically called a spathe, has a long stem-like growth, the spadix (or 'Jack'), containing the reproductive elements.

female sexuality (straight or lesbian sexuality? I'd say bisexual/ pansexual, mapping O'Keeffe's own orientation), while Mapplethorpe's convey blatantly queer male tropes. Apparently floral ethos is all in the eye of the beholder.

232

74 Paul Harfleet, *Fucking Faggot!* (Queen Street, Blackpool, 2014, photographed as part of The Pansy Project).

In contrast to such flowering-and-empowering queer identities, though, gay men have also been disparaged by such homophobic slurs as 'pansy' (mocking flamboyant queer affect), 'daffy' (daffodils, polymorphic, can mate with their own sex) and 'lavender boys' (the colour commonly represents gay themes). These verbal assaults have been known to become marching orders for physical assaults, queer-bashing hate crimes.

Paul Harfleet's 'The Pansy Project', begun in 2005, combats and reconfigures the floral slur. He documents homophobic public assaults around the world and then plants a pansy, just one – without going through 'official channels' to get any civic permission – in the soil nearest to where the persecution occurred. Harfleet then posts a photograph of the flower on his website to memorialize 'a frequent reality of gay experience, which often goes unreported to authorities and by the media. This simple action operates as a gesture of quiet resistance; some pansies flourish and others wilt in urban hedgerows.' His first pansy marked his own traumatic experience in Manchester, and launched his performative mission by exploring how people subjected to such abuse felt at the precise location where it happened. Harfleet has planted almost three hundred memorial pansies, each 'named' for the slur experienced on that spot.

What interested me was the way that the locations later acted as a prompt for me to explore the memories associated with that place. I wanted in some way to manipulate these associations, in order to feel differently about the location and the memories it summoned. I became interested in the public nature of these incidents and the way one was forced into reacting publicly to a crime that often occurred during the day and in full view of passers-by. I had observed that the tendency to place flowers at the scene of a crime or accident had become an accepted ritual and I considered a similar response. Floral tributes subtly augment the reading of a space that encourages a passer-by to ponder past events at a marked location, generally understood as a crime or accident; my particular intervention could encourage a passer-by to query the reason for my own ritualistic action.

Placing a live plant felt like a positive action, it was a comment on the abuse; a potential 'remedy'. The species of plant was of course vitally important and the pansy instantly seemed perfect. Not only does the word refer to an effeminate or gay man: the name of the flower originates from the French verb *penser* (to think), as the bowing head of the flower was seen to visually echo a person in deep thought. The subtlety and elegiac

quality of the flower was ideal for my requirements. The
action of planting reinforced these qualities, as kneeling in
the street and digging in the often neglected hedgerows felt
like a sorrowful act.[17]

It is moving and inspiring to see how prejudices that cruelly impli-
cate flowers may be redirected, undone. Flower imagery that is
used stupidly, as a slur, can be almost magically redeemed simply
by using it thoughtfully, as Harfleet's 'Pansy Project' exemplifies.
Love wins; flowers win.

If (after all this) you are still considering getting flowers
for a man who can't stomach anything even a tiny bit flowery, a
good alternative might be a Beef Jerky Bouquet – meat seems like
the opposite of flowers – from The Manly Man Company, where
'FLOWERS NEVER TASTED SO GOOD!'

> Our arrangements are 100% edible and truly are made
> for that rugged one of a kind, hammer swinging, IPA
> drinking, duck hunting, beast of a man-animal you call
> yours. Each broquet's vase is a Manly Man pint glass . . .
> Flower is made with 100% beef. Stem sections are made
> from a mouthwatering blend of beef, pork and spices.[18]

'Broquet' – get it?

The Story of Ferdinand (1936), a beast fable for children written
by Munro Leaf and illustrated by Robert Lawson, rejects gendered
flower restrictions. Ferdinand is a Spanish bull – a solid, masculine
creature, but also a gentle one, who refuses to fight: 'All the other
little bulls he lived with would run and jump and butt their heads
together, but not Ferdinand. He liked to sit just quietly and smell

75 The way to a man's heart is through his stomach: 'flowers' masculinized as food.

the flowers.' Concerned that Ferdinand is too gentle, his mother encourages him to romp around, but he responds, '"I like it better here where I can sit just quietly and smell the flowers." His mother saw that he was not lonesome, and because she was an understanding mother, even though she was a cow, she let him just sit there and be happy.'

Stung by a bee – always a hazard of smelling flowers! – Ferdinand starts bucking and snorting wildly, giving the misleading impression of a tough combatant, but when men abduct him for the bullring, to monetize this masculinity, he regains his peaceful composure. 'When he got to the middle of the ring he saw the flowers in all the lovely ladies' hair and he just sat down quietly and smelled. He wouldn't fight and be fierce no matter what they did. He just sat and smelled.'[19]

236

Although Leaf denied any political allegory, the book's timing and setting led to its reception as an enormously popular text of resistance to the Spanish Civil War. Mahatma Gandhi admired it, as did Eleanor Roosevelt. Burned in Nazi Germany and unavailable in Spain until after Francisco Franco's death, the book outsold *Gone with the Wind* in the USA.[20]

Ernest Hemingway, a human who preferred his bulls violent and bloody (and not the sort who was himself inclined to stop and smell the flowers) parodied Ferdinand in a 1951 story, 'The Faithful Bull':

> One time there was a bull whose name was not
> Ferdinand and he cared nothing for flowers. He loved
> to fight and he fought with all the other bulls of his
> age, or any age, and he was a champion … He was always

76 The Iberian cork oak Ferdinand enjoys, *Quercus suber*, blooms with resplendent bright yellow strings of flowers.

ready to fight and his coat was black and shining and his
eyes were clear.

Hemingway's bull 'fought wonderfully and everyone admired him
and the man who killed him admired him the most'.[21] But Leaf's
Ferdinand lives happily ever after, surrounded by flowers: 'And
for all I know he is sitting there still, under his favorite cork tree,
smelling the flowers just quietly. He is very happy.'[22]

The Story of Ferdinand celebrates gender nonconformity.
'Ferdinand refuses to fight in the bullring, simultaneously mocking traditional Spanish masculinity and escaping the Banderillos,
Picadores, and matador who intend to slaughter him. His gender
variance – manifest in his preference for peace and flowers – makes
him unworthy as a competitor and saves his life.' Leaf's moral,
according to education scholar Katie Sciurba, is: 'Be true to your
identity, and you will live a tranquil life.'[23] Or as I read the lesson,
through my own lens, flowers *can* delight men – taurine as well as
human, Spanish as well as British, American or Barbadian. (Barba-
dians of all gender identities seem prone to affirm their botanical
heritage: their national flower, *Caesalpinia pulcherrima*, bears the
common name 'pride of Barbados'. I endorse such rhetorically
emphatic appellations to encourage citizens' exultation in their
flowers' splendour.)

Flowers of femininity

If men are culturally and semiotically alienated from flowers,
women are pervasively enveloped in them. Flowers' cycles mirror
women's cycles, and botanical fertility mirrors female fertility. As
chary as one must be about giving flowers to men, there is nothing

more appropriate than giving a woman flowers constantly; she may put them on her table, or wear them in her hair or on her wrist, or even (especially in less hygienic eras) nuzzled between her breasts (sorry, *bodice*) as a 'nosegay'.

When Thomas Campion writes 'There is a garden in her face / Where roses and white lilies grow,' he is composing a *blazon*, a literary form that poeticizes flowers as metaphors for women. Campion was a contemporary of William Shakespeare, whose Sonnet 130, 'I have seen roses damasked, red and white, / But no such roses see I in her cheeks,'[24] parodies this tradition that many other poets of their age embraced with florid fervour. Edmund Spenser's *Amoretti* (Sonnet 64) is a full-blooming iteration of this genre:

> Comming to kisse her lyps, (such grace I found).
>> Me seemd I smelt a gardin of sweet flowres:
>> that dainty odours from them threw around
>> for damzels fit to decke their louers bowres.
> Her lips did smell lyke vnto Gillyflowers,
>> her ruddy cheekes, lyke vnto Roses red:
>> her snowy browes lyke budded Bellamoures
>> her louely eyes lyke Pincks but newly spred,
> Her goodly bosome lyke a Strawberry bed,
>> her neck lyke to a bounch of Cullambynes:
>> her brest lyke lillyes, ere theyr leaues be shed,
>> her nipples lyke yong blossomd Iessemynes,
> Such fragrant flowres doe giue most odorous smell,
>> but her sweet odour did them all excell.[25]

Women are very much like flowers, these poets propose. As much as I like flowers (and women), still, this is a dangerous equivalency.

Flowers objectify women as pretty and delicate, thus 'essentializing' them (that is, suggesting that all women have a single common, essential quality that is flower-like) in ways that delimit them, script them.

Indeed, women are not merely *like* flowers: women *are* flowers, pure and simple. Ask Lily, Rose, Violet, Myrtle, Flora, Florence, Blossom, Heather, Jasmine, Iris, Marigold, Poppy or Daisy. Shoshana in Hebrew and Sawsana in Arabic mean Lily, becoming Suzanne in English and Zsa Zsa in Hungarian. Rosa, Rhoda, Ruusu and Rosalie

77 Sir Joshua Reynolds, *Anne Dashwood*, 1764, oil on canvas. A nosegay makes the nose gay, as floral scents mask some not-so-gay bodily odours.

78 Allan Ramsay, *Lady in a Pink Silk Dress*, 1762, oil on canvas. Nosegays appear near, or even in, a woman's bosom, as if her cleavage is the vase.

are Rose in Spanish, Greek, Finnish and French. Nasreen in Persian and Eglantine in French are wild roses. Iolantha is Russian for Violet. Yasmeen in Arabic and Mallika in Sanskrit are Jasmine; Padma is Sanskrit for pink lotus, Kamala for red lotus. Leilani in Hawaiian means 'heavenly flower'. Fiorenza is 'flower' in Italian. Sakura in Japanese is a cherry flower, and Keiko is a September flower. The Scandinavian names Linna, Lynae and Linnea (among other variants) all mean 'small pink flower', referring to the twin-flower (*Linnaea borealis*) that has the impressive stature of having been botanical taxonomist Carl Linnaeus' favourite flower.

My colleague Lynée Gaillet hadn't known her first name derived from the twinflower, but when I informed her she ecstatically told me 'Gaillet' is a small yellow flower: *Galium verum*, or *gaillet jaune* in French, also known in English as curweed or lady's bedstraw. (Speaking of gender, I wonder how a lady's bedstraw differs from a gentleman's? I suppose the gentleman's is probably somehow better, in accordance with the patriarchy.) Lynée is a good sport when I now, on occasion, call her 'small pink flower, small yellow flower': she blooms with pride.

Even before Georgia O'Keeffe's paintings made this connection inescapably obvious, a woman's vulva has often been compared to a flower, which it may resemble in form; see especially the genus *Clitoria*. Besides being named for flowers, women are also described as being 'deflowered' (an odd, sexist and largely antiquated phrase) when they first have sexual intercourse. 'A young bride is like a plucked flower; but a guilty wife is like a flower that had been walked over,' Honoré de Balzac writes in *Honorine*.[26] If his wife-flower equiv-alency is obtuse and ridiculous, still it exemplifies men's common compulsion to see women, and especially their sexual experiences, in floral analogies.

79 *Clitoria ternatea*, aka butterfly pea, or Asian pigeonwings. Practitioners of traditional Chinese medicine use it to augment the female libido and treat sexual ailments.

Breaking a woman's hymen is like plucking a flower, presumably, after which she blossoms forth as a woman. 'Flower' referred to virginity at least as far back as the fourteenth century. 'Fall and Passion' from the Kildare Lyrics (c. 1300), describes Mary's virgin birth: 'Maid bere heuen king . . . þer for sso ne les noȝt hir flure' ('A maid bore heaven's king [but] did not for that reason lose her flower'). In John Gower's *Confessio Amantis* (1393) a maiden pleads, 'O Pallas noble quene . . . Help, that I lese nought my flour' ('help, that I do not lose my flower').[27] So 'defloration' signifies the 'loss' of virginity, the flower. A woman's first heterosexual experience in possessive, inconsiderate, patriarchal cultures (whether in the past or today) is likely to be painful and traumatic; referring to it as 'defloration' could be a way to soften that reality, flowering it over.

In Nigeria, Yoruba courtships connote defloration as the bridegroom's family delivers a letter to the bride's family that reads: 'Our son was walking past your garden one day and saw a flower, and he needs your permission to cut the flower'; the wedding ceremony features many evocations of cut flowers, focusing on their transience before they perish.[28]

Just as women are named after flowers, flowers in turn are also named after women: granny's bonnet, busy Lizzie, poor Annie, black-eyed Susan (which has a common racist variant), Queen Anne's lace, fair-maid-of-France, mother-of-the-evening, lady's slipper, lady's mantle, lady's smock, lady's eardrop, naked lady, hooker's lips. *Atropa belladonna* (deadly nightshade) is a poisonous flowering plant; *bella donna* means pretty woman, evoking the practice of using belladonna to dilate a woman's eyes so she is more attractive to men.[29] If some of these names are not manifestly offensive, several of them are, and certainly the roster as a whole is striking.

It is not hard to see gender objectification at play, significant semiotic evidence for how florifying women invites sexism and misogyny. There are a few, but just a few, men's names that grow out of flowers – Rajiv (lotus), Roosevelt (rose field), Florian – and also a small number of male flower names: bachelor buttons, Jacob's ladder, white man's foot, Jack-in-the-bush, cockscomb and naked man orchid (which is absolutely worth Googling). We might agree to gender devil's nettle (also known as old man's pepper) and devil's plague as male, but we cannot by that logic designate witch hazel as female: its name derives from the Middle English word *wiche* (pliant).

In nosegay paintings (illus. 77 and 78), the women and flowers seem to be harmonious, complementary. But Edgar Degas' *A Woman Seated Beside a Vase of Flowers* presents a less comfortable scenario. The flowers seems to be expanding out of control: the tableau simply offers too many blooms, and not enough woman. The dahlias, asters and gaillardias seem to be squeezing her right off the edge of the canvas, encroaching onto her sleeve, her neck, her hat – it's not clear where exactly the flowers end and the woman begins.

Is she just distracted, or anxious? What worries her? Why does she look away from the vase? Is she savvy to the hypergendering of flowers? Do they suck up her womanhood, essentialize her, over-power her? Or maybe she is just thinking about something else (which might seem heretical to hardcore floraphiles: how could she possibly contemplate anything else when there are *all those flowers*

80 Blooms overwhelm the woman in Edgar Degas' *A Woman Seated Beside a Vase of Flowers*, 1865, oil on canvas.

there?). Possibly she is allergic to flowers – Degas, who did not produce many flower paintings, suffered such allergies himself – and her odd facial expression simply foreshadows a sneeze.[30] I am not sure exactly what this image means, or what 'inference there-from' to draw. But I think it is safe to take it as a caution: beware that flowers may not always be as welcome as they may seem; one may have too much of a good thing.

Flowers and biology, sexuality, fertility

Nehemiah Grew, the aptrynomic father of plant anatomy, first proposed a sexual theory of plant reproduction in 1684, which botanist William Hofmeister confirmed in 1851. In *Flora Unveiled: The Discovery and Denial of Sex in Plants*, biologists Lincoln and Lee Taiz write that cultural biases about human gender and sexuality hindered the scientific understanding of plant sexuality for centuries. Grew's hypothesis resulted in 'almost pornographic descriptions of what goes on in flowers' that 'outraged pious people and polarized the debate even further'. Believing that all plants were female, people could not imagine them 'having sex'.[31]

Following Hofmeister's breakthrough, Charles Darwin's observations on botanical sexuality 'helped decipher the function of the flower in the plant's reproductive system', art historian Nira Tessler writes. 'Once the flower was recognized as the plant's sexual organ – with various stages of development, from bud to bloom to wilting – it was only natural for it to be perceived as analogous to a woman's female organs and body, and as a metaphor' for her life cycle.[32]

Women's association with flowers can be unfortunate: the ancient custom of footbinding, for example, 'prevalent in China from the twelfth century and eradicated only in the twentieth, sought to constrict women's feet from girlhood into tiny "golden lotuses" . . . Songs, poems and plays of China in the Mongol era refer to "lotus blossom" feet of just three inches.'[33] It is ironic – indeed, profoundly disturbing – that labelling a barbaric practice with a flowery term made it seem (to some people) acceptable, even beautiful.

Freud interpreted flowers as symbols of menstruation when a patient dreamed of coming down from a high place with a branch full of red camellias that were falling off.[34] In Amharic, menstruation is called *yewor abeba*, or 'monthly flower'. Eastern texts recognize more than a dozen varieties of menstrual fluid 'and all of these terms end with *puspa* (Sanskrit, "flower"), a common designation for the red menstrual flux and flow'.[35] In the Andaman Islands, 'girls acquire an additional name at puberty drawn from a tree or plant which is flowering at that time,' Jack Goody writes; her community '[thinks] of her as having blossomed . . . so she is given her flower-name which is no longer used after she gives birth'.[36] In many cultures menstruation has been, and sometimes still is, described as the time when a woman 'has her flowers', and menopause was called a 'cessation of flowers'.

Leviticus 15:24 warns: 'if any man lie with her at all, and her flowers be upon him, he shall be unclean seven days; and all the bed whereon he lieth shall be unclean.'[37] If men are mostly advised to avoid flowers in general, as Teleflora and the Manly Man Company indicate, then these menstrual 'flowers' must be especially treacherous in light of all the misogynistic taboos men have promulgated about women's monthly cycles. Perhaps it is precisely these metaphorical womanly flowers – bloody menstrual flow – that have ruined actual flowers for men. Men's aversions towards flowers provide all the more impetus to deflower women, not so much to *take* their flowers (we don't want them anyway), but to *take them away*: to obliterate them. Once impregnated, a woman will no longer have her flowers for nine months, making her less threatening as a source of Levitican uncleanliness.

But against all these derogatory cultural fixations, there are also empowering associations of flowers and female eroticism, as in the Indian figure of the Padmini (lotus-woman) whose sexual organ, her yoni, is 'like a flower and loves to absorb the sun's rays – that is, to be seen in daylight – and the caress of strong hands. Her juices have the fragrance of a freshly blossoming lotus flower.'[38] In Eve Ensler's *The Vagina Monologues*, a woman speaks of learning to embrace her own sexuality: 'My vagina is a flower, an eccentric tulip, the center acute and deep, the scent delicate, the petals gentle but sturdy.'[39]

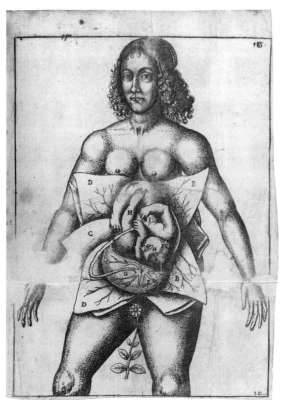

81 A flower signifies fertility in this illustration of a pregnant woman from Jane Sharp, *The Midwives Book; or, The Whole Art of Midwifery Discovered* (1671).

Natalie Joffe describes in her article 'The Vernacular of Menstruation' how flowery euphemisms arose because discussing menstruation was considered impolite.[40] 'Flowers' would have been an untroubling word to discuss a natural process that men construed as mysterious, toxic and disgusting. Jane Sharp, a seventeenth-century midwife, explained that the term alluded to the fact that fruit follows flowers; menstruation was a sign of fertility and babies might follow.[41]

A great many cultural texts interweave associations of women, flowers, fertility, sexuality and the perceived dangers men fetishize or fear in female biology. When Pluto rapes Persephone while she is gathering narcissi, the flowers that fall from her tunic symbolize her loss of innocence. The writings of Charles Baudelaire and Edgar Allan Poe display a repugnance for flowers that correlates with a disdain for women. When the American billionaire Robert Kraft was arrested in a massage parlour on prostitution charges, a legal writer explains why the establishment's name, Orchids of Asia Day Spa, made him presume it was a brothel:

> When a day spa is called 'Massage Envy' or something generically Asian like 'Tokyo Spa' there's nothing overtly suspect. However what, exactly, are the 'orchids' in this name? It seems to me that the name directly commodifies the women who work there. They are the 'pretty flowers' the customer is intended to consume, meaning unless it's actually a florist, something is amiss.[42]

The term 'flower girl' has long been a synonym for a prostitute and is still in common usage in Japanese and Chinese cultures, alongside many others around the world..

No consistent logic explains how, precisely, women are flowers/ flowered/deflowered: is it the whole woman that is the flower, or a part of her, or is it something that her body produces? Is the florified woman pure or corrupt, angel or whore? As with the Victorian 'language of flowers', there is no denotative precision, no unilateral 'translation' of a certain flowery signifier into an exact meaning. Instead the extensive symbolic intertwining of women and flowers offers writers, especially male writers, a great deal of free play. In this discourse of the flowery female, it may seem as if the writer or artist is using flowers for women – for describing and imagining and accessorizing them – but he may also be using them *against* women. The trope is full of contradictions: although menstruation was supposed to be a symbolic manifestation of the floral female, for example, some scientists propounded that a woman who touched actual flowers during her period would kill them. The Austrian professor Béla Schick believed he had identified 'menotoxin', the poison in menstrual flow that destroys cut flowers (also ruining bread dough and spoiling wine):

> On the afternoon of August 14, 1919, I received about ten long-stemmed roses that looked very fresh; they were dark red and had hardly begun to open. In order to keep them fresh, I gave them to a maid to put into water. I was not a little surprised to find the next morning that all the roses had wilted and dried up . . . I presumed that this was not some sort of deception and asked the maid . . . She replied that she knew yesterday that the flowers would die; she shouldn't have touched them, because she was menstruating. Every flower that she handles during this time dies.[43]

Modern holistic medicine offers more positive botanical connections to menstruation. An article entitled '7 Herbs and Flowers That Can Do Wonders for Your Period' recommends evening primrose oil (an anti-inflammatory) to manage PMS symptoms and reduce mood swings; lavender aromatherapy for helping with migraines, alleviating anxiety and reducing uterine contractions during painful periods; and yarrow to help women who have fibroids or experience heavy bleeding.[44] Such practices have an ancient lineage: in traditional Chinese medicine, a tea made from the roots, leaves and flowers of Chinese roses has long been used to treat menstrual discomfort and disorders.

Another historical link between flowers and reproduction involves abortion. In the eleventh century the Tunisian-Italian scholar and physician known as Constantine the African identified iris, rue, willow and stinking ferula as effective herbs for inducing menses. Before that Muhammed ibn Zakariya Al-Razi, a tenth-century Persian medical scholar, wrote that a cinnamon, rue and wallflower broth could be used for the same purposes.[45] Herbal guides 'were quite explicit, stating that wallflower mixed in honey and wine, applied to the vagina "takes the foetus from the womb" and that pennyroyal could "bring foorth [sic] dead fruit"'.[46] *Flos pavonis*, or the peacock flower, which stands at nearly 3 metres (9 ft) tall with brilliant red and yellow blossoms, is another ancient abortifacient. Botanical illustrator Maria Sibylla Merian recounts in her 1705 book that 'The Indians, who are not treated well by their Dutch masters, use the seeds [of this plant] to abort their children, so that their children will not become slaves like they are. The Black slaves from Guinea and Angola have demanded to be well treated, threatening to refuse to have children. They told me this themselves.'[47] (The peacock flower is also known as 'the pride of Barbados', the national flower I admired earlier for its straightforward braggadocio.)

Such information about flowers and health was 'knowledge passed from woman to woman, often outside the boundaries of traditional medical discourses and, therefore, forever confined to a moral realm of danger and superstition', writes Stassa Edwards, a scholar of gender; it was not recorded in men's scientific treatises during the age of European empire, despite explorers' and merchants' keen interest in pharmaceutical plants. Women who shared and practised such flowery medicine might have been killed as witches.[48]

Rivera's flowers and female empowerment

Diego Rivera created a large series of paintings that spotlights race, class and gender, depicting flower sellers who are almost all women, peasants from Mexico's indigenous underclass. Despite their poverty Rivera imbues them with an air of aesthetic and spiritual exaltation, which seems to be associated with their intimate proximity to the calla lilies (almost always this particular flower) that they gather and sell. Rivera's scenes harmoniously counterpoise the vendor and the product, the woman and the flower. While these sellers seem as professionally dutiful as many others we have seen, they convey an especially keen sense of biophiliac intensity: a deep and fundamental connection to these flowers. It is not just a job for them. And if these women are likely as poor as the European flower girls, still, because of Rivera's devout respect for them, they seem somehow immune to the economic hardships that the London and Paris vendors could not escape; their appearances do not betray, as the European paintings did, their precarious impoverishment.

Contemporary female flower workers describe a sense of pride in their occupation according to Greta Friedemann-Sánchez's ethnography. Though her research was conducted in a different country (Colombia) and time (2006), the dignity she depicts maps well onto Rivera's subjects. Before the women had jobs on flower farms, Friedemann-Sánchez writes, they felt 'their individuality, their humanity, and their identities as women are erased or do not count when the space they occupy day and night is exclusively

82 Diego Rivera, *The Flower Vendor (Girl with Lilies)*, 1941, oil on masonite.

the household'. Overworked with mundane caretaking chores for their families, they commonly experienced domestic abuse; men controlled their homes and their lives. But the women she interviewed reported that 'work at the flower farms makes them feel integrated into a community and as complete individuals. They say that their individuality is recognized by their supervisors and that their work is valued. They see value in their own work and feel that their self-worth is affirmed and recognized by others.' These women discovered 'a worldview that did not exist for them before, one in which they are valued both by themselves and by others. The word people constantly use to describe this change is *valoración*', or self-esteem.[49] But as empowering as this account appears, remember too the dangers for women working in the flower industry – both historical and contemporary – recounted in the previous chapter. These women may be figuratively ripe for plucking and deflowering – which is to say, literally, vulnerable to sexual exploitation.

We mostly cannot see the women's faces in Rivera's paintings, so we appraise their relations to their flowers via the connections he draws out between their bodily forms and the flowers' forms, their postures and the flowers' postures, their colouring (skin, clothing) and the flowers', their parts (feet, toes, arms, braids) and the flowers' (stems, bracts, spathes and spadices). Rivera conveys a conviction that the women's aura – proud and strong, self-assured, eloquent, inherently beautiful – parallels these strong, stately flowers. The flowers seem almost to grow out of the sellers, or along with them: all part of the same garden.

Calla lilies were imported alongside the people who were taken from Africa and brought, enslaved, to Mexico, adding a particularly Marxist resonance to Rivera's focus on that flower. Linnaeus erred in calling this species a lily (it was later reclassified as zantedeschia). Nor is it its genus, Calla, but we persist in the tongue-tripping misnomer. 'Calla', from the Greek *kallos*, means 'beauty', which is accurate at least aesthetically if not botanically. Freud discussed its sexual symbolism as he interpreted this flower's form,[50] and (likely as a result of his attention) it became a prominent subject in modern art: Georgia O'Keeffe painted so many that she was known as 'the lady of the lilies' (penile counterparts, possibly, to her many yonic flowers, though some see in calla lilies an intersexual fusion of both male and female genital shapes). Robert Mapplethorpe's photography features an overtly sexualized portrayal of these flowers as well; Marsden Hartley, Man Ray, Joseph Stella, Imogen Cunningham and

Ansel Adams have also used calla lilies in their art, often with erotic undertones, as has Salvador Dalí in his bizarre canvas *The Great Masturbator*. The flower's cultural resonance is sacred as well as profane: in the Easter service, calla lilies signify resurrection, the cone-like flower evoking a trumpet that heralds victory.

Rivera's paintings mutually celebrate both flowers and sellers: 'The Indian girl, kneeling before her pile of calla lilies – a flower associated with funerals and death – constitutes an ode at once to the beauty of Mexico's native cultures and to the suffering of her native peoples.'[51] Rivera asks his viewers to think about the sellers' indigence, but it is for him an ennobling poverty, compared to the buyers' decadent wealth. These women work hard, and according to

83 Diego Rivera, *The Flower Vendor*, 1942, oil on masonite.

84 Diego Rivera, *The Flower Carrier*, 1935, oil on masonite.

conventional Marxist analysis they are exploited; but they perform their work with poise and do not appear alienated. In the flowers they touch so intimately they seem to perceive a transcendent beauty, and even reap some of this beauty for themselves. (A person who works around flowers – at least before their odours were bred out of them – would smell flowery at the end of the day; similarly, we can imagine, these woman acquire some sort of metaphysical effluvium that attaches to them.) They are often kneeling, perhaps in subjugation, but also as if in prayer, worshipping the lilies' spirit along with its evocation of their own.

The Flower Vendor actually includes a male figure, albeit just a few slivers of one: a tiny wedge of his bald head peeks through amid the lilies, and if you look carefully (you won't notice at first) you can see his hands on the basket's rim. At the base of the basket his feet are a bit more prominent. He is helping the woman carry these flowers, but Rivera suggests that she doesn't really much need the help and barely registers his presence, as we, too, hardly perceive him. In this business, men's intrusions are negligible, marginal.

What I like most about the class-consciousness of Rivera's images is the incredible fecundity, the massive quantity of flowers that the sellers have, compared to the buyers who will get only eight or a dozen of these stems. These women have *all* the flowers, and I think Rivera sees that as an affirmation of the sellers' virtue and their consummate appreciation of the valuable beauty the calla lilies exude. These women deserve all these flowers, which is why such scenes of gathering the voluminous floral crop are the ones Rivera chooses to enshrine. While these flowers will ultimately decorate the homes of customers who are wealthier and whiter than these women, the painter never deigns to show this bourgeois clientele, and as we reflect on his masterpieces I think we, too, forget about them. Rivera freezes capitalistic time in the moment when these sellers have full possession of the calla lilies, and our admiration for these strange, bright crowds of flowers extends to the women who bring them to market.

Most of Rivera's paintings of flower sellers depict all women – or just a bit of a man, as above. One, however, *The Flower Carrier*, features a more prominent man. Compared to the women, this man seems notably less integrated with the flowers and with his work. He is not, like the women, part of the flower arrangement; he is separate, awkward, almost prostrate. He does not seem to derive bliss from the flowers as Rivera's women do. Possibly because he is male, he is asked to carry a heavier load than the women, which is why he seems more burdened by his cargo. Or perhaps, being male, he simply does not appreciate the flowers' beauty. There is a weird disconnect in this image: surely the flowers are not extremely heavy, even in large quantities? And yet he seems almost overcome, while the standing woman, who helps support the basket, seems better able to manage this shipment. Rivera consistently depicts a unique, gendered, almost supernatural affinity between women and flowers; this man, who looks uncomfortably misfitting in his job, emphasizes all the more how closely Rivera's women and flowers coexist.

Race and flowers, racist flowers

The human history of racial injustice and persecution inflects flowers in many ways. In Chapter Three I discussed how people of colour are more likely to live in areas vulnerable to the environmental hazards of floriculture, compared to the mostly white communities for whom the flowers are grown. Another blatant example of how flowers have been tainted by racist prejudice is the significant number of common names for species that include racially derogatory slurs, which I decline to recount here because they are simply too offensive and too idiotic. The n-word has been used for at least a dozen flower names, and the South African equivalent, the k-word, for as many as 75; these numbers grow much larger when slang, regional, folkloric and other colloquial designations are accounted.

When colours are part of a flower's name or description, it has been common to use the n-word to describe darker shades of a given colour, or darker variants of flowers that grow in many colours. Flowers with any black features are prone to be described, either formally or colloquially, with racist slurs. Many plants with 'Indian', or a slur for native peoples, in their names are weeds or other unfavoured flowers.

The determination of 'weeds' reflects an arbitrary logic and ethos, which parallels the arbitrary and prejudicial construction of racial, gendered and class-based otherness. In German, the word 'weed,' *Unkraut*, means un-herb, 'echoing the Nazi term for a Jew, *Unmensch*, an un-person', writes Nina Edwards. If weeds are commonly characterized as unwanted and ugly trespassers, these may embody contingencies of cultural bias: 'the idea of the weed is a slippery one, constantly changing according to different needs, fashions and contexts.'[52] ('What is a weed?' asks Ralph Waldo Emerson: 'A plant whose virtues have not yet been discovered.'[53])

In 'Racist Relics: An Ugly Blight On Our Botanical Nomenclature', Melvin Hunter describes slurs for African, African American, Native American, Australian Aboriginal, Chinese, Jewish and other cultures that feature in flowers' names. Many of these have been changed in the last generation or two, but many others endure. An effort in the 1990s to convince horticultural writers and editors to abandon racist names faced considerable resistance: 'I feel it would stress the sociological implications at the expense of the botanical,' one editor wrote; another said, 'The subject is inappropriate and appears to create a quarrel where there isn't one at present . . . your charge of racism is a little dramatic.'[54]

Most of the offending terms are in flowers' common names, but there are also examples of scientific names that convey racist slurs. A botanist who writes about a African succulent with an offensive name – the k-word was 'Latinized' as part of its binomial nomenclature – sidesteps ethical responsibility as he explains: 'I apologize for using a racist term . . . but I didn't name this plant.'[55] I would

259

suggest that he could refuse to use the word, interrogate the racist discourse and suggest an alternate name.

While flowers are beautiful and innocent enough to resist a good deal of human folly, still they are not immune to our immorality, and if people work hard enough it is possible to drag flowers down to the level of human malice. I wonder why, exactly, a plant would come to be called by a racist name. Perhaps people who use slurs already in other aspects of their speech just want to use more of them, and the denotation of a flower (or a town, lake, or another geographical landmark, many of which also bear racist names) offers bigots yet another opportunity to use language cruelly. The same was true about offensively gendered common names for flowers: calling them 'hooker's lips' or 'naked ladies' not only *reveals* social prejudices but also simultaneously *advances* such biases, providing yet one more way to demean women.

A woman depicted with flowers generally connotes positive virtues: she is meant to be seen as beautiful. Even if floristry is just her job, still, she must be talented and sensitive to be able to perform such work. Victorian flower girls are an exception – for them, the bouquets may be a mark of shame, signifying that they are too naive, or too poor, or too lascivious, to forestall their deflowering.

For Black women, too, holding flowers may not confer the automatic graces that white women with flowers enjoy. Two famous images, painted by white French men, show figures who do not seem very pleased with their flowers, which makes sense because the flowers are not for them. These servants are intermediaries for the flowers, which will be given, finally, to someone else. While the flowers are beautiful, that beauty ironically accentuates the sadness: it is beauty these women cannot have themselves, except fleetingly. It might even seem dangerous for them to betray any sense of delight exactly because the flowers are not theirs: they could be intentionally suppressing any sign of pleasure, fearing that the intended recipient would view that as a threatening transgression of their subjugated position.

Édouard Manet's *Olympia* depicts a nude prostitute, a pale white woman, lying on a chaise alongside a black cat. Hovering behind, a Black maid holds a bouquet of flowers, presumably from the courtesan's customer. Wrapped in cheap newsprint, the bouquet 'would fade quickly', as Therese Dolan reads the tableau, 'not long after the sexual encounter itself was completed and the client departed. Like the remains of a consumed meal, they would soon be discarded as their beauty vanished [*sic*].'[56] Possibly Manet intends our perspective on the scene to enact a 'male gaze' suggesting that I, the viewer, am supposed to be Olympia's client, and her maid takes the flowers from me to put in a vase so I can get on with my business.

Manet's composition pays homage to Titian's sixteenth-century *Venus of Urbino*, though it also deconstructs that masterpiece. Titian's nude is unironically and purely seductive; Manet's is promiscuous and bored. If the earlier portrait idealizes the artistic tradition of divine feminine beauty, the later one subverts that tradition (and unsurprisingly faced derision at its debut). Olympia is meant to be seen as real, and indecent: aesthetically banal. If Titian expected the viewer to revel in his subject's pure and inviting feminity, Manet challenges us to endure his figure's uncomfortable stare. Two of Manet's disruptions especially suit my purposes: first, Venus's maids in the background are white, while Olympia's is Black. And second, Venus holds a small cluster of roses – flowers with which she is traditionally associated, that symbolize the fruitful passion of licit love – while Olympia does not even hold her flowers herself, as if she is unworthy to do so.

Manet paints both the maid and the cat very dark; they are hard to see clearly against the dark green backdrop. Their colour contrasts with Olympia's whiteness and several other creamy white objects: the pillow, sheets and shawl; the maid's livery; the flowers' wrapping; and several of the flowers themselves. In addition to the large bouquet of flowers the maid holds, there is a creamy pink flower (a hibiscus, I'd say, though others see an orchid or camellia) behind Olympia's ear, and the shawl's fabric is decorated with small red and purple flowers. It is a heavily flowered scene as well as a heavily racialized scene, and those two themes are intricately related.

The model for Olympia was Victorine-Louise Meurent, who was a painter herself and whose nude form appears also in Manet's

85 Édouard Manet, *Olympia*, 1863, oil on canvas.

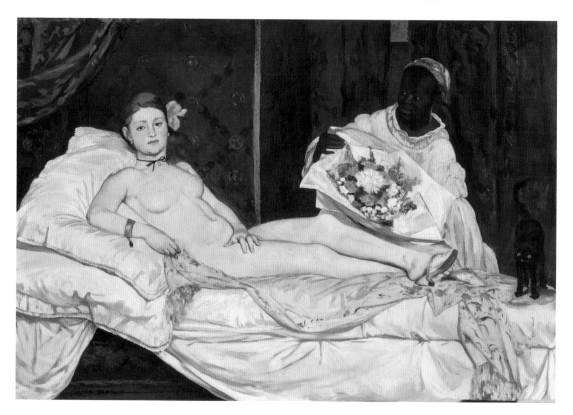

Le déjeuner sur l'herbe. The maid's identity was not known until recently; although her name appeared in an easily accessible document, nobody had bothered to find out who she might be until a few years ago. Manet's studio notebook listed 'an appointment from 1862 with a model he described as "Laure, très belle négresse". Her address was a 10-minute walk from the artist's studio in northern Paris, where the Impressionists lived and worked, a neighbourhood with an influx of Black migrants after the French abolition of territorial slavery in 1848.'[57] In a 2019 Musée d'Orsay exhibition intended to redress past sensibilities that rendered people of colour anonymous and invisible, *Olympia* was renamed *Laure* – but only temporarily for the show's duration, which strikes me as perfunctory and inadequate.

86 Titian, *Venus of Urbino*, c. 1534, oil on canvas.

Some critics share my impression that the maid's presence resonates with glaring racist exploitation because she is subordinate, subaltern — as people of colour often are in the white imagination. 'Forget "tonal contrast",' writes [artist] Lorraine O'Grady. 'We know what she is meant for . . . Olympia's maid, like all the other "peripheral Negroes", is a robot conveniently made to disappear into the background drapery.'[58]

But there are also less damning readings. Denise Murrell, a curator at the Metropolitan Museum of Art, sees the figure as 'emblematic of a new Black working class that Manet saw around him every day'.

> 'Part of what was radical about *Olympia* was the way
> that he chose to portray this Black woman,' . . . who wears
> the plain, shapeless dress of the French proletariat.
> 'She's not bare-breasted or in the gorgeously rendered
> exotic attire of the harem servant', typical of how
> Black women were depicted in history paintings
> at the Paris salons. 'Here she almost seems to be
> a friend of the prostitute, maybe even advising
> her: "Look, think twice before you turn this man
> away. Take these flowers, girl! You gotta get paid."'[59]

The image of Laure 'is frequently oversimplified as a racist stereotype', Murrell writes in her project to recover 'the full complexity and enduring influence of the figure's problematic nuance'.[60] Art historian Griselda Pollock, too, sees the image as 'an anti-Orientalist or de-Orientalising work', because Laure is not depicted, as most Black women in that period would be, in an African headdress as an exotic other, nor fetishized for her 'blank darkness' or 'venal sexuality'. Manet 'gives us a way to locate this figure . . . in metropolitan modernity', she writes.[61]

In giving Laure almost equal pictorial space to Olympia, Manet 'was drawing attention to an aspect of contemporary society that bourgeois critics may have preferred to ignore; the presence of a small but highly visible population of free Black people who had come to the city following the abolition of slavery in French colonies in 1848'.[62] Part of the audience's shock came from Manet's subversion of the default expectation that the Black character would appear more depraved. 'It was the white female body within *Olympia* that was read as naked, dirty, dead; and sexually uncontrollable. Juxtaposed with the fully clothed demure presence of the Black maid, Manet effectively reversed and problematized the stereotypical racial position to which these two bodies were generally assigned.'[63]

Perhaps the flowers here are less ironic, and more powerful, than they first appear – perhaps they truly enhance, delight and empower Laure's character in some way, and she is more than just the robotic appendage of a white woman's bouquet. Perhaps she actually uplifts (or preserves) the flowers in some sense, since they are, in her hands, at a remove from the intended recipient, Olympia, whose emotional ennui might diminish the flowers' *joie de vivre*. Perhaps Laure protects the blossoms from becoming *fleurs du mal*, and the correct 'inference therefrom' is that her possession of the bouquet signals a Black figure's transcendence of traditional two-dimensional roles in European painting.

Or perhaps, finally, as enigmatically stimulating as Manet's painting is, these are just bad flowers reflecting the bad social dynamics that afflict women and Black people, and especially Black women. Perhaps the profusion of flowers is meant to mock: in their beauty, we are invited to judge, by contrast, the unloveliness of the two women, one 'fallen' and one Black.

Manet's friend Frédéric Bazille composed a pair of paintings quite similar to each other, *Young Woman with Peonies* (illus. 87) and *African Woman with Peonies*, both of which feature the same (unidentified) model, presumably a servant, in the same outfit, with most of the same flowers. In *Young Woman with Peonies* they are gathered in a basket while the other painting shows the woman arranging them in a large vase. The most significant difference is that in *Young Woman with Peonies* the woman stares at the viewer directly, head-on, with a powerful and accusatory glance, holding up a few peonies for us to see or (if we dare) to take. Bazille's companion painting renders her face in three-quarter profile, so the viewer does not meet her eye to eye. In the great many representations I have studied of people handling flowers, rarely do they convey such passionlessness. This woman seems astoundingly unmoved by the large basket of colourful, lush flowers in her arms. She doesn't connect with them; they don't connect with her. Like Laure, perhaps, she does not allow herself to become too fond of something she cannot truly have.

An acolyte of Manet's (appearing in studies for *Le déjeuner sur l'herbe*, though he did not make the final cut), Bazille is thought to have painted these portraits in homage to his mentor and in dialogue with *Olympia*. In addition to reprising the Black woman holding flowers, the specific flowers themselves suggest a connection: peonies, one of Manet's favourite flowers (they appear in Laure's bouquet, too), grew in his Gennevilliers garden. Manet and Bazille shared their peony passion with many other people, real and imaginary. Peonies were Apollo's flower. According to one myth, the flower is named for Paeon, physician to the gods and a

student of Aesculapius, the god of medicine. When Paeon healed Pluto with a milky liquid from the peony's root the jealous Aesculapius tried to kill him, so Pluto transformed him into a peony to keep him safe.

Virgil and Ovid note the peony's restorative powers: seeds from the flower worn around the neck were thought to ward off evil. John Hall, a Stratford physician and Shakespeare's son-in-law, treated epilepsy with extracts from the flower, writes medical editor M. Therese Southgate in a paean to peonies. In the nineteenth and twentieth centuries these flowers

87 Holding flowers seems distasteful in Frédéric Bazille's *Young Woman with Peonies*, 1870, oil on canvas.

were taken up by the poets and novelists. From Keats
to Amy Lowell, D. H. Lawrence and Siegfried Sassoon,
even to Carl Sandburg – every poet who ever created a
garden apparently planted peonies in beautiful colors.
Amy Lowell's are crimson, Sandburg's delicate pink,
Lawrence's 'ghostly-white.' Dostoevsky's are red, like
a face full of shame. Henry Adams, on the other hand,
when he recounted his education, had always seen the
peony simply as color, an archetype perhaps. Until he
was a 'fullgrown man,' he writes, '[my] idea of color was
a peony, with the dew of early morning on its petals.'

But it is to the artist that the peony rightly belongs,
perhaps even more than to Apollo or the physicians.
With its shaggy, bulbous head and shades of red ranging
from a deep sanguine, like mined rubies, to soft, delicate
pinks like a baby's skin, even to whites like ghosts, the
peony begs to be painted. If the garden is its ancestral
home, the canvas is where it has finally settled. Peony
paintings were especially popular in 19th-century Paris.
Berthe Morisot, Cézanne, Bazille, Braque, even Picasso
tried their hands at them.[64]

Resplendent and richly storied flowers par excellence (and sol-
idly on my own top-five list), peonies couldn't be brighter, fluffier
or more captivating as they transform overnight from tight,
plump, spherical buds into extravagant, bombastic, strong- and
sweet-smelling broad-petalled blossoms that seem, in their dainty
delicacy, as if they are destined to dissipate after a day or two,
although they will surprise you by persevering in their spirited
exuberance for well over a week.

To return to Bazille's peony-holder: look at her dour demean-our. She seems angry, hurt, disempowered, even mean: not innately nasty, I think, but as if the world's vicissitudes have soured her spirit. (In this regard, she reminds me of Toulouse-Lautrec's flower seller, see illus. 61, and Mayhew's, see illus. 63.) She stands alien-ated from the sublime cultural drift of flowers that white women so easily imbibe. The colourful floral bounty we see here, and the tableau, and the way she holds the flowers, and the mood they spark – all the 'inferences therefrom' we have been gathering bloom by bloom throughout our strange, bright crowd – are askew. She is an outsider, and it is precisely this heap of flowers that confirms her marginality. 'I didn't want any flowers', we might easily imagine her saying (as Sylvia Plath did) because even if she has them, they are not for her. It may be better to have no flowers at all than to have them only temporarily, holding them (as Laure was too) only as an intermediary, from someone else and for some-one else. Imagine cooking a feast and not being allowed to eat it, or working as an usher at a symphony hall but not being able to hear the concert: so close to, but so far from, enjoying the delight that others may easily experience.

I am cautiously receptive to the possibility that both artists *intended* to depict these Black women in an enlightened spirit of multicultural inclusion. Nevertheless, the predominant visual impact shows women of colour who cannot enjoy a simple, imme-diate, untroubled engagement with flowers. Perhaps Manet and Bazille did not realize at the time – what is more clearly apparent to us today – how discomfited their Black subjects look; or perhaps they did.

Do the white male artists believe they know better than the Black female models how richly the flowers may ennoble them, if they would just stand still and pose while they are transformed into art? Do Manet and Bazille mean for these flowers to be post-racial (as we might term it today), implying that racism is over and thus assuaging the viewers' and the painters' guilt? Even if so, it remains the case that the Black women in these paintings, along with Black women audiences and anyone who empathetically understands their historical condition, must see that these flowers are at best problematic, and at worst emblematic of every other cultural object that conditionally connotes value and elegance: accessible to those who are rich, white and empowered, but attenuated, if not wholly inaccessible, for those at the other end of the social continuum.

But if flowers can succumb to racist and sexist contexts, they can also transcend them. I conclude with flowers that betoken celebrations of women's racial and cultural identity, emanating from floral fashion featured in Washington, DC's National Museum of African American History and Culture. Mae Reeves, one of Philadelphia's first Black businesswomen, owned a famous establishment called Mae's Millinery Shop from 1940 to the end of the century, where her creations were the diametric opposite of the racist and sexist flowers surveyed above. Her flowered hats proclaim – loudly, with a visual impact rivalling Emily Dickinson's tonal register of shouting flowers – flair, pride, resolve. Reeves presents flowers at their best: bright and ecstatic.

Florified to the hilt, Reeves broadcasts all the passion that a flower may embody. Her millinery recalls the unbridled admiration that Virginia Woolf conveys. The hats are a stage, or a canvas, upon which are displayed consummately positive and life-affirming flowers that her clientele adored, unbowed by the Jim Crow era's racism, just as Clarissa Dalloway, though overwhelmed

88 Mae Reeves's black and pink velvet beehive hat with pink artificial roses, from Mae's Millinery Shop, Philadelphia.

by patriarchy, managed to find bliss by selecting and revelling in her own flowers. Prominently featured in the Museum's Power of Place exhibition – 'reflecting the resiliency of African Americans in making places for themselves and overcoming the challenges they faced' – Mae's Millinery offers 'a place story of creativity, community and entrepreneurship'.[65]

Reeves's elaborate custom-made hats were assembled from layers of bright pink chiffon, pink velvet-ribbon hat bands and artificial flowers with large rounded petals, sometimes profusely begemmed. They embodied dignified, self-assured festivity for her regular customers as well as such superstar clients as Ella Fitzgerald, Lena Horne, Eartha Kitt and Marian Anderson; socialites from illustrious white families, such as the DuPonts and the Annenbergs, also patronized her shop.

Reeves's hats might be spotted at parties and weddings, graduations and other formal ceremonies, but they were primarily for church. 'Countless Black women would rather attend church naked than hatless,' write Michael Cunningham and Craig Marberry in *Crowns: Portraits of Black Women in Church Hats*.

> For these women, a church hat, flamboyant as it may
> be, is no mere fashion accessory; it's a cherished African
> American custom, one observed with boundless passion
> by Black women of various religious denominations.
> A woman's hat speaks long before its wearer utters a
> word. It's what Deirdre Guion calls 'hattitude . . . there's
> a little more strut in your carriage when you wear a nice
> hat. There's something special about you.' When the Apostle
> Paul wrote decreeing that a woman cover her head when
> at worship, he could not have imagined the flamboyance

with which African American women would comply. For generations, Black women have interpreted Apostle Paul's edict with boundless passion and singular flair, wearing platter hats, lampshade hats, why'd-you-have-to-sit-in-front-of-me hats, often with ornaments that runneth over.[66]

89 Mae Reeves's pink chiffon mushroom hat with artificial flowers, from Mae's Millinery Shop, Philadelphia.

Adorning the head for worship dates back to African traditions. Hats featuring bright, bold, textured designs, and no stinting on decorative flowers, exemplified how Sunday church services 'provided African American women who worked as domestic servants or in other subservient roles the only real chance to break away from their drab, dreary workday uniforms'.[67]

Even when flowers fall prey to bad people and bad ideas that threaten to exploit, corrupt, co-opt or otherwise diminish them, I find, they finally take the day; you can't keep a good gardenia down. Mae Reeves and her clientele were privy to the inexhaustible floral potential that Alfred Lord Tennyson describes:

Flower in the crannied wall,
I pluck you out of the crannies,
I hold you here, root and all, in my hand,
Little flower – but if I could understand
What you are, root and all, and all in all,
I should know what God and man is.[68]

To know a flower is to know everything; to 'understand' it means stripping away a human cultural context that too easily implicates flowers in foot-binding, period-shaming, virginity fetishes, sexual exploitation, essentialism and other misogynies, homophobia, racism, classism: all the hegemonies that leverage flowers to advance tawdry human prejudices. Jorge Luis Borges distils Tennyson's sensibility into an even simpler apophthegm: 'if we could understand a single flower we would know who we are and what the world is.'[69] That premise inspires my determination to expose people's worst practices with respect to flowers, and to rescue flowers from those practices and practitioners: from ourselves.

274

5

FLOWERS OF WAR

Where have all the soldiers gone, long time passing?
Where have all the soldiers gone, long time ago?
Where have all the soldiers gone?
Gone to graveyards, everyone.
Oh, when will they ever learn?
Oh, when will they ever learn?

Where have all the graveyards gone, long time passing?
Where have all the graveyards gone, long time ago?
Where have all the graveyards gone?
Gone to flowers, everyone.
Oh, when will they ever learn?
Oh, when will they ever learn?

PETE SEEGER AND JOE HICKERSON[1]

Forgive me, distant wars, for bringing flowers home.
WISŁAWA SZYMBORSKA[2]

As innocently peaceful as flowers seem (and generally are), they can also be weaponized. The Cirraean War in the sixth century BCE featured the first recorded instance of chemical warfare, which was waged with flowers. Forces of the Great Amphictyonic League besieged Cirrha, whose citizens had harassed pilgrims travelling to the sacred Delphic temple nearby, and contaminated the water supply with crushed hellebore. Sometimes called

Christmas rose or Lenten rose, hellebore is highly toxic: it is a strong emetic, alongside other dangerous properties. The ancient Greek word ἐλλέβορος (*helléboros*) may come from *heleîn*, meaning 'to injure', and *bora*, 'food'; or possibly, it may derive from *ellos*, 'young deer', so the word would mean 'food of deer', who were considered adept at recognizing medicinal plants. Whatever the etymology, the sabotage left Cirraeans suffering severe diarrhoea and unable to defend themselves. The League captured the city easily, and slaughtered its residents.[3]

90 *Atropa belladonna* – 'bella donna', or deadly nightshade – contains highly toxic roots, berries and leaves with hallucinogenic properties that made it popular at ancient orgies.

Romans, too, used flowers for war: Pliny the Elder writes in his *Natural History* that warriors dipped their spears in deadly nightshade (which he called *dorycnion*, 'spear drug') to make the weapons all the more lethal when they pierced their victims.[4] A Scottish military campaign centuries later used the same flower, which Linnaeus would later name *Atropa belladonna* after Atropos, the Greek Fate who held everyone's life in her hands, snipping the thread when one's time had come. Duncan I, the eleventh-century king who inspired the Shakespearean character in *Macbeth*, poisoned an invading Danish army during a truce by serving them bottles filled with liquid nightshade. The Danes drank the concoction heartily – notwithstanding their toxicity, the berries taste sweet – and died instantly.[5]

One might think that warfare and flowers would be incompatible, mutually exclusive, but in fact there are many strange conjunctions. People may invoke floral beauty to temper or mask the ugliness of war, to memorialize its devastation, to express pacifist opposition. Flowers inflect warfare commonly enough that we must draw some 'inferences therefrom', as Emily Dickinson has charged us.

Notwithstanding the Greek, Roman and Scottish altercations, botanical specimens themselves are rarely instruments of military aggression: rather, they usually feature more figuratively. Often they are nominative, as in the Wars of the Roses, the Opium Wars, the Aztec Flower Wars, Hungary's Őszirózsás Forradalom (Aster Revolution) after the First World War, Portugal's 1974 Revolução dos Cravos (Carnation Revolution). In Georgia, the 2003 Rose Revolution marked a peaceful transition from lingering Soviet-era control to independence as demonstrators holding red roses burst into parliament demanding the ousting of President Eduard

Shevardnadze. Declaring a state of emergency, he tried to mobilize troops but resigned when the military refused to support his government. The roses were inspirational and strategic: how could anyone impugn the cause of a revolution conducted florally?

In the Aster Revolution, a mostly peaceful action that brought down the Habsburg dynasty, Budapest's citizens joined dissident soldiers who stuck flowers in their caps to show support for the new government. The flowers in this kind of conflict provide no actual combat strength but they convey the power of symbolic unity, channelling the resilience and fecundity that flowers manifest in their natural habitat. If an army's guns seem significantly more fearsome because everyone in ranks is holding one, a floral protest employs a different type of object to make a similar point: everybody is wearing flowers, accentuating the resistance movement's size and solidarity. Blooms are delicate, yet they survive nature's storms. A lone aster is a frail specimen, but a field full of them shows the strength of innumerable individuals, whether people or flowers, joined together in a single expression. When everyone in a large, bright crowd wears asters in their caps, their triumph seems inevitable. One cannot ignore a field of flowers, nor a (battle)field of flowered rebels who invoke a meadow's tranquillity and assured beauty to oppose guns and mayhem.

Lisbon's Carnation Revolution began as a military coup of soldiers who opposed dictatorship and soon became a popular campaign of civil resistance. As in Hungary's and Georgia's flower-named revolts, Portugal's saw minimal violence. Are flowers somehow amulets of protection? Or perhaps these are self-selecting revolutions in which the rebels, sensing that lethal military reprisal is unlikely, feel comfortable arming themselves with merely flowers. Still, I like to think that the aesthetic and psychological force of the flowers plays some part in such triumphs of non-violent florified resistance. When the Portuguese regime fell, rebels celebrated in the streets by putting carnations on soldiers' uniforms and in their rifle muzzles. The carnations here were not calls to revolution, as the Hungarian asters had been, but, rather, joyous symbols of victory.

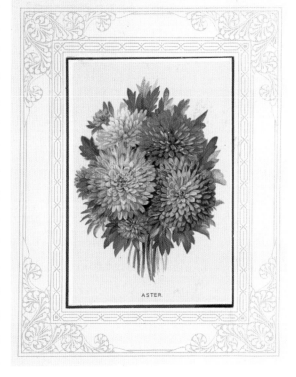

92 Asters add a cheery burst of colour to both revolutions and decorative arrangements in J.H.S.'s 1877 anthology *Floral Poetry and the Language of Flowers.*

Flowers of resistance are not just nominative, but strategic. The buds and blooms are so patently peaceful that it is as if the protestors are daring the soldiers to shoot them, aware that the visuals would depict such an assault as monstrous cowardice

93 Every year on 25 April, the Portuguese celebrate the Carnation Revolution's anniversary in Lisbon's Largo do Carmo square: the site of the resistance.

and would likely provoke a backlash that would humiliate the military forces.

Instead of fighting fire with fire, floral revolutionaries decline to perpetuate the horrific violence that pervaded the larger conflagrations (the First World War, the Second World War and the Cold War) from which these conflicts were offshoots. Facing a surreal contest of rifles versus flowers, those carrying the guns find themselves too shamed, or too sensible, to fire them. Perhaps protestors choose flowers over armaments because they lack the means to mobilize competitive weaponry for themselves; or perhaps they believe so strongly in their cause that they feel they don't need guns. Outfitted with innocuous flowers, the rebels convey a sense of transcendent immanence, cowing a desperate regime into a retreat that their conventional arms might delay but not forestall.

Opium and Aztecs

Should the nineteenth-century Opium Wars be considered as part of this anthology of flower combat? ('Anthology': from Greek ἀνθολογία – *anthologia, anthos* 'flower' + *logia* 'collection', denoting compiled 'flowers' of writings, which is to say, the best and the brightest.) Opium came from poppies, which proliferated among strange, bright crowds of Indian and Turkish flowers, blossoming at the centre of a decades-long geopolitical conflict. Following the logic of imperial commerce, Europeans believed they had the right to flood China with massive quantities of opiates that addicted millions, wreaking extensive social, political and economic damage in what became a narcotized society. The Chinese disagreed. The Opium Wars may seem attenuated, many steps away from the poppies that seeded this long, deadly series of battles. The flowers grew far from where the wars were fought, and the drug production generated an end-product very unlike a flower.

But Amitav Ghosh's historical novel about the wars, *Flood of Fire*, imagines an evocative, direct flowery connection eliding all the imperial, capitalist distractions that intercede between the poppies and the war. Ghosh depicts a Chinese tycoon in an opium den addressing his supplier:

> Now it was Mr Chan's turn with the pipe. After he had
> finished, he laid it on the table and leant back against
> a bolster. 'Do you know why I have a yen for the smoke,
> Mr Reid? It is because I am a gardener by profession.
> I love flowers – and this smoke is the essence of the
> kingdom of flowers.' His voice drifted away.[6]

Does opium smoke actually have a floral essence? Other accounts more commonly describe a smell like 'old tires or melted plastic' or 'undercooked brownies with an odd fishy edge';[7] 'The air is sultry and oppressive. A stupefying smoke fills the hovel.'[8] But Mr Chan explicitly foregrounds flowers as he consumes the opium, even though it hardly resembles the original source by the time it has become a narcotic commodity. Opium gum that oozes slowly out of the poppy's bulb is processed, dried and heated to a black-tar morphine as unsightly as the original poppy flower is exquisite. Perhaps that's precisely why a person might want to imagine flowers while ingesting this dangerously addictive, debilitating synthetic concoction. (Toilet paper, in a loosely similar semiotic parallel, often features embossed floral designs.)

The poppy returns to the military panorama in the twentieth century, not as *casus belli* but symbolizing another conflict that,

94 This graphic illustration of 'In Flanders Fields' (1921) intertwines images of flowers and war.

like the Opium Wars, realigned the world: the First World War. The plant's medicinal power – the pleasant, dreamy release from pain – loosely links these two very different iterations of the poppy as a war flower. For the opium trade, the poppy was harvested for its actual chemical properties: its seed-pod's milk was literally enmeshed in commercial trade and the consequent militarism. After the Great War the flower functioned as a memorial, a balm for Europe's devastation – as if a dose of opium, or even just the symbol of analgesic relief that the poppy evokes, might help alleviate the pervasive psychological and emotional pain. (It would be derelict to overlook the most famous flowers-of-war poem, by John McCrae: 'In Flanders fields the poppies blow / Between the crosses, row on row,' it begins, and concludes, 'If ye break faith with us who die / We shall not sleep, though poppies grow / In Flanders fields.'⁹)

The poppy's symbolism as a war flower also reflects the fact that it is 'a hardy flower, one that grows well on shattered ground'.[10] Poppies bloom 'in upturned soil. Poppy seeds are very durable and can lie dormant on a field for years, but only when someone, or something, uproots the ground will they flower,' Robert Hemmings writes in his essay on war poetry. 'The volume of high explosive shellfire in Flanders during the war years, or cannon fire a century before, ensured there was a constant violent tilling of the fields, which ensured a bountiful crop of both poppies and traumatic memories.'[11] Poppies worn on Remembrance Day have no narcotic properties whatsoever as they are artificial – silk, often made by disabled veterans and sold to benefit the families of dead or maimed soldiers.[12]

Fifteenth-century Aztecs conducted flower wars, *guerra florida* in Spanish, *xōchiyāōyōtl* in Nahuatl, perhaps better rendered in English as 'flowery wars'. The term described a ritualized low-level practice war, or preparation for war, like a tournament, with staged battles that resembled sport or scrimmaging rather than conquest. While much about these wars is uncertain, the winner may have been predetermined, and the losing side did not lose as much as they would have in a full-scale war: they were not vanquished or decimated. Real weapons were used, though not the most potent ones. Opposing warriors met at a pre-selected location with equal ranks of soldiers and burned incense before going into action. One motivation for these exercises may have been acquiring victims for human sacrifices (an enterprise seen as more spiritually noble, less horrible, than it seems to us today).[13]

The term xōchiyāōyōtl includes the root xōchitl, meaning flower, but that word also connotes an expansive scope of flowery sensibilities and activities. Xōchipilli, the 'flower prince', is the god of – in addition to flowers – games, beauty, dance and song in Aztec mythology, illuminating the connection between flowers and the choreographed contest of the flowery wars. The Aztec connotation of flowers was intricately cognate with ideas about art and humanity, and a flowery war might be considered a celebration of life as well as death.

95 Fresh stems of red ginger flowers adorn a statue of the ancient Aztec flower god Xōchipilli.

Flowery projectiles

The Bailiwick of Jersey in the Channel Islands began an annual 'Battle of Flowers' festival in 1902 with real flowers serving as projectiles in a fake battle. The floral carnival began with a procession of horse-drawn floats through St Helier. When that concluded, the Battle commenced: a free-for-all between the parade's participants and spectators who dismantled the floats to provide floral 'ammunition'. 'At times the flowers flew in veritable showers,' according to a news report from the 1902 Battle. The furious flinging of flowers took place each year for half a century until that part of the festival was discontinued in 1964, though the event, still staged annually, retains its military moniker.[14] I asked its events director, Jackie

284

96 Following Jersey's first Battle of Flowers, the faux-floral-militarism spread to the Continent as Cannes introduced its own version in spring 1905. The local newspaper informs: 'At exactly two o'clock the first flowery projectiles are launched, spinning through the air before achieving their goal.'

Donald, if recent Battles have seen any impromptu outbreaks of floral projectiles, even just an occasional one-off nostalgic recurrence of the tussie-mussie tussles, or heliotropic havoc, of yore. Any crocus fracas? Frangipani free-for-all? Begonia barrage? Petulant petunias? 'No, sadly not,' she replied. 'It's another health and safety issue that has stopped many of the fun things.'[15] Concerns about injurious thorns or a stem that might put someone's eye out have elicited nanny-state prudence.

But back in the day, an account from the 1909 Battle gives a keen sense of the skirmish:

> Staid old men become again as romping children, the
> stern official throws off his robe of dignity and austerity,
> and even the cleric forgets for a moment that he has a
> distinguishing collar which gives him away. If one threw
> a bunch of flowers at a fellow on an ordinary day we should
> most probably be summoned for assault, but with the Battle
> of Flowers everything is different.[16]

Of all the varied things people do with flowers, throwing them at each other is certainly unusual. (Search YouTube for 'Pathé, Jersey Battle of Flowers' to see the furor in all its cinematic glory; you'll find it near the end of each year's newsreel, after the parade winds down. The 1957 Battle, one of my favourites, saw especially raucous combat!) Unusual practices are the most tantalizing aspects of these strange, bright crowds of flowers, however. I intend no disrespect for more genteel and conventional floral customs, but things get especially interesting, both botanically and anthropologically, when flower aficionados venture outside the box, outside the vase, with enthusiastic eccentricities.

It seems highly unlikely that Jersey's Battle of Flowers inspired Banksy's iconic flower-throwing mural, *Flower Bomber* (also known as *Rage, the Flower Thrower*), painted in Beit Sahur, near Bethlehem, in 2003. But still it is interesting to compare and contrast phenomena, however disparate, that have a salient common aspect.

Flower Bomber is monochromatic except for the flowers, which retain their vital brightness in an otherwise grim, black-and-white world. A man in a baseball cap, his face partially covered to prevent him from being identified, plants his feet and takes aim: as if to throw a bomb, or a Molotov cocktail, in some protest or skirmish. But the bomb is replaced with a bouquet of flowers. The man almost looks as if he doesn't realize that he is not holding a weapon in his hands: as if, perhaps, Banksy substituted the flowers for the bomb unbeknown to the 'bomber'. It would be dramatically ironic: the viewers see that he is armed with just flowers, but he himself doesn't know this, suggesting a fantasy that artists can imagine (and thus effectuate) the erasure of violence. Or perhaps the man does realize that he is throwing only flowers, and the point then might be that he has a much richer sense of the power of flowers than most other people do. Perhaps flowers are the only weapon he has available . . . or perhaps he could throw whatever he wants, and he has pointedly chosen flowers.

I think we are meant to be uncertain about the 'correct' reading of this image. Banksy invites us to mull all these possibilities that are unlikely and surreal, but better than the scene would be without flowers – just another conflict marked by the usual violence. The bouquet signifies the possibility of beauty, the ability to choose beauty, however improbable this choice may be. And even if it is improbable, still, it is our choice, our ethics, that makes it so. Something implausible could become true if we simply chose differently. Anyone *could* pick up a bouquet of flowers, as Banksy has painted here, and throw it at the people on the other side.

The person depicted is presumably Palestinian, facing off against Israeli military forces who occupy his homeland. Determined rage resonates in his eyes, his posture and what we can imagine about his battle. The idea that a bouquet of flowers would

97 Banksy, *Flower Bomber*, 2003.

suit his purposes here is remote, but this, we acknowledge with a sigh of resignation (or we embrace with epiphanic bliss) is artistic licence. Flowers appear in wars because everything else – gunpowder, bayonets, atomic bombs, rocks, grenades – has been used forever, and those weapons are not working. Or maybe they *are* working, the military might argue, in the sense that they are efficiently facilitating destruction and death, but from an ethical human perspective, Banksy suggests, they are failures. Let's try flowers instead – what could it hurt?

Whether in Palestine, Jersey or Cannes, I'd imagine throwing flowers must feel strange and somewhat futile: their floppy petals and leaves are not aerodynamically designed to be propelled through the air like javelins or footballs. They will drop clumsily a short distance from where they were thrown, probably the worse for wear after their flight: unsuitable for display or any other practical use. One common venue for tossing flowers is at an artistic performance, especially ballet or opera. It's easier to throw them in a theatre with banked seats – gravity helps counteract aerodynamic deficiencies. There is a protocol for tossing theatre flowers: remove thorns and aim the flower, stem forward, towards the intended performer. Even then, 'many times flowers accidentally land in the lap, shoulders or on the heads of the musicians in the orchestra pit,' Bolshoi dancer Anastasia Babayeva says. 'The thoughtful musicians almost always assist by quickly and quietly tossing the flowers onto the stage.'[17] Flowers usually fly at classical but not modern dance performances, and they are almost always for women artists only; but in the 1960s Margot Fonteyn charmed audiences when she would pluck one flower from a bouquet thrown onstage for her and hand it to her partner, Rudolf Nureyev.[18]

Flowers of protest

'Suppose they gave a war and nobody came,' read signs carried by anti-Vietnam War protestors (adapting a Carl Sandburg poem).[19] Or suppose people came, but armed with flowers?

Imagine one troop of combatants with tear gas and M16s, and the other side packing carnations or chrysanthemums. In the past century this has happened often. These flower-fighters don't throw their flowers like the Jerseyfolk; instead, they place them, precisely and delicately, in their opponents' guns (or sometimes their own). Putting flowers into rifle barrels conjoins a fragile life force with a devastating lethal counterforce. It seems like a quixotic attempt to vanquish military violence, safeguarding humanity by blocking the holes where the bullets would come out. In a match-up of flowers against guns, the flowers would seem primed for defeat. The bullets can shoot out anyway; flowers won't prevent that. And yet the confrontation is so striking, such a powerful contrast, that the soldiers ordered to pull the trigger (and those who give the orders) might think twice before firing. An ethical, cognitive resistance to violence blossoms when flowers face guns.

The roots of putting flowers in guns date to the early twentieth century. *Il parts la fleur au fusil* (he leaves with a flower in his gun barrel) was a common French expression during the First World War, describing infantry recruits marching off with no idea what horrors lay ahead. Families and girlfriends, holding back tears, would place flowers in the young men's rifles to provide one last moment of calm domesticity – as if the Berthier carbines slung over their shoulders were just so many elaborate bud vases – and to sublimate the danger for a few more moments as soldiers paraded through villages on their way to the front. The phrase connotes an impending loss of

98 As the French 303rd *régiment d'infanterie* heads off towards the front, *ils partons les fleurs au fusils.* Ricardo Florès, illustration from *Le Rire* (1915).

innocence, and an improbable hope that things might turn out all right: perhaps the guns will not be fired in combat after all, and can remain as merely flower-holders. With a mix of courage and denial, everyone keeps a stiff upper lip as the flower in the rifle stock provides the focal point for this pretence.

A half-century later, American protests against the Vietnam War commonly featured flowers in guns, inspired by photojournalist Bernie Boston's image from the 1967 March on the Pentagon. The closely cropped photograph he called *Flower Power* zooms in from above on the protest's front line. A few 'hippies' and 'yippies' face off against a force of armed, helmeted soldiers from the 503rd Military Police Battalion, who form a semicircle around the demonstrators to prevent them from climbing the Pentagon steps (with the ultimate intention of levitating the building).

A young man in a baggy turtleneck sweater, later identified as eighteen-year-old George Harris III, approaches the soldiers (whose presence, especially because of their rifles, fills most of the frame) holding a handful of carnations that he inserts into the bore of each rifle's barrel. He seems to be going down the line soldier by soldier, rifle by rifle, flower by flower. In the moment captured here, having already flowered one gun and in the process of doing a second, he appears to have enough flowers on hand to fill all the rifles around him.

A video recording of this scene shows that after the second rifle has been flowered and Harris moves on to the next one, the soldier whose face is most prominent in the top left corner removes the flower from the first gun.[20] Harris seems consummately comfortable, methodical and on-message with his flowers; the video shows that the soldier, by contrast, looks awkward as soon as he takes out the flower. He doesn't seem to know what to do with it, and after deflowering that first rifle he looks as if he just doesn't want to touch any more flowers. I imagine that he resigns himself to the engagement, and to letting the peaceniks do what they want, unimpeded. The soldiers seem to understand that they are being mocked, and they probably resent the triumphant protestors. But if they had worried that violence might erupt from this confrontation, they may be relieved that now the milieu does not seem angry. The flower-action seems strange, silly, dramatic, even histrionic, but not dangerous.

(Another fun floral fact about George Harris III: years after his fifteen minutes of fame at the Pentagon, he founded a psychedelic gay liberation theatre collective. His cabaret act, a glittery drag musical extravaganza, featured the protestor formerly known as Harris, now rechristened Hibiscus, at the helm of the troupe he called Hibiscus and the Screaming Violets.)[21]

The Pentagon demonstration grew out of the USA's long-standing non-violent protest movement, an extensive campaign Martin Luther King Jr, Rosa Parks, John Lewis, Fannie Lou Hamer and many others had led during the past decade as they fought for civil rights. Boston's photograph captures a poetic air, a touch of the absurd, reflecting a privilege that African American activists simply didn't have. These white protestors had the luxury of making a flashy statement with significantly less risk than Black

99 *Flower Power*, a photograph by Bernie Boston taken during the anti-Vietnam War March on the Pentagon 21 October 1967.

demonstrators faced of police dogs, water cannon, mob assaults or incarceration.

The idea of 1960s flower protests began with Beat poet Allen Ginsberg, who later described what he saw when he looked at *Flower Power*:

> a somewhat timid, tender kid, but courageous, with his
> flower, poking it into the barrel of a soldier who was
> the same age, but in the wrong place at the wrong time,
> sweating and worried, holding his rifle up against his
> fellow brother, a college boy, an image of flower power.
> Flower power meant more than just walking around with
> flowers in your hair. It really meant the power of earth

292

itself. The dissolving of the authority of the Pentagon was symbolized by that moment of putting a flower in.[22]

In 1965 Ginsberg began organizing anti-war and free-speech protests in Berkeley. After several had been squelched, sometimes violently, by police and the pro-war Hells Angels, he decided to change the mood of his demonstrations, devising techniques to defuse anxiety:

the parade can embody an example of peaceable health which is the reverse of fighting back blindly. Announce in advance it is a safe march, bring your grandmother and babies . . . 'We aren't coming out to fight and we

100 *The Ultimate Confrontation: The Flower and the Bayonet*, a photograph by Marc Riboud taken at the same march on the same day.

simply will not fight.' We have to use our imagination.
A spectacle can be made, an unmistakable statement
outside the war psychology which is leading nowhere.'

His ideas included:

> Masses of flowers – a visual spectacle – especially
> concentrated in the front lines. Can be used to set
> up barricades, to present to Hells Angels, Police,
> Politicians, and press and spectators whenever needed
> or at parade's end. Masses of marchers can be asked
> to bring their own flowers. Front lines should be
> organized and provided with flowers in advance.[23]

Ginsberg stationed poets, artists, mothers and professors in
the front lines. Besides flowers, carry harmonicas, tambourines
and banjos, he advised, along with sparklers, toy soldiers and candy
bars to give to the police. At the first sign of possible violence, he
wrote, people should start singing 'I Wanna Hold Your Hand' and
dancing, or doing calisthenics, or reciting the Lord's Prayer. These
protests are tinged – no, doused – with the spirit of the times: free
love, free speech, flower children (as they would come to be called)
holistically resisting mainstream politics and values.

By the time of the 1967 March on the Pentagon, protests regularly featured such groovy resistance techniques. The term 'flower
power' was Abbie Hoffman's coinage: 'Personally, I always held my
flower in a clenched fist,' he wrote.[24] The Flower Power Day Rally
in May 1967 was Hoffman's rebranding of Armed Forces Day, and
he called his troop of protesters the Flower Brigade. Hoffman
may have been combining Ginsberg's flower concept with Stokely

Carmichael's phrase 'Black Power'.[25] If young social rebels found this floral identity empowering, their antagonists in 'the establishment' mocked it: 'As fads go, Flower Power was less than impressive,' the rock critic Nik Cohn wrote. 'Everyone wore kaftans and beads and bells. Everyone spoke in hushed tones of San Francisco and Monterey, of acid and Love and the Maharishi.'[26] In the same vein, novelist Kingsley Amis described the vibe as 'just another fun thing and now thing, like these clothes they all wear and theatre in the nude and flower power and environmental art.'[27] But the believers believed. 'The cry of "Flower Power" echoes through the land,' Hoffman wrote. 'We shall not wilt. Let a thousand flowers bloom.'[28]

A wilted flower, of course, has lost its power. Hoffman inspires his crowds of marchers to be strong, fresh, bright (and also *strange*, in the eyes of many Americans), and at their peak for the protest, just like the floral ammunition they carry. The allusion to Chairman Mao, too, is interesting: 'Let a thousand flowers bloom' is a common misquotation of Mao Zedong's maxim from a 1957 speech: 'Letting a hundred flowers blossom and a hundred schools of thought contend is the policy for promoting progress in the arts and the sciences and a flourishing socialist culture in our land.'[29] Mao offered the U.S. counterculture a popular reference point for ideological resistance to capitalist/imperialist/militarist sensibilities, and his own famous flower metaphor dovetailed with Hoffman's rhetoric. For Western leftists of the era, Mao's paean to cultural and intellectual diversity seemed especially credible as it came packaged in such an organic flower metaphor, a Zen-like resonance infusing his blooming field. One hundred flowers were perhaps insufficiently fecund for American appetites, so the crop increased tenfold in translation.

For Mao's critics, this slogan's flowery scent of tolerance was a craven deception to disguise a totalitarian iron fist. From the vantage point of our own times, there is no evidence that Mao was at all sincere about freedom of expression, or that he held any genuine affection for flowers. Nevertheless, visitors to his Tiananmen Square mausoleum today buy a single white chrysanthemum (or to show more fervent devotion, an entire bouquet) to leave at the foot of his statue. In a devious business practice that seems fitting for the devious leader, the flowers are then collected and resold.

Flower power (whether Hoffman's or Mao's version) may easily suit the purposes of propaganda. However much beauty and truth inheres in flowers, their presence does not guarantee the authenticity and probity of the image, or the idea, to which they are connected. As tempted as I am to attribute a noble ethos to flowers, the plants themselves are, finally, amoral: they will do as they are told. But however disingenuous Mao's liberalism was, however false his political promises, still, his 1957 slogan was a pretty nice turn of phrase. The idea that intellectual diversity is like (and could be inspired by) a field of profusely blooming flowers is an excellent way to imagine how creative human individuality mirrors our ecosystem's non-human life forces.

Preparing for Flower Power Day, Hoffman set out his Flower Brigade's botanical tactics: 'We were poorly equipped with flowers from uptown florists. Already there is talk of growing our own. Plans are being made to mine the East River with daffodils. Dandelion chains are being wrapped around induction centers. Holes are being dug in street pavements and seeds dropped in and covered.'[30] I am fairly certain that this is a joke. I doubt Hoffman really tended flowers to stock his rallies; but the imagery and messaging, like Chairman Mao's, were nevertheless cleverly appealing.

Flowers were a key prop for Hoffman's guerrilla theatre tactics, his performative activism.

Bernie Boston's photograph has been re-staged ad infinitum. Another famous image from the same rally was the French photographer Marc Riboud's photograph of a young woman, Jan Rose Kasmir, entitled *The Ultimate Confrontation: The Flower and the Bayonet*. While it is similar to Boston's photo, this scene focuses more intently on the chrysanthemum Kasmir holds near – not inside – the soldiers' rifles. She seems to be smelling the flower, devoutly attuned to its power and only that, ignoring the guns. Perhaps she was going to insert the flower inside the rifle barrels as George Harris did, but hesitated at the last moment, mesmerized by the flower and not wanting to let it go. Perhaps she is trying to mesmerize the soldiers aligned in battle stance immediately in front of her. Maybe she imagines the chrysanthemum as a shield.

It is hard to imagine that Lisbon's 1974 Carnation Rebellion, full of rampant rifle-flowering, wasn't directly inspired by Boston's

101 During the Arab Spring's Yemeni Revolution in 2011, soldiers displayed plastic flowers that they had placed in their rifles themselves.

and Ribaud's images, which were re-enacted ritually at protest after protest. The scene is still being repeated at protests around the world in causes ranging from the Arab Spring and Tunisia's Jasmine Revolution to Occupy and Black Lives Matter. Soldiers and police are now, presumably, prepared for such floral tactics, as they would not have been back in 1967; sometimes, as in the Yemeni Revolution of 2011, the soldiers co-opt the rhetoric by self-flowering.

A recent iteration of the flowered gun, a digital creation made to resemble a Palestinian mural (artist unknown, but in the 'school of Banksy'[31]), depicts a small boy inserting a flower into a heavily

102 A digitally created 'mural', artist unknown, recirculates the powerful image of a flower in a gun.

armed soldier's rifle. In most other versions of this interaction guns are aimed at civilians but here, instead, the gun points down. The soldier, presumably Israeli, kneels to allow the boy, presumably Palestinian, easy access to the gun barrel that would otherwise be a difficult stretch for him. We might expect the boy to look vulnerable, but he seems unafraid. (Gun-flowerers frequently convey this sense of boundless tranquillity.) The play of light on the boy's shirt and shorts echoes the camouflage pattern on the soldier's uniform: it is as if they are both on the same side, which would be highly unlikely in real life, but this harmony is depicted in a way that seems credible in the moment we witness their meeting. Although their 'sides' have different nationalities, different political objectives, and vastly different amounts of power, still they are both human.

It is as if the boy has brought the soldier – humbled, tamed – to his knees. The soldier seems drained of threat because of the flower, the boy's poise, his own genuflection. The colours are grey-scale, white and dull khaki, except for the small boy's small flower, with its small but striking burst of yellow.

The flower is the power, the magic, of this scene. Connecting the two human figures, it signifies a profound potential transformation from battle to truce, from violence to peace. Jan Rose Kasmir and turtlenecked George Harris III showed how a flower in a gun embodies a kind of transcendence that celebrates humanity over destruction. This is a good tradition, a triumph of flowers. These transformative flowers against violence are quite possibly the best of all the strange, bright crowds we have encountered.

Where have all the flowers gone?

Flowers come and go in cycles: germinating and sprouting, growing, blooming, pollenating and fertilizing (reproducing), going to
seed, dying off (as it may seem, though life continues in the next
cycle as seeds, tubers, bulbs and shoot systems defy death), and
returning. Wars, which disrupt life's rational and comfortable cycles,
might seem anathema to flowers and flowery representation. On
the other hand, cynics will note, wars, too, are often cyclical – they
recur one after another; one conflict ends, sort of, and then another
one arises out of its ashes. Do wars ever actually end in resolution,
or do they only go dormant for a period until the next one sprouts
up again in the same place?

   In 'Where Have All the Flowers Gone?' (1955),[32] Pete Seeger
and Joe Hickerson interleave the cycles of flowers with the cycles
of war. The form is itself a cycle, a 'circular song' that ends up where
it started and keeps going around as long as people want to keep
singing, suggesting that the cycles it describes are similarly never-
ending. Girls pick the flowers, then boys pick the flowery-beautiful
girls (by marrying them). Next, wars pick the boys as soldiers. The
language Seeger uses to describe this phase of the cycle is 'gone
to soldiers': the young men have *gone off* to be soldiers, but some
of them will also be *gone as* soldiers – gone to their deaths. After
that, the soldiers (cut down in war) are gone to graveyards, and
finally, the flowers come again and reclaim the graveyards with
their blossoms. The flowers ultimately endure, implying (by Seeger's
logic) that the people do, too: when the flowers bloom, more young
women will come to pick them, which will attract more young men,
and so the cycle of reproduction will continue. The fecundity of
flowers resembles the fecundity of humanity.

But the trope of disappearance underlies Seeger's formulaic depiction of this fecund cycle: 'Where have all the . . . gone?' The cycle is ironic in its regularity. Flowers are nice, love is nice, war is terrible, but then the flowers come back, and flowers are nice. Or are they? Are they deceptively masking war's true horror? People often plant, tend and derive succour from flowers growing in cemeteries and other sites scarred by violence or death. Is this restorative, or does it distort, tenderly but dishonestly, what has really happened? Flowers are not supposed to delude us, they are supposed to teach us – or, as Emily Dickinson insists, they invite us to learn from them (which amounts to the same thing), to make inferences. Seeger's subversive folk song certainly leaves powerful inferences to be drawn.

'Where Have All the Flowers Gone?' became the score for many anti-war protests, a favourite of flower children expressing flower power. It is an international anthem of flowery pacifism: Mexicans sing '¿Dónde están las flores?'; in Poland, 'Gdzie są kwiaty z tamtych lat?'; 'Söyle Çiçekler nerde?' in Turkey; 'Para onde foram todas as flores?' in Portugal. When Marlene Dietrich sang a characteristically smoky, sultry version, 'Sag mir, wo die Blumen sind?' during one of her infrequent post-war visits to Germany, 'the old Nazis were out to run her down: "don't listen to this woman, she sang for the soldiers fighting us!" But her rendition reached number one on the German Hit Parade.'[33] Israeli audiences wildly applauded Dietrich's 1962 performance of this song, which ended that country's taboo on performing in the German language.[34]

Written at the peak of the Cold War, Seeger implicitly took aim at the global threats of the day (geopolitical realignment, nuclear proliferation, aggressive military destabilization) via the conspicuously modest trope of flowers: simple and delicate, but in their own way, as we have seen again and again, ineluctably powerful. Foregrounding the eternal regeneration inherent in flowers, Seeger tacitly connotes the relative insignificance of war. The specific details of military violence do not merit acknowledgement in this song, which is pointedly about flowers. Granted, it's not just about flowers, but it tries as hard as it can to tell a story of flowers rather than a story of war. War is evoked not in typical martial extravagance, but in two lonely nouns – *soldiers, graveyards* – and a simple verb, *gone*. Seeger leaves us to fill in the rest of the story ourselves (if we choose to . . . or, not). 'In its simplicity and kind tune,' writes Francesca Aloisio, a scholar of international relations, '[the song conveys] a sense of boredom about everything that war involves'.[35]

As the song circles towards the end and then back again to the beginning, the first stanza announces that the flowers are gone again – though that is a 'glass-half-empty' reading: on the other hand, they must have first come back again if they are gone again. We may consider this a depressing song, because young men keep going to wars; or we may hear it as soothing because the flowers always come back (albeit sometimes growing out of the young men's corpses), and the cycle continues: the cycle of love and violence, of denuded fields (flower fields and battlefields) and replenishment. The crux of the song blossoms in its first line: when flowers are gone, we wonder where they are; we miss them. Our ethos towards flowers – nurturing and cherishing them, valuing them or failing to do so – is our ethos towards life. A life full of flowers is a kind life, embodying a proper embrace of humanity, nature and cyclical sustainability.

In this lyric about war and flowers depicted alongside each other, like many other such juxtaposed encounters I explore in this chapter, the flowers come out on top: they are more interesting, more important, more compelling. They are the moral of this story, or they are somehow coterminous with – symbolic of – the moral. The 'proper' singer of this song will have both flowers and war going up against each other in her mind, but the flowers will win out, if for no other reason than that the song begins and ends with flowers, and recommences with flowers; the flowers are cleverly poised to triumph here.

'Gone' may denote either a passive or active absence. Are the flowers gone because someone removed them, or the wind blew them away, or the ground became infertile? Or, did they somehow *intentionally* leave, scorning and abandoning humanity in our militaristic insanity? The word connotes alienation, but also connection, as one thing is 'gone' to another, which replaces it, carrying on something that it got (or something that was taken) from the thing that came before. That connection is emphasized, repeatedly and ritually, as the question about where something has gone is always followed by an answer, beginning with the words 'Gone to'. Whether Seeger intends us to think of the flowers going passively or actively, 'gone' rings as a word of action. The song is about what *we* do, where we go (which somehow parallels where flowers go, where they have gone); it describes our choices as individuals and our movements as collectives.

'When will they ever learn?' is the published text of this lyric. But later in his life (after he had sung this song over and over, but soldiers nevertheless kept going to graveyards) Seeger changed 'they' to 'we': 'When will *we* ever learn?' This seemingly minor modification resounded powerfully with audiences who were expecting 'they,' and got unexpectedly implicated in the first-person pronoun, sucked into the moral universe of Seeger's war flowers.

A century before Pete Seeger, Emily Dickinson, too, linked botanical and military cycles. Her poem about Civil War carnage depicts a figurative parallel between disappearing flowers and disappearing soldiers:

> They dropped like Flakes –
> They dropped like Stars –
> Like Petals from a Rose –
> When suddenly across the June
> A Wind with fingers – goes –
>
> They perished in the Seamless Grass –
> No eye could find the place –
> But God can summon every face
> On his Repealless – List.[36]

If someone I loved had died in a war, I don't know if I would be comforted or offended by the soft poetic expression that he had 'dropped . . . Like Petals from a Rose'. I might find it affected, inauthentic, gratuitous: stylized in a way that trivializes the bloodshed. Perhaps, though, thinking about flowers is an effective way of displacing and sublimating, and thus soothing, the trauma of loss. It is a long stretch to think of people who have dropped away from life – who have been *taken away from life*, or, in Seeger's terminology, who are *gone* – as being like the petals that have dropped away from a flower, but perhaps contemplating such improbable similes is a useful exercise for strengthening people's emotional and spiritual capacities in ways that help mourners deal with the tragedies of war.

For many other American Civil War poets, too, the language of flowers blossomed, but in different ways for Northern and

Southern women, literary critic Eliza Richards writes. Northern readers and writers usually had the luxury of separating the home front from the battlefield, while Southerners, living in the throes of violent conflict, could not; the immediate proximity of actual warfare made their flower poetry less comforting.

For example, the Northern poet Elizabeth Akers Allen turns to flowers for reassurance in her poem 'Spring at the Capital': 'Down-looking in this snow-white bud, / How distant seems the war's red flood! / How far remote the screaming wounds, the sickening scent of human blood!' The speaker 'notes the incongruity between the tranquil scenario before her and the violence she knows is taking place' at a distance.[37]

Southern women were more likely to turn away from the tradition of floral poetry, and what flower poems do exist are dark, replete with 'violence that destroys actual flowers as well as their emblematic counterparts . . . presenting dead flowers to the reader' and 'pointedly choosing plants that don't blossom when commemorating the dead'. Richards writes: 'Flowers break under the enormous burden of maintaining or restoring moral order,' quoting Kentucky poet Agnes Leonard's macabre vision of flowers and carnage horrifically conjoined in her poem 'After the Battle': 'Thickly on the trampled grasses / Lay the battle's awful traces, / Mid the blood-stained clover blossoms / Lay the stark and ghastly faces.' For the Southern poets who were so disturbingly close to the battlefields (which might recently have been fields of flowers), 'war's violence destroys everything that once enabled pastoral vision.'[38]

Flowers of the Second World War

It is better to light a single candle, the saying goes, than to curse the darkness. This determination animates Kenneth I. Helphand's *Defiant Gardens: Making Gardens in Wartime*, about 'gardens made by victims – soldiers, prisoners, and internees – who refused to be victimized' in such venues of war as the trenches of the First World War and the ghettoes of the second, European prisoner-of-war camps and Japanese-American internment camps: places where people craved flowers to help resist the evil that surrounded them. They were oases 'created in extreme conditions' that stood 'not in harmony but in opposition to their locations'.[39] Probably most importantly, these gardens provided vegetables, farmed for subsistence, but they also included flowers plentifully. Even if they had no pragmatic (nutritional) value, these flowers emphatically defied the violence and fear in the world immediately around the people who nurtured botanical connections to a land that was otherwise in chaos. Representing 'sites of assertion and affirmation',[40] flowers helped mitigate these landscapes of disempowerment and destruction.

'These are gardens against the odds' that 'seem out of place', Helphand writes. 'Defiant gardens are places of peace,'[41] arising in circumstances where the 'biophilia' that E. O. Wilson has identified – a human need to affiliate with life, a compulsion that sustains our spirit – is especially attenuated, and especially vital for survival. War and gardening are, as Helphand construes them, two opposing phenomena that can take place, paradoxically, in a single setting. Wars are insane and appalling; flower gardens are comprehensible, pleasing, full of sensory richness and pleasure; they 'assuaged the horrific conditions' for people suffering in trenches or camps, representing their 'wish for the comforts of home . . . and the desire for life, peace, a future'.[42]

Confined inside the Warsaw Ghetto, Mary Berg wrote in her diary: 'A little garden like ours is very dear to us. The spring this year is extraordinary. A lilac bush under our window is in full bloom.'[43] As Nazis tried to alienate Jews from the world and from the earth, ghetto gardens represented a mode of resistance, Helphand writes, a 'small but potent reminder of a life free from deprivation and humiliation'. In the spring of 1943 Herman Kruk noted, as gardens appeared throughout the Vilna Ghetto, 'Instead of flowers over us, we will make our courtyards bloom for the time being.'[44]

In 1942 the United Kingdom's War Artists' Advisory Committee commissioned the avant-garde artist David Bomberg to paint an underground bomb store at RAF Fauld. Sited in a former Staffordshire mine, it was one of the country's largest stores of munitions with a capacity to hold 20,000 tonnes of explosives. (Two years after Bomberg worked there the depot blew up, killing 68 people, when an accidental detonation ignited the largest explosion ever recorded in Britain.) Bomberg's paintings and drawings from the bomb store are now considered his best work, but at the time the WAAC disliked the portfolio. They accepted only a few (and displayed none) of the many paintings he had done, refusing to extend the commission. The committee found his work too dark; they wanted art that would comfort audiences rather than troubling them.[45]

Seeing his frustration, his wife, Lilian, brought home some flowers and suggested he paint them. At first he refused, but eventually took to the task with intensity: Lilian describes how 'he used to go every day early to Covent Garden to buy the flowers himself [like Clarissa Dalloway!] . . . He only painted flowers, and very much enjoyed doing it. He always arranged them himself, in the

same vase, against the same curtain.' Bomberg produced a series
of canvases resounding with paradox: they celebrate a coexistent
beauty and violence in the flowers, which seem to be bursting out
of their vases. A fellow artist recalled Bomberg saying, in a conversation cut short by menacing sirens, 'even flowers can be
painted so as to remind us all of the terror in the human breast.'[46]
The flower pictures 'share the explosive energy of the bombstore
subjects and indicate Bomberg's renewed interest in painting'.[47]

308

While the strange, bright violence in these paintings is clear enough to viewers today, that mood would have been even more striking to audiences during the war, for whom omnipresent danger went without saying.

In a fascinating case study of how war and flowers intersect, the artist's feelings about combat are channelled directly into flowers and expressed through flowers. Unable to paint the ominous (and obvious) military subjects he preferred, Bomberg refocused his attention on a more palatable subject, into which he encoded his anxieties about warfare. He showed, simply and irrefutably, that flowers could bear the symbolic resonances of danger and destruction: they could convey war. His art demonstrates how one paints flowers in a way that exacts such immediate, intense reactions as this from a reviewer of his 1943 exhibition: 'these are veritable explosions in oil colour; No. 25 goes off with an almost audible bang.'[48] What makes these flowers explosive? Most flowers aren't: they are quiet, delicate, mannered, perhaps even arrogantly impervious in their placid eloquence. The rest of the world may fumble with its troubles and turmoil, they seem to preen, but we flowers will simply relax in a vase, sedately and prettily.

Bomberg's flowers provoke the question of whether there may be more explosive potential than we initially suspect – more energy, and even more violence – lurking beneath the surface in *all* flowers: hiding somewhere among the innocuous petals and buds? After all, we have seen that flowers may contain poison (both natural toxins and synthetic pesticides) and drugs; thorns and cankers; classism, homophobia, racism and sexism; carbon footprints that ravage vulnerable ecologies. More than a bit of potential danger, upheaval, even derangement (remember Baudelaire, Plath, *Little Shop of Horrors*) may emanate from flowers.

Bomberg's canvases confirm that flowers may indeed be weaponized, with volatile warring energies, good and bad, yin and yang, compressed within. Bomb-flowers would seem to be bad flowers; and yet, during the Second World War, as Bomberg's world was being blitzkrieged by Nazis, perhaps bombs (at least, *Allied* bombs) weren't as objectionable. He might have seen in them, and in his symbolic flower-bombs, some sense of empowerment and defence against Hitler's Germany. (Could it be at all relevant that Bomberg literally carries a 'bomb' in his surname?) The bomb stores he had painted were bleakly depressing. Perhaps he transferred that energy, that bomb-power, to flowers – figurative bomb stores – making him more productive and more successful as an artist by conjoining, idiosyncratically, the power of a massive dynamite blast with the power of delicate beauty.

What makes Bomberg's flowers bomb-like? Most prominently, the colours: the sharp yellows and reds that pervade these images are the colours of fire and explosion. It's not just that those colours are so prevalent in his paintings, it's the way they are composed: in streaks, intermixed, intermingled, just as a close-up image of an explosion will show yellow ribbons in the red. Spiky and angular, like weaponry or fragmented bombshell casings, these flowers have bursts – or, they *are* bursts. Other floral representations have been imagined, metaphorically, as bursts of colours, but Bomberg literalizes this – or he comes as close to doing so as one can on a painted canvas, which, of course, cannot literally explode.

(John Hersey's renowned 1946 *New Yorker* essay 'Hiroshima' confirms that bombs can resemble flowers, or can at least be imagined as flower-like. When he interviewed survivors about the moment they saw the blast on that horrible day, most could not even imagine what it was: 'Dr Machii said, "It must have been a

Molotoffano hanakago" – a Molotov flower basket, the delicate Japanese name for the "bread basket," or self-scattering cluster of bombs.'[49])

In Bomberg's *Flowers* (illus. 103), the bright red flower at left and the blurrier red flower at centre are like two bombs – the left one is just exploding, while the other seems to have done so a few seconds earlier and now leaves a fading burst of fire and smoke. More red blotches like bombs in the distance emanate from the vase, which resembles a cannon or a gunpowder store in both form and function.

Other flowers are yellow, but with traces of red: they, too, are projectiles, missiles, of a slightly lesser intensity, or perhaps closer to dissipating after having exploded. The canvas is a fusillade of fireworks. The colours transcend the precise boundaries of the flowers: the entire table is yellow, as if the yellow energy has spread across it in the way a fire spreads, and the yellow and red wall behind the flowers, too, reflects the contagious dynamic of constant cascades of bombs, which many viewers would have experienced at first hand in carpet-bombing attacks across Britain. The scene is aflame. Behind the reds and yellows are streaks of black, evoking the smoke and char that linger after the fires die down. A few other blotches of red and yellow around the centre of the arrangement have little clarity as flowers because they are in the process, in the instant, of exploding.

An important compositional aspect of Bomberg's flowers lurks in their forms: their stems, their angles, their directionality. The stems encourage our eyes to follow the flowers as they burst upwards: they symbolize the trajectory, making us feel and see a sense of power. When one sees bombs, one immediately wonders: where exactly are they headed? Where will they fall? Will they hit me? A key painterly technique involves directing how viewers' eyes move around the canvas; here, the method is like tracking bombs.

Speed, too, is an important dynamic of Bomberg's flower paintings. Many canvases in museums, especially floral scenes, invite a slow, quiet, methodical, contemplative appraisal. Not these: the viewer experiences and responds to these quick, loud, instant flares with the immediacy and intensity they embody. We are completely engaged with movement; there is no stillness (and precarious life) in these 'still-life' compositions.

Bomberg wanted to contribute to the war effort by depicting in his art what was happening in the world. When his initial vision was unappreciated, he became devious. He found a way to present audiences something they have always looked at – flower arrangements – and through that transmit some of the reality, the dangerous turmoil, of his moment. As he made his morning rounds through Covent Garden, I wonder if he told the florists he was transforming their raw materials into explosives. I imagine not: I like to think it was his secret, up until the moment when the flowers detonated on his canvases.

A flower for 9/11

Another Banksy artwork illustrates a flower à la Bomberg, that is, a bursting flower that connotes a bursting explosion. As in *Flower Bomber*, Banksy explores the imaginative space, the semiotic free play, in the confluence of flowers and violence. Visiting New York City in 2013 he painted a 9/11 tribute in lower Manhattan's Tribeca neighbourhood, not far from where the World Trade Center stood. A small, rough silhouette of the instantly recognized towers is rendered all in charcoal black, except for a flower placed where

American Airlines Flight 11 hit the North Tower. The flower *represents* the burst of fire, the image seared into our minds, but it also *displaces* that explosion. Shocking and disturbing, Banksy's image, *Twin Towers*, offers a strange conjunction of beauty and terror. Many New Yorkers found this image profane, irreverent, ridiculous. I agree that it is somewhat ridiculous, which is exactly what I find so powerful about it: who else could have made this tragedy ridiculous? Even if only briefly, aesthetically, imaginatively, Banksy drains the terrorists of their power to shock us with evil. The flower is the focal point, a springboard for a meditation, perhaps a fantasy, about how the world would be if people did not hate and hurt each other.

It is odd to realize (as we do in Bomberg's paintings, too) how much the flower looks like the explosion, and signifies the explosion: how unexpectedly easy it is to see both flower and explosion in the same instant. Flowers don't usually look like explosions, do they? It is a kind of *trompe l'oeil*: if an artist draws a flower in a place where the viewer expects to see an explosion, then the context helps make the case for the similarity of these images, at least

104 Strangely and brightly, the flower in Banksy's 2013 New York mural *Twin Towers* alludes to the horrific 9/11 attack. The flower, which appears three-dimensional, is actually flat.

in terms of form, colour, visual energy. And having seen this similarity, you cannot unsee it. The chrysanthemum's yellow-orange colour, tinged (as if scorched) with black edges, and the geometrically 'exploding' petals, could be either a flower or something so profoundly unlike a flower as to make it seem impossible to conflate these images in any way, and yet that is just what Banksy has done here.

Does such an aesthetic ploy trivialize the attack? I can see how people might feel that it would, but I don't think this is Banksy's point. Rather, this depiction is aspirational, intended to provoke the viewer's deliberations. It is a fantastically absurd expression – but at the same time, poignantly moving – of how art can depict something different, can wish for (and can actually fulfil that wish, by creating) something other than what actually happened. Like the (ridiculous) idea of holding a war to which nobody came, or to which people came armed with flowers: suppose something inconceivable happened to the World Trade Center and it was harmless? If, instead of horrible, it was pretty, what would that look like? (Like this: an enormous flower.) A flower as big as a dozen floors of a skyscraper would be impossible; but wouldn't it be amazing if a flower *could* be supersized? (It can be in art: remember Jeff Koons's failed floral gigantism in Paris, and Eduardo Catalano's more popular botanical colossus in Buenos Aires.) Banksy's surreal mural plays with the flower/bomb binary to posit that our ethical presence in the world is a series of choices between life and death, beauty or terror.

When we first see this image (which is now gone, like the towers themselves) and realize what is going on, our memories of the attack shift. Artists can make this happen: they can switch something out for something else as easily as if they were cutting and pasting. They can play with images, artifice, in ways that make us see reality with more expanded possibilities. What happened is not limited to what happened. Banksy uses this flower to make us think about violence, and representations of violence, and ways of changing, transmuting, pacifying those representations (and, by implication, the reality of that violence itself). It is shocking to equate the flower, imagistically, with the devastating panorama of death wreaked on 9/11. Yet, at the same time, it may seem calming, transcendent, to depict the scene of this trauma in a way that does not deign to allow the explosion to happen: that forestalls it, overwrites it or imagines it otherwise. That may be a transgression of what memorial art is supposed to do, or it may be a therapeutic way to embrace healing. As in several of Banksy's most powerful works, the flower is the fulcrum, the aporia, the amulet, the portal to the wonderland, or perhaps the 'secret weapon' (I like that . . . and I think Banksy would too) for an artistic phenomenon that may facilitate an astounding perceptual and ethical transfiguration.

The Wars of the Roses

The Wars of the Roses are the most prominent flower-named conflict in history because the world's premier playwright dedicated nearly one-quarter of his canon, eight plays, to telling the story (with more dramatic flair than historical accuracy) of the red-rosed Lancastrians vs the white-rosed Yorkists. The plays propagate a hothouse of extended horticultural metaphors describing late medieval England as a decaying garden amid the chaos of civil war, as, for example, when Hotspur chides:

Shall it for shame be spoken in these days,

Or fill up chronicles in time to come,

That men of your nobility and power

Did gage them both in an unjust behalf,

As both of you – God pardon it! – have done,

To put down Richard, that sweet lovely rose,

And plant this thorn, this canker, Bolingbroke?[50]

Bolingbroke became King Henry IV when he usurped his nephew King Richard II's throne, a move Shakespeare denounces. And the flowers? Poetically expressive and vivid, Shakespearean

105 Henry Arthur Payne's *Plucking the Red and White Roses in the Old Temple Gardens, c.* 1908, a mural in the Palace of Westminster, depicts Shakespeare's busy scene filled with much angst and many roses.

roses are always a treat: not to be sneezed at. But they are also, I think, ironic and delusory – they are not quite the point. Should audiences be worried about flowers when England's survival is at stake? Certainly the English have always loved their gardens, taking floriculture very seriously. But perhaps the roses are a distraction. As the histories play out, it almost seems as if the wars have been reduced to a gardening competition.

Of course this is how figurative language always works, especially in Shakespeare's writing. Planting a flawed rose while disrespecting the sweet, lovely specimen it replaces metaphorically embodies the failure to respect royal lineage that (as Hotspur foresees) precipitated carnage between the Houses of York and Lancaster. But extensive floral display becomes a heavily burdened vehicle; can one have too much of a good thing? The flowery language overblossoms with resplendent fecundity:

> I see no reason, if I wear this rose,
> That any one should therefore be suspicious
> I more incline to Somerset than York:
> Both are my kinsmen, and I love them both.[51]

> Then will I raise aloft the milk-white rose,
> With whose sweet smell the air shall be perfumed;
> And in my standard bear the arms of York
> To grapple with the house of Lancaster.[52]

>   I cannot rest
> Until the white rose that I wear be dyed
> Even in the lukewarm blood of Henry's heart.[53]

The red rose and the white are on his face,

The fatal colours of our striving houses:

The one his purple blood right well resembles;

The other his pale cheeks, methinks, presenteth:

Wither one rose, and let the other flourish;

If you contend, a thousand lives must wither.[54]

A massive military campaign germinates from this conflict's origins, which flourish in the eloquent (and wholly fictitious) Temple Garden confrontation:

SOMERSET

Let him that is no coward nor no flatterer,

But dare maintain the party of the truth,

Pluck a red rose from off this thorn with me.

WARWICK

I love no colours, and without all colour

Of base insinuating flattery

I pluck this white rose with Plantagenet.

SUFFOLK

I pluck this red rose with young Somerset

And say withal I think he held the right . . .

VERNON

Then for the truth and plainness of the case.

I pluck this pale and maiden blossom here,

Giving my verdict on the white rose side.

SOMERSET

Prick not your finger as you pluck it off,

Lest bleeding you do paint the white rose red

And fall on my side so, against your will.

The richly florid repartee cannot be stemmed:

PLANTAGENET

Now, Somerset, where is your argument?

SOMERSET

Here in my scabbard, meditating that

Shall dye your white rose in a bloody red.

PLANTAGENET

Meantime your cheeks do counterfeit our roses;

For pale they look with fear, as witnessing

The truth on our side.

SOMERSET

No, Plantagenet,

'Tis not for fear but anger that thy cheeks

Blush for pure shame to counterfeit our roses,

And yet thy tongue will not confess thy error.

PLANTAGENET

Hath not thy rose a canker, Somerset?

SOMERSET

Hath not thy rose a thorn, Plantagenet?

PLANTAGENET

Ay, sharp and piercing, to maintain his truth;

Whiles thy consuming canker eats his falsehood.

SOMERSET

Well, I'll find friends to wear my bleeding roses,

That shall maintain what I have said is true,

Where false Plantagenet dare not be seen.[55]

Shakespeare, who considered these rose-warriors ruinous forces in English history, depicts them as fops who disguise their blood

lust with artful poetry. The conceits are delusory: vastly more blood will be spilled than the drops from thorn pricks that trouble Somerset. When noblemen act as if the wars are merely about flowers, or political affiliation is comparable to floral preferences, then they have lost sight of the forest for the trees. At the scene's end, Warwick more sensibly anticipates the course of the wars:

And here I prophesy: this brawl to-day,
Grown to this faction in the Temple-garden,
Shall send between the red rose and the white
A thousand souls to death and deadly night.[56]

Shakespeare tests his audiences: are they dazzled by the botanical wordplay in rose garden intrigues, or can they keep their attention on the significantly more dire matters ('Now is the winter of our discontent . . .') of national stability? Such an awareness is especially timely if the reigning monarch lacks an heir, as was the case when Shakespeare wrote these plays. Roses are vivid symbols, both politically and dramatically, but they may be too neat, too pat – too symbolic, even.

It is a botanical and ethical triumph when flowers can help prevent war by diverting people's attention away from weapons and soldiers and towards something more pacific, as with Hungary's asters, Georgia's roses and the 1960s U.S. flower brigades. Banksy's Palestinian flowers, although they have not yet succeeded in bringing peace to the Middle East, still aspire to non-violence, and inspire people to seek their better selves. Bomberg's flowers tell truths, however disturbing, about the spirit of the times.

But Shakespeare's roses lack any of these motivations or socially uplifting consequences. The wars are destined to happen anyhow after the Temple Garden scene (because Shakespeare's country-people believed the fifteenth-century English aristocracy were corrupt failures, and also simply because, historically, the wars had already taken place). These flowers are uniquely impuissant, compared to the other fields of war-flowers I have surveyed, because they don't forestall the battles; they don't enlighten people looking for a better way of handling conflict and trying to defuse violence.

Instead Shakespeare just accepts the oncoming bloodshed, even whetting our appetite for the dramatic carnage ahead, and overlays that with a flurry of flowers that are pretty, but not useful; compelling and memorable, but not ethically honest.

Most of what Shakespeare believed about these wars was inaccurate. Modern historians have spent considerable energy correcting him, and now believe the Wars of the Roses would have been a minor historical footnote had they not been enshrined in drama. The actual conflicts were nothing like the coherent overarching narrative that Shakespeare sets out (though we cannot be too critical of the Bard for creating a compelling story from a messier reality: that was his job).

They were not even called 'Wars of the Roses' until the nineteenth century, and they were much shorter in duration than the Elizabethans believed – only a few decades, if that; not the entire fifteenth century. Despite Shakespeare's outrage at their venality, the wars were not unusually deadly or destabilizing; trade and agriculture suffered minimally.[57] Depicting the combatants as being divided into two discrete camps oversimplifies a more complex historical situation. And while the Yorkists did sometimes use white roses in their emblems and Lancastrians (less often) used red ones, they both had many other badges as well; Shakespeare greatly exaggerated the unity of their image branding.[58]

If Shakespeare was simply reiterating the received wisdom of his time, still, he had an ulterior motive in crafting the histories as he did. He was invested in promoting the legitimacy of the Tudor line – the family of his patron, Queen Elizabeth – in contrast with the Yorkists' and Lancastrians' impolitic dynastic struggles. The story Shakespeare told of England's medieval blunders bolstered the Tudor myth of having righted a badly foundering ship.[59]

As the conflict resolves at the end of *Richard* III, the white rose and the red rose blend together – a botanically credible metaphor about cultivating variegated flowers – to form the Tudor rose. Although the roses of York and Lancaster were less meaningful emblems than Shakespeare depicts, the Tudor rose of reconciliation was actually established by King Henry VII after the wars ended, exactly as depicted in *Richard* III:

> We will unite the white rose and the red:
> Smile heaven upon this fair conjunction,
> That long have frown'd upon their enmity![60]

I suggested that these warring roses present audiences a test to see whether they could accurately adjudicate history through the fog of propaganda and other window-dressing. But Shakespeare, too, arguably falls into his own trap, a comfortable distraction – he is *so good* with flowers! – of foregrounding the symbols, the prettiness, which may dissuade both the audience's and the playwright's attention to historical accuracy. If flowers monopolize our attention too intensively, we may not have enough room in our minds to consider the larger picture.

War is always somehow mischaracterized, and the Wars of the Roses are among the most distorted wars ever in literature. Is our cultural fascination with this conflict due to the fact that we remember it so prominently in flowers, enflowered? Roses are exceptionally seductive, and Shakespeare was an exceptionally talented playwright who was especially enamoured of roses, so there is vast opportunity for flights of fancy. Did Shakespeare get seduced by the rose garden (and do we, even today?) as he constructed a version of history to squeeze into an intricate and extravagant floral design?

Flowers may obscure or palliate, decorating a brutal reality lurking beneath. In Shakespeare's garden scene, the plucking of flowers daintily symbolizes the deaths of human beings. What a marvel it would be if combat really were simply about the supremacy of one coloured rose over another, the pricking of fingers on thorns rather than the spilling of blood on the battlefield, the cutting of flowers rather than lives.

REFERENCES

INTRODUCTION

1 Lewis Carroll, *Through the Looking-glass, and What Alice Found There*, illustrations by John Tenniel (London, 1871), p. 28.

2 Immanuel Kant, *Critique of Judgment*, trans. Werner Pluhar (Indianapolis, IN, 1987), p. 49.

3 Virginia Woolf, *Mrs Dalloway* (London, 1925), p. 3.

4 Okakura-Kakuzō, *The Book of Tea* (London, 1906), pp. 124–5.

5 Malcolm de Chazal, *Sens-Plastique*, trans. Irving Weiss (New York, 1979), p. 55.

6 Okakura, *The Book of Tea*, pp. 126–7.

7 Rabindranath Tagore, *The Complete Poems of Rabindranath Tagore's Gitanjali*, ed. S. K. Paul (New Delhi, 2006), p. 45.

8 Vita Sackville-West, *In Your Garden* (London, 1951), p. 149.

9 Jessica Shaw, 'A Long Night of "Flower Flashing" with Lewis Miller', *New York Times*, 20 June 2020, www.nytimes.com.

10 Woolf, *Mrs Dalloway*, p. 11.

11 Ibid., p. 33.

12 T. S. Eliot, *Collected Poems, 1909–1962* (New York, 1971), p. 176.

13 Emily Dickinson, *The Poems of Emily Dickinson*, ed. Thomas H. Johnson (Cambridge, MA, 1955), p. 132 (poem 180).

14 Penelope Lively, *Life in the Garden* (New York, 2017), p. 4.

15 James Cullen, *The Identification of Flowering Plant Families* (Cambridge, 1997), p. 15.

16 Henry Salt, *The Call of the Wildflower* (London, 1922), pp. 43–4.

17 John Ruskin, *Modern Painters*, V [1860], in *The Library Edition of the Works of John Ruskin*, ed. Edward Tyas Cook and Alexander Wedderburn, VII (London, 1905), p. 119.

18 Ralph Waldo Emerson, 'Hamatreya', www.poetryfoundation.org.

19 Oliver Wendell Holmes Sr, *The Autocrat of the Breakfast Table* (Boston, MA, 1858), p. 269.

20 Dickinson, *Poems*, p. 746 (poem 1058).

21 Efrat Huss et al., 'The Meaning of Flowers: A Cultural and Perceptual Exploration of Ornamental Flowers', *Open Psychology Journal*, X (2017), pp. 140–53.

22 William Burger, *Flowers: How They Changed the World* (Amherst, NY, 2006), p. 33.

23 Tomo Kosuga, 'Nobuyoshi Araki', www.vice.com, 1 July 2008.

24 Debra Prinzing, *The 50 Mile Bouquet: Seasonal, Local and Sustainable Flowers* (Pittsburgh, PA, 2012), p. 11.

25 Alejandra Reyes-Velarde, 'Instagram-hungry Crowds Are Destroying the Super Bloom', *Los Angeles Times*, 14 March 2019, www.latimes.com.

26 Ibid.

27 Molly McHugh, 'The Instagram Obsession with Flowers Is Killing Them', *The Ringer*, 1 March 2019, www.theringer.com.

28 Britany Robinson, 'Our Super Bloom Obsession Is Ruining the Wildflowers', *The Dyrt*, 19 March 2019, www.thedyrt.com.

29 While there are many forgeries of Hitler's paintings, this one has an authoritative provenance: Samuel Morgenstern's stamp on the back. A Hungarian Jew who lived in Vienna while Hitler was painting, Morgenstern was 'the most loyal buyer of Hitler's paintings', according to Brigitte Hamann in *Hitler's Vienna: A Dictator's Apprenticeship* (Oxford, 1999), p. 356.

30 Jan Friedmann, 'Flowers for the Führer in Landsberg Prison', *Der Spiegel*, 23 June 2010, www.spiegel.de.

31 Adolf Hitler, *Mein Kampf* [1925], trans. James Murphy (London, 1939), p. 12.

32 Marilyn Reid, *Mythical Flower Stories* (Newtonmore, Highland, 2005), p. 40.

33 Mike Whicker and Ilse Dorsch, *Flowers for Hitler: The Extraordinary Life of Ilse Dorsch* (Evansville, IN, 2016), pp. 13–14.

34 Charles Baudelaire, *Les Fleurs du mal* [1861], trans. William Aggeler, in *The Flowers of Evil* (Fresno, CA, 1954).

35 Joris-Karl Huysmans, *Against Nature* (Blacksburg, VA, 2008), pp. 70, 73.

36 Clare Ortiz Hill, *The Roots and Flowers of Evil in Baudelaire, Nietzsche, and Hitler* (Chicago, IL, 2006), p. xv.

37 Ibid., p. 75.

38 Leonard Woolf, *Downhill All the Way: An Autobiography of the Years 1919-1939* (London, 1967), p. 254.

1 FLOWERY WRITING

1 W. H. Davies, *The Poems of W. H. Davies* (London, 1934), p. 422.

2 Emily Dickinson, *The Poems of Emily Dickinson*, ed. Thomas H. Johnson (Cambridge, MA, 1955), p. 664 (poem 903).

3 Mark Twain, *The Diaries of Adam and Eve* (London, 2009), p. 14.

4 'History of the VW Beetle', www.heritagepartscentre.com, accessed 15 July 2020.

5 Sara Lacey, 'Do Men Buy the Volkswagen Beetle?', 30 December 2014, www.cars.com.

6 Umberto Eco, *The Name of the Rose* [1980] (New York, 2014), pp. 542–3.

7 National Public Radio, 'Two Decades Later, Indigo Girls' Voices Still Strong', www.npr.org, 20 March 2007.

8 Marcus Tullius Cicero, *Letters to Friends* (Cambridge, MA, 2015), p. 158.

9 Dylan Thomas, *The Poems of Dylan Thomas* (New York, 1971), p. 90.

10 W. B. Yeats, *The Collected Poetry of W. B. Yeats* (New York, 1996), p. 27.

11 H. D., *Collected Poems, 1912–1944* (New York, 1983), pp. 21, 26, 14.

12 Denise Levertov, *This Great Unknowing: Last Poems* (New York, 1999), p. 11.

13 Dickinson, *Poems*, p. 1113 (poem 1621).

14 Ibid., p. 278 (poem 348).

15 Jeffrey Masson, *When Elephants Weep: The Emotional Lives of Animals* (New York, 1995).

16 Dickinson, *Poems*, p. 1114 (poem 1624).

17 Mark Mescher and Consuelo De Moraes, 'Role of Plant Sensory Perception in Plant–Animal Interactions', *Journal of Experimental Botany*, LXVI/2 (1 February 2015), pp. 425–33.

18 Marine Veits et al., 'Flowers Respond to Pollinator Sound Within Minutes by Increasing Nectar Sugar Concentration', *bioRxiv*, 28 December 2018, www.biorxiv.org.

19 Itzhak Khait et al., 'The Sounds of Plants – Plants Emit Remotely-detectable Ultrasounds That Can Reveal Plant Stress', *bioRxiv*, 28 December 2018, www.biorxiv.org.

20 Ed Yong, 'Plants Can Hear Animals Using Their Flowers', *The Atlantic*, 10 January 2019, www.theatlantic.com.

21 'A Flower Will Be Named after Ballerina Polina Semionova', *Dance Spirit*, 15 August 2013, www.dancespirit.com.

22 William Shakespeare, Sonnet 18, www.shakespeares-sonnets.com, accessed 15 July 2020.

23 William Wordsworth, *Selected Poems and Prefaces* (Boston, MA, 1965), p. 191.

24 Dorothy Wordsworth, *Journals of Dorothy Wordsworth*, ed. Mary Moorman (New York, 1971), pp. 109–10.

25 Randy Malamud, *Reading Zoos: Representations of Animals and Captivity* (New York, 1998); *Poetic Animals and Animal Souls* (New York, 2003); *An Introduction to Animals and Visual Culture* (New York, 2012).

26 Letter to Lord Byron from 'Miss Pepper,' 28 July (no year given), MS.43523, John Murray Archive & Publishers' Collections, National Library of Scotland.

27 Dickinson, *Poems*, p. 314 (poem 402).

28 Dickinson's Herbarium may be seen in the beautifully curated digital version at 'The Emily Dickinson Collection', https://library.harvard.edu, accessed 15 July 2020.

29 Judith Farr, *The Gardens of Emily Dickinson* (Cambridge, MA, 2004), p. 9.

30 Ibid., p. 11.

31 Marta McDowell, *Emily Dickinson's Gardens: A Celebration of a Poet and Gardener* (New York, 2005), p. 24.

32 Maria Popova, 'Emily Dickinson's Herbarium: A Forgotten Treasure at the Intersection of Science and Poetry', 23 March 2017, www.brainpickings.org.

33 Farr, *Gardens of Emily Dickinson*, p. 3.
34 Dickinson, *Poems*, p. 1048 (poem 1519).
35 Henry David Thoreau, *The Journal of Henry David Thoreau, 1837–1861* (New York, 2009), p. 212.
36 Theodora Van Wagenen Ward, ed., *The Letters of Emily Dickinson* (Cambridge, MA, 1958), p. 907.
37 Dickinson, *Poems*, p. 149 (poem 214).
38 Ibid., p. 56 (poem 70).
39 Ibid., p. 96 (poem 134).
40 Okakura-Kakuzō, *The Book of Tea* (London, 1906), pp. 134–5.
41 Dickinson, *Poems*, p. 477 (poem 620).
42 Farr, *Gardens*, p. 11.
43 Dickinson, *Poems*, p. 664 (poem 903).
44 Ibid., p. 862 (poem 1241).
45 Ibid., p. 707 (poem 978).
46 Ibid., p. 189 (poem 265).
47 Ibid., p. 746 (poem 1058).
48 At www.thefreedictionary.com, accessed 15 July 2020.
49 Ezra Pound, 'In a Station of the Metro', *Poetry*, II/1 (April 1913), p. 12.
50 Philip Larkin, *Collected Poems* (New York, 1988), p. 58.
51 Sylvia Plath, *The Collected Poems* (New York, 1981), pp. 160–61.
52 Okakura, *The Book of Tea*, p. 124.
53 Efrat Huss et al., 'The Meaning of Flowers: A Cultural and Perceptual Exploration of Ornamental Flowers', *Open Psychology Journal*, X (2017), pp. 140–53.
54 Plath, *Collected Poems*, p. 162.
55 Celia Fisher, *Tulip* (London, 2017), p. 32.
56 Marjane Satrapi, *Persepolis 2* (New York, 2004), p. 127.
57 Robert Browning, *Selections from the Poems and Plays of Robert Browning*, ed. Myra Reynolds (Chicago, IL, 1909), p. 85.
58 Virginia Museum of Fine Arts, www.vmfa.museum/connect.
59 Amy Stewart, *Flower Confidential* (Chapel Hill, NC, 2007), p. 56.
60 Dickinson, *Poems*, p. 1007 (poem 1456).
61 T. S. Eliot, *Collected Poems, 1909–1962* (New York, 1971), p. 16.
62 Ibid., pp. 17–18.
63 Ibid., p. 18.
64 T. S. Eliot, 'The Metaphysical Poets', *Times Literary Supplement* (20 October 1921).
65 William Shakespeare, *Hamlet*, Act IV, sc. 5.
66 Ibid.
67 Eliot, *Collected Poems*, p. 9.
68 Ibid., p. 26.
69 Ibid., p. 45.
70 Ibid., p. 53.
71 Geoffrey Chaucer, 'Prologue', *The Canterbury Tales* (1387–1400), lines 1–4.
72 *Oxford English Dictionary*, flower, n.; flour, n.
73 Saul Bellow, *Herzog* (New York, 1964), p. 15.

74 Eliot, *Collected Poems*, p. 54.

75 Ibid., p. 176.

76 Ibid., p. 180.

77 Ibid., p. 182.

78 Ibid., p. 184.

79 Gail Harland, *Snowdrop* (London, 2016).

80 Alfred Lord Tennyson, *The Princess, A Medley*, in *The Works of Tennyson* (New York, 1913), p. 161.

81 Eliot, *Collected Poems*, pp. 193–4.

82 Estimates count 140–200 million copies sold in three hundred languages and dialects.

83 Adam Gopnik, 'The Strange Triumph of "The Little Prince"', *New Yorker*, 29 April 2014, www.newyorker.com.

84 Antoine de Saint-Exupéry, *The Little Prince*, trans. Richard Howard (San Diego, CA, 2000), p. 22.

85 Ibid., pp. 23–5.

86 Ibid., pp. 46–7.

87 Ibid., p. 54.

88 Ibid., pp. 63–4.

89 Ibid., p. 71.

90 Gopnik, 'The Strange Triumph of "The Little Prince"'.

91 Saint-Exupéry, *The Little Prince*, p. 67.

92 Ibid., p. 76.

93 Stacy Schiff, 'How a Beloved Children's Book Was Born of Despair', *Literary Hub*, 6 April 2018, www.lithub.com.

94 Geoffrey Chaucer, 'Prologue', *The Legend of Good Women*, lines 41–59, available at http://mcllibrary.org. A modern English rendering of the passage, trans. A. S. Kline (2008), is available at www.poetryintranslation.com:

>   of all the flowers in the mead,
>   Love I most the white and red I see,
>   Such as men call daisies in our town.
>   For them I have so great an affection,
>   As I have said, at the start of May,
>   That in my bed there dawns no day
>   When I'm not up and walking in the mead
>   To see this flower to the sun freed,
>   When it rises early on the morrow;
>   That blissful sight softens all my sorrow,
>   So glad am I when I am in its presence
>   To show it all and every reverence,
>   As she that is the flower of all flowers,
>   Whom every virtue and honour dowers,
>   And ever alike fair and fresh of hue,
>   And I love it, and ever the love renew,
>   And ever shall until my heart shall die;

Though I swear not, and this I tell's no lie,
No creature loved hotter in his life.

2 FLOWERY ART

1 'First of all, I must have flowers.'
2 Frederic George Stephens, *Memorials of William Mulready*, R.A. (London, 1890), p. 36.
3 Theodore Roethke, 'The Stony Garden', *Poetry*, CXIII/2 (November 1968), p. 105.
4 Vincent van Gogh, letter to Theo van Gogh (765), 30 April 1889, www.vangoghletters.org.
5 See my earlier books on animals in art, literature and culture: *Poetic Animals and Animal Souls* (New York, 2003); and *An Introduction to Animals and Visual Culture* (New York, 2012).
6 Fergal MacErlean, 'First Neanderthal Cave Paintings Discovered in Spain', *New Scientist*, 10 February 2012, www.newscientist.com.
7 Ewen Callaway, 'Is This Cave Painting Humanity's Oldest Story?', *Nature*, 11 December 2019, www.realclearscience.com.
8 Paul Bahn, *Cave Art: A Guide to the Decorated Ice Age Caves of Europe* (London, 2007), pp. 81–5.
9 Caroline Ransom, *The Tomb of Perneb* (New York, 1916), p. 78.
10 Kelly Richman-Abdou, 'How Flowers Blossomed into One of Art History's Most Popular Subjects', 16 March 2018, www.mymodernmet.com.
11 Auguste Rodin and Paul Gsell, *Art*, trans. Romilly Fedden (Boston, MA, 1912), p. 48.
12 Paul Hulton and Lawrence Smith, *Flowers in Art from East and West* (London, 1979), p. x.
13 Arthur Wheelock Jr, *From Botany to Bouquets: Flowers in Northern Art* (Washington, DC, 1999), pp. 19–20.
14 Vienna, Kunsthistoriches Museum, 570; see www.khm.at/en.
15 Arianne Faber Kolb, *Jan Brueghel the Elder: The Entry of the Animals into Noah's Ark* (Los Angeles, 2005), p. 2.
16 Ibid., pp. 51–2.
17 Alastair Sooke, 'Why these Dutch Flower Paintings Bear no Resemblance to Reality', *Daily Telegraph*, 6 April 2016, www.telegraph.co.uk.
18 Wheelock, *From Botany to Bouquets*, p. 9.
19 'Kalamkari', www.utsavpedia.com, accessed 18 July 2020.
20 William Morris, *The Collected Works of William Morris*, XXII (Cambridge, 1914), p. 259.
21 Palampore, *c.* 1700–1725, Metropolitan Museum of Art, New York, 2010.337.
22 Martyn Rix, *The Golden Age of Botanical Art* (London, 2013).
23 Chen Hengke, *Narcissus and Orchid*, 1920, Metropolitan Museum of Art, New York, 1986.267.105.

24 Etienne Denisse, *Flore d'Amérique* (Paris, 1843–6), p. 197.

25 Hu Yuan, *Herbaceous Peony*, 19th century, Metropolitan Museum of Art, New York, 1986.267.33.

26 Ding Fuzhi, *Lychees*, 1941, Metropolitan Museum of Art, New York, 1986.267.255.

27 Wu Xizai, *Apricot*, 19th century, Metropolitan Museum of Art, New York, 1986.267.20.

28 Paul Sorene, 'The Art of the Photogram: The Most Wonderful Camera-less Photographs', 19 January 2016, https://flashbak.com.

29 Ansel Adams, in *The Fortnightly* [San Francisco], 1/5 (5 November 1933), p. 25; quoted in Natalie Dupêcher, 'Eugène Atget', www.moma.org, accessed 18 July 2020.

30 Bayard's images are not black-and-white, but rather monochromatic sepia or purple-brown in tone.

31 Hulton and Smith, *Flowers in Art from East and West* p. ix (emphasis in original).

32 Abigail Cain, 'These 100-year-old Glass Flowers Are So Accurate, They Rival the Real Thing', 20 October 2017, www.artsy.net.

33 'The Archives of Rudolph and Leopold Blaschka and the Ware Collection of Blaschka Glass Models of Plants', Harvard University Herbaria and Libraries, https://botlib.huh.harvard.edu, accessed 18 July 2020.

34 'Glass Flowers Always in Bloom', Harvard Museum of Natural History, https://hmnh.harvard.edu, accessed 18 July 2020.

35 Cain, 'These 100-year-old Glass Flowers'.

36 Okakura-Kakuzō, *The Book of Tea* (London, 1906), pp. 137–8.

37 Randall Griffin, *Georgia O'Keeffe* (London, 2014), p. 47.

38 Tate Modern, Georgia O'Keeffe Room Guide, www.tate.org.uk.

39 Georgia O'Keeffe, 'About Myself', in *Georgia O'Keeffe: Exhibition of Oils and Pastels*, exh. cat., An American Place, New York (New York, 1939), pp. 2–3.

40 Hannah Ellis-Petersen, 'Flowers or Vaginas? Georgia O'Keeffe Tate Show to Challenge Sexual Cliches', *The Guardian*, 1 March 2016, www.theguardian.com.

41 Giovanni Aloi, *Why Look at Plants? The Botanical Emergence in Contemporary Art* (Leiden, 2019), p. 256.

42 Mat Collishaw, www.seditionart.com, accessed 19 July 2020. A digital recording of an actual burning flower may be seen here in all its splendour.

43 Aloi, *Plants*, pp. 255–6.

44 *The Lady's Not for Burning* is a 1948 verse play about a medieval witch-hunt.

45 Virginia Woolf, *Mrs Dalloway* (London, 1925), p. 13.

46 Alexandra Jones, 'Devil's Trumpet: A New Acquisition in the V&A's Silver Galleries', 23 October 2017, www.vam.ac.uk/blog.

47 Omar Khayyam, *The Rubaiyat*, trans. Edward Fitzgerald (London, 1856), p. 6, stanza 26.

48 Peter Sturman, 'Spreading Falling Blossoms: Style and Replication in Shen Zhou's Late Calligraphy', *Tsing Hua Journal of Chinese Studies*, XL/3 (September 2010), pp. 365–410.

49 Shax Riegler, 'Change Agent: Everyday Objects Become Wondrous Artworks in Artist Ann Carrington's Clever Hands', *Architectural Digest* (November 2017), pp. 56–8.

50 Ibid.

51 Ibid.

52 Elizabeth Blair, 'Jeff Koons Gives France a Giant Bouquet of Flowers, But It Comes with a Price', 2 December 2016, www.npr.org.

53 Henry Samuel, 'Paris Finally Finds a Home for Jeff Koons' Giant Tulips after Purist Claims They Would Lower the Tone', *Daily Telegraph*, 12 October 2018, www.telegraph.com.

54 Naomi Rea, 'French Art Luminaries Reject Jeff Koons's Flashy Gift to Paris as a "Cynical" Act of "Product Placement"', 23 January 2018, https://news.artnet.com.

55 Lauren Collins, 'Jeff Koons Unveils His Iffy "Bouquet of Tulips" for Paris', *New Yorker*, 15 October 2019, www.newyorker.com.

56 Elizabeth Palermo, 'Why Do Flowers Close Up at Night?', *Live Science*, 22 May 2013, www.livescience.com.

57 Geoffrey Chaucer, *The Legend of Good Women*, trans. A. S. Kline, www.poetryintranslation.com, accessed 19 July 2020.

58 Andrea Shea, 'What the Giant, Polyester Lotus Flower at the MFA Says about Life in Asia's Megacities', 11 April 2016, www.wbur.org.

59 Katherine Kuh, *The Author's Voice* (New York, 1970), pp. 190–91.

60 Roxana Robinson, *Georgia O'Keeffe: A Life* (New York, 1989), p. 278.

3 FLOWER SELLERS

1 Ralph Waldo Emerson, 'Gifts', in *Essays: First and Second Series*, ed. Joel Porte (New York, 1996), p. 305.

2 'The Wild Bunch', *The Economist*, 17 December 2014, www.economist.com.

3 Rabindrath Tagore, *Stray Birds* (New York, 1916), p. 47.

4 Edna St Vincent Millay, 'Afternoon on a Hill', in *Renascence and Other Poems* (New York, 1917), p. 42.

5 Francis Thompson, *The Mistress of Vision* (Aylesford, Kent, 1966), p. 19.

6 Mehmet Murat Ildan, personal blog, https://muratildanquotations.wordpress.com, accessed 19 July 2020.

7 Mary Mann, *The Flower People* (Boston, MA, 1875), p. 38.

8 Ibid., p. 28.

9 The $75 billion figure appears in 'Global Floriculture Market Revenue to Register CAGR of 5.0% Over Next 10 Years', www.prnewswire.com, 25 April 2018. Dun & Bradstreet's 2019 Florists Industry Profile puts the revenues at $100 billion; see www.firstresearch.com, 21 October 2019.

10 Nick Marino, 'A Perfumer's Fragrant Flower Salad', *New York Times*, 5 June 2019, www.nytimes.com.

11 Dave Hone, 'Moth Tongues, Orchids and Darwin: The Predictive Power of Evolution', *The Guardian*, 2 October 2013, www.theguardian.com.

12 Yangyang Cheng, 'A Coronavirus Care Package from China', *New York Times*, 25 June 2020, www.nytimes.com.

13 Efrat Huss et al., 'The Meaning of Flowers: A Cultural and Perceptual Exploration of Ornamental Flowers', *Open Psychology Journal*, x (2017), pp. 140–53.

14 John Kell, 'Mother's Day Is like the Super Bowl for Florists', www.fortune.com, 8 May 2015.

15 '6 Reasons To Buy Yourself Flowers', www.obsessedbyportia.com, 15 February 2017.

16 Amy Stewart, *Flower Confidential* (Chapel Hill, NC, 2007), p. 6.

17 Ibid., pp. 7–10.

18 'The Wild Bunch'.

19 Okakura-Kakuzō, *The Book of Tea* (London, 1906), pp. 128–9.

20 Celia Fisher, *Tulip* (London, 2017), pp. 89–90.

21 Ibid., p. 125.

22 Ibid., p. 86.

23 Bobby Ward, *A Contemplation upon Flowers: Garden Plants in Myth and Literature* (Portland, OR, 1999), p. 20.

24 I note, however, that there is ambiguity about even the forget-me-not: not in terms of what the flower 'means' but about which flower precisely is denoted by that common name. Robert Hemmings writes, 'While the name forget-me-not is now widely attributed to the *Mysotis palustris*, a flower with sky-blue petals with yellow centres, there is disagreement over which botanical species the name applies to. Vernon Rendall notes that the name once applied to the "dullish looking" ground pine, which was so named "because its persistent smell could not be forgotten".' Robert Hemmings, 'Of Trauma and Flora: Memory and Commemoration in Four Poems of the World Wars', *University of Toronto Quarterly*, LXXVII/2 (Spring 2008), pp. 738–56.

25 Ibid., p. 744.

26 'R.', 'Bring Flowers', *American Ladies' Magazine*, IX/7 (July 1836), p. 403.

27 Fanny Downing, 'Memorial Flowers', music by Mendelssohn Coote (New Orleans, LA, 1867). To make this more acceptable for publication elsewhere in the USA, the second line became 'Which hides my children from my view'.

28 'The Wild Bunch'.

29 For a more sustained personal screed, see my recent book *Email* (New York, 2019) in Bloomsbury's Object Lessons series.

30 Reviews from www.trustpilot.com and www.yelp.com.

31 Dun & Bradstreet, '2019 Florists Industry Profile', www.firstresearch.com, 21 October 2019.

32 Henry Mayhew, *London Labour and the London Poor* (London, 1861), vol. I, p. 137.

33 Ibid., p. 135.

34 Ibid., p. 134.

35 Octave Uzanne, *The Modern Parisienne* (London, 1912), pp. 183–4.

36 See C. Sussnap: *Robert Thompson Crawshay, c. 1860*, Cyfarthfa Castle Museum & Art Gallery, www.artuk.org, accessed 21 July 2020.

37 George Bernard Shaw, *Pygmalion* (London, 1916), Act I.

38 Gertrude Stein, 'Sacred Emily,' in *Geography and Plays* (Boston, MA, 1922), p. 187.

39 Megan Lowthers, 'On Institutionalized Sexual Economies: Employment Sex, Transactional Sex, and Sex Work in Kenya's Cut Flower Industry', *Signs: Journal of Women in Culture and Society*, XLIII/2 (2018), p. 457.

40 Ibid., pp. 458–9.

41 The Life Is Good bouquets are advertised (July 2020) in orange, yellow, pink and hot pink combinations, with or without a vase.

42 Patricia Hampl, *The Florist's Daughter* (Boston, MA, 2009), p. 63.

43 Society of American Florists, https://safnow.org.

44 See www.inlieuofflowers.info.

45 Ibid.

46 Candice Shoemaker and Diane Relf, 'Flowers for Funerals – They Are Important', www.inlieuofflowers.info.

47 Jenny Scalaon, 'SAF Tackles 18 Cases of Harmful Mother's Day Floral Publicity', Society of American Florists, 17 May 2017, www.safnow.org.

48 Society of American Florists, 'Rutgers: Flowers Improve Emotional Health', www.aboutflowers.com.

49 Ashley Seager, 'Air-freight Flowers Greener than Dutch Hothouses, say Kenyans', *The Guardian*, 14 February 2007, www.theguardian.com.

50 Peter Goodman, 'Brexit Could Leave Wedding Bouquets Stuck at the Border', *New York Times*, 14 November 2018, www.nytimes.com.

51 Ibid.

52 Kathleen Buckingham, 'Love Hurts: Environmental Risks in the Cut-flower Industry', 9 February 2016, www.policyforum.net.

53 'Cut Flowers – A Major yet Little-known Source of Toxic Pesticides', 11 February 2014, www.mercola.com.

54 Charles Bergman, 'A Rose Is Not a Rose', January/February 2008, www.audubon.org.

55 Florverde standards for the sustainable production of flowers and ornamentalism, May 2018, www.florverde.org.

56 Debra Prinzing, *The 50 Mile Bouquet: Seasonal, Local and Sustainable Flowers* (Pittsburgh, PA, 2012), p. 9.

57 Debra Prinzing, media release for *The 50 Mile Bouquet*, www.debraprinzing.com, accessed 20 July 2020.

58 Prinzing, *The 50 Mile Bouquet*, p. 14.

59 Miriam Zoila Pérez, 'A Second Life for Flowers', *New York Times*, 10 March 2020, www.nytimes.com.

60 Lori Weidenhammer, *Victory Gardens for Bees: A DIY Guide to Saving the Bees* (Madeira Park, BC, 2013), p. xiii.

61 Ibid., pp. 11–12.

62 Prinzing, *The 50 Mile Bouquet*, p. 45.

63 Michael Tortorello, 'Wooing and Celebrating with Seasonal,
   Sustainable Blooms', *New York Times*, 28 March 2012, www.nytimes.com.

64 Prinzing, *The 50 Mile Bouquet*, pp. 51–5.

4 FLOWERS, GENDER, SEXUALITY, RACE AND CLASS

1 Rapum Kambili, ed., *14 (An Anthology of Queer Art): We Are Flowers* (2017),
   p. 9; available at www.brittlepaper.com, accessed 22 July 2020.

2 Sigmund Freud, 'Dream of the Botanical Monograph', *The Interpretation
   of Dreams*, trans. A. A. Brill (New York, 1913), p. 143.

3 'And so the conversation slips / Among velleities and carefully caught
   regrets . . .'; T. S. Eliot, 'Portrait of a Lady', in *Others: A Magazine of the
   New Verse* (September 1915).

4 *Oxford English Dictionary*, 'velleity', n.1.

5 Jennifer Davies, *Saying it with Flowers: The Story of the Flower Shop*
   (London, 2000), p. 21.

6 Flower Resource Guide: 'Flowers for Men', www.fromyouflowers.com.

7 FTD ProFlowers, www.proflowers.com/manly-flowers-man.

8 Teleflora, Flowers for him, www.teleflora.com/flowers-for-him.

9 'What Are the 5 Best Flowers to Give to Men?', www.floraqueen.com.

10 Louise Smithers, 'Flowers That Will Actually Add Masculinity to Your
   Home', 20 October 2016, www.dmarge.com.

11 Tyler, the Creator, 'Garden Shed' and 'Where this Flower Blooms',
   https://genius.com.

12 Kambili, ed., *14 (An Anthology of Queer Art)*.

13 Jonathan Van Ness, *Over the Top: A Raw Journey to Self-love* (New York,
   2019), p. 1.

14 Sappho, 'I Have Not Had One Word from Her', trans. Mary Barnard,
   www.thissideofsanity.com.

15 Tony Scupham-Bilton, 'Flower Power: Violets',
   6 April 2012, http://queerstoryfiles.blogspot.com.

16 Maisie Skidmore, 'Robert Mapplethorpe's Sensual Flowers', *AnOther*,
   29 March 2016, www.anothermag.com.

17 Paul Harfleet, The Pansy Project, https://thepansyproject.com.

18 'Beef Jerky Flower Bouquet', The Manly Man Company, https://
   manlymanco.com.

19 Munro Leaf, *The Story of Ferdinand* (New York, 1936).

20 Bruce Handy, 'How "The Story of Ferdinand" Became Fodder for
   the Culture Wars of Its Era', *New Yorker*, 15 December 2017, www.
   newyorker.com.

21 Ernest Hemingway, 'The Faithful Bull', *Holiday* (March 1951), available
   at www.xoxosoma.com.

22 Leaf, *The Story of Ferdinand*.

23 Katie Sciurba, 'Flowers, Dancing, Dresses, and Dolls: Picture Book
   Representations of Gender-variant Males', *Children's Literature in
   Education*, XLVIII (2017), p. 290.

24 William Shakespeare, Sonnet 130, www.shakespeares-sonnets.com.

25 Edmund Spenser, *Amoretti and Epithalamion* (London, 1595), Sonnet LXIV
64.

26 Honoré de Balzac, *Honorine* [1843], trans. Clara Bell (London, 1901).

27 *Oxford English Dictionary*, 'flower,' n., 6c.

28 Yemisi Aribisala, 'The Beauty and Burden of Being a Nigerian Bride',
New Yorker, 19 September 2019, www.newyorker.com.

29 Miss Cellania, '5 Classic Poisons and the People Who Used Them',
3 November 2009, www.mentalfloss.com.

30 Richard Whelan, *Impressionist Flowers: Art of the Bouquet* (Cobb, CA, 1998),
p. 69.

31 Tim Stephens, 'New Book Explores Why the Discovery of Sex in
Plants Took So Long', 19 January 2017, www.news.ucsc.edu.

32 Nira Tessler, *Flowers and Towers: Politics of Identity in the Art of the American
'New Woman'* (Newcastle, 2015), pp. 3–4.

33 Jennifer Potter, *Seven Flowers and How they Shaped Our World* (New York,
2013), p. 23.

34 Janice Delaney, Mary Jane Lupton and Emily Toth, *The Curse: A Cultural
History of Menstruation* (Urbana, IL, 1988), pp. 190–91.

35 Rufus C. Camphausen, *The Encyclopedia of Erotic Wisdom* (Rochester, VT,
1991), p. 124.

36 Jack Goody, *The Culture of Flowers* (Cambridge, 1993), pp. 18–19.

37 King James Version.

38 Naomi Wolf, *Vagina* (New York, 2013), pp. 209–10.

39 Eve Ensler, *The Vagina Monologues* [1996] (New York, 2008), p. 43.

40 Natalie Joffe, 'The Vernacular of Menstruation', WORD, IV/3 (1948),
pp. 181–6.

41 Alice White, 'How to Handle Your Period: Ten Pieces of (Bad) Advice
from History', 30 October 2017, https://wellcomecollection.org.

42 Joe Patrice, 'Is It Racist to Assume Bob Kraft's Massage Parlor Was
Obviously a Brothel?', 26 February 2019, https://abovethelaw.com.

43 Museum of Menstruation, 'Menotoxin: A Short, Incomplete
Introduction to the "Poison" in the Menstrual Flow', www.mum.org,
accessed 19 July 2020.

44 Aisha Moktadier, '7 Herbs and Flowers that Can Do Wonders for Your
Period', 28 May 2018, www.vix.com.

45 Stassa Edwards, 'The History of Abortifacients', 18 November 2014,
www.jezebel.com.

46 Amy License, 'His Story, Her Story', 11 December 2012, http://
authorherstorianparent.blogspot.com.

47 Edwards, 'History of Abortifacients'.

48 Ibid.

49 Greta Friedemann-Sánchez, *Assembling Flowers and Cultivating Homes:
Labor and Gender in Colombia* (Lanham, MD, 2006), pp. 95–6.

50 Barbara Buhler Lynes, *Georgia O'Keeffe and the Calla Lily in American Art,
1860–1940* (New Haven, CT, 2002), p. 18.

51 Diego Rivera, *The Flower Vendor (Girl with Lilies)*, Norton Simon
Museum, Pasadena, CA, www.nortonsimon.org.

52 Nina Edwards, *Weeds* (London, 2015), p. 7 and cover.

53 Ralph Waldo Emerson, *Fortune of the Republic* (Boston, MA, 1878),
     p. 3.

54 Melvin Hunter, 'Racist Relics: An Ugly Blight on Our Botanical
     Nomenclature', *The Scientist* (25 November 1991), p. 13.

55 Ibid.

56 Therese Dolan, 'Fringe Benefits: Manet's Olympia and Her Shawl',
     Art Bulletin, XCVII/4 (December 2015), pp. 409–29.

57 Hilarie M. Sheets. 'New Attention for Figures in the Background',
     New York Times, 25 October 2018, www.nytimes.com.

58 Lorraine O'Grady, 'Olympia's Maid: Reclaiming Black Female
     Subjectivity', in *New Feminist Criticism: Art/Identity/Action*, ed. Joanna
     Frueh et al. (New York, 1994), pp. 152–70.

59 Sheets, 'New Attention'.

60 Denise Murrell, 'Seeing Laure: Race and Modernity from Manet's
     "Olympia" to Matisse, Bearden and Beyond', PhD thesis, Columbia
     University, 2014.

61 Darcy Grimaldo Grigsby, 'Still Thinking about Olympia's Maid',
     Art Bulletin, XCVII/4 (December 2015), pp. 430–51.

62 Cath Pound, 'The Hidden Figures Revealed by Art', BBC Culture,
     21 March 2019, www.bbc.com. Slavery was abolished in French
     colonies in 1794 but was reinstated in 1802 under Napoleon Bonaparte,
     before finally being eliminated in 1848.

63 Charmaine Nelson, *Racism, Eh?: A Critical Inter-disciplinary Anthology of
     Race and Racism in Canada* (Concord, ON, 2004), p. 380.

64 M. Therese Southgate, 'Still Life with Peonies', *Journal of the American
     Medical Association*, CCXCV/5 (1 February 2006), p. 476.

65 Smithsonian National Museum of African American History and
     Culture, 'Power of Place', https://nmaahc.si.edu/power-place, accessed
     19 July 2020.

66 Michael Cunningham and Craig Marberry, *Crowns: Portraits of Black
     Women in Church Hats* (New York, 2000), p. 4 and cover.

67 Dan Aubrey, 'Crowns: From Page to Stage', U.S.1 *Princeton Info*, 14 March
     2018, https://princetoninfo.com.

68 Alfred Lord Tennyson, 'Flower in the Crannied Wall', in *Tennyson's
     Poetry*, ed. Robert W. Hill Jr (New York, 1971), p. 282.

69 Jorge Luis Borges, *A Personal Anthology* (New York, 1967), p. 136.

5 FLOWERS OF WAR

 1 Pete Seeger and Joe Hickerson, 'Where Have All the Flowers Gone?'
     1955, rev. 1960, https://genius.com.

 2 Wisława Szymborska, 'Under One Small Star', in *View with a Grain of
     Sand: Selected Poems*, trans. Stanisław Barańczak and Clare Cavanagh
     (New York, 1995), p. 91.

 3 Adrienne Mayor, *Greek Fire, Poison Arrows, and Scorpion Bombs: Biological and
     Chemical Warfare in the Ancient World* (Woodstock, NY, 2003), pp. 100–101.

4 Louise Cilliers and F. P. Retief, 'Poisons, Poisoning and the Drug Trade in Ancient Rome', *Akroterion*, XLV (2014), p. 91.

5 William DeLong, 'Beware the Deadly Nightshade – The Beautiful Plant that Can Kill You', 5 March 2018, https://allthatsinteresting.com

6 Amitov Ghosh, *Flood of Fire* (London, 2016), p. 396. This is the third of Ghosh's Ibis Trilogy; *Sea of Poppies* (2009) and *River of Smoke* (2012) also explore the roots of the Opium Wars.

7 Carl Swanson and Lissa Townsend, 'Opiate of the Masses', *New York*, XXXIII/33 (28 August 2000), p. 35.

8 Dr Weirde, 'Chinatown's Opium Dens', www.foundsf.org, accessed 23 July 2020.

9 John McCrae, 'In Flanders Fields', *Punch* (8 December 1915).

10 Matthew Leonard, *Poppyganda: The Historical and Social Impact of a Flower* (London, 2015), p. 44.

11 Robert Hemmings, 'Of Trauma and Flora: Memory and Commemoration in Four Poems of the World Wars', *University of Toronto Quarterly*, LXXVII/2 (Spring 2008), p. 743.

12 Leonard, *Poppyganda*, p. 52.

13 Barry Isaac, 'The Aztec "Flowery War": A Geopolitical Explanation', *Journal of Anthropological Research*, XXXIX/4 (1983), pp. 415–32.

14 'Jersey Battle of Flowers Parade', www.battleofflowers.com.

15 Personal email to author, 10 September 2018.

16 'Early History of the Jersey Battle of Flowers', www.theislandwiki.org.

17 Bill Conville, 'The Arts and Elegance of Flower Tossing', 5 March 2019, www.mainlineneighbors.com.

18 Judith Mackrell, 'How Ballet Fell for Flower-giving', *The Guardian*, 18 December 2012, www.theguardian.com.

19 In *The People, Yes* (1936), a girl watching troops on parade says, 'Sometime they'll give a war and nobody will come.' Carl Sandburg, *Complete Poems* (New York, 1950), p. 464.

20 Described by Allen Ginsberg in *It Was 20 Years Ago Today* (1987, dir. John Sheppard). An excerpt listed as 'Story Behind Flower Power' can be seen on www.youtube.com, accessed 23 July 2020 (see 2:24 mark).

21 Robert Heide, 'Regarding Hibiscus, the Flower Power Man', 18 December 2017, www.pleasekillme.com.

22 'Story Behind Flower Power' (from 2:00).

23 Allen Ginsberg, 'Demonstration or Spectacle as Example, as Communication or How to Make a March/Spectacle', *Berkeley Barb*, I/15 (19 November 1965).

24 Abbie Hoffman, *Soon to Be a Major Motion Picture* (New York, 1980), p. 99.

25 Andrew Grant Jackson, *1965: The Most Revolutionary Year in Music* (New York, 2015), pp. 247–9; excerpt as 'November 19: Allen Ginsberg invents "flower power"', 5 November 2014, https://1965book.com.

26 Nik Cohn, *Pop from the Beginning* (London, 1969), p. 221.

27 Kingsley Amis, *Girl, 20* (London, 1971), p. 152.

28 Marty Jezer, *Abbie Hoffman: American Rebel* (New Brunswick, NJ, 1993), pp. 93–105.

29 Elizabeth Knowles, ed., *Oxford Dictionary of Modern Quotations* (Oxford, 2007), p. 214.

30 Jezer, *Abbie Hoffman*, p. 105.

31 Internet sources commonly attribute this mural to Banksy; however, when I contacted Banksy's organization directly they informed me he did not create it. Personal email to the author, 9 October 2018.

32 Seeger's original 1955 version comprised just the first three verses. Five years later singer Joe Hickerson proposed adding the final two, which Seeger eagerly included, always sharing a writer's credit and a share of royalties with him.

33 Aviva Shen, 'Pete Seeger: Where Have All the Protest Songs Gone?', *Smithsonian Magazine*, April 2012; rev. as 'From the Archives: Pete Seeger on What Makes a Great Protest Song', 3 May 2019, www. smithsonianmag.com.

34 Steven Bach, *Marlene Dietrich: Life and Legend* (Minneapolis, MN, 2011), p. 406.

35 Francesca Aloisio, 'Where Have All the Flowers Gone?', 26 June 2015, www.wordsinthebucket.com.

36 Emily Dickinson, *The Poems of Emily Dickinson*, ed. Thomas H. Johnson (Cambridge, MA, 1955), p. 318 (poem 409).

37 Eliza Richards, 'The Civil War Language of Flowers', in *A History of Nineteenth-century American Women's Poetry*, ed. Jennifer Putzi and Alexandra Socarides (Cambridge, 2017), p. 252.

38 Ibid., pp. 255–6.

39 Kenneth I. Helphand, *Defiant Gardens: Making Gardens in Wartime* (San Antonio, TX, 2006), p. ix.

40 Ibid., p. 1.

41 Ibid., p. 211.

42 Ibid., pp. 17, 47–8.

43 Ibid., pp. 71–2.

44 Ibid., pp. 104–5.

45 David Bomberg, *Bomb Store*, www.tate.org.uk, accessed 19 July 2020.

46 Andrew Moore and Christopher Garibaldi, eds, *Flower Power: The Meaning of Flowers in Art* (London, 2003), p. 86.

47 David Bomberg, *Flowers*, www.tate.org.uk, accessed 19 July 2020.

48 Moore and Garibaldi, *Flower Power*, p. 86.

49 John Hersey, 'Hiroshima', *New Yorker* (23 August 1946).

50 William Shakespeare, *1 Henry IV*, Act I, sc. iii.

51 William Shakespeare, *1 Henry VI*, Act IV, sc. i (King Henry VI).

52 William Shakespeare, *2 Henry VI*, Act I, sc. i (York).

53 William Shakespeare, *3 Henry VI*, Act I, sc. ii (Richard).

54 William Shakespeare, *3 Henry VI*, Act II, sc. v (King Henry VI).

55 William Shakespeare, *1 Henry VI*, Act II, sc. iv.

56 Ibid.

57 A. J. Pollard, *The Wars of the Roses* (New York, 2001), pp. 8–15.

58 Shakespeare's version is only slightly less contrived than that of W. C. Sellar and R. J. Yeatman in their satirical masterpiece *1066 and*

All That (London, 1930), p. 47: 'Noting suddenly that the Middle Ages were coming to an end, the Barons now made a stupendous effort to revive the old Feudal amenities of Sackage, Carnage, and Wreckage and so stave off the Tudors for a time. They achieved this by a very clever plan, known as the *Wars of the Roses* (because the Barons all picked different coloured roses in order to see which side they were on).'

59 John Gillingham, *The Wars of the Roses: Peace and Conflict in Fifteenth-century England* (London, 1981), p. 11.

60 William Shakespeare, *Richard III*, Act v, sc. v.

FURTHER READING

Aloi, Giovanni, *Why Look at Plants? The Botanical Emergence in Contemporary Art* (Leiden, 2019)

Boddy, Kasia, *Blooming Flowers: A Seasonal History of Plants and People* (New Haven, CT, 2020)

Buchmann, Stephen, *The Reason for Flowers: Their History, Culture, Biology, and How They Change Our Lives* (New York, 2015)

Burger, William, *Flowers: How They Changed the World* (Amherst, NY, 2006)

Davies, Jennifer, *Saying it with Flowers: The Story of the Flower Shop* (London, 2000)

Goldgar, Anne, *Tulipmania: Money, Honor, and Knowledge in the Dutch Golden Age* (Chicago, IL, 2007)

Goody, Jack, *The Culture of Flowers* (Cambridge, 1993)

Greenaway, Kate, *Language of Flowers* (London, 1884)

Hulton, Paul, and Lawrence Smith, *Flowers in Art from East and West* (London, 1979)

Leonard, Matthew, *Poppyganda: The Historical and Social Impact of a Flower* (London, 2015)

Potter, Jennifer, *Seven Flowers: And How They Shaped Our World* (London, 2014)

Prinzing, Debra, *The 50 Mile Bouquet: Seasonal, Local and Sustainable Flowers* (Pittsburgh, PA, 2012)

Reaktion Botanical series (London, 2012–present), more than two-dozen titles

Stewart, Amy, *Flower Confidential* (Chapel Hill, NC, 2007)

Ward, Bobby, *A Contemplation upon Flowers: Garden Plants in Myth and Literature* (Portland, OR, 1999)

Wheelock, Arthur Jr, *From Botany to Bouquets: Flowers in Northern Art* (Washington, DC, 1999)

PHOTO AND COPYRIGHT ACKNOWLEDGEMENTS

(photo Rik Klein Gotink)/© 2021 Artists Rights Society (ARS), New York – c/o Pictoright, Amsterdam: 43; Kunsthistorisches Museum, Vienna: 30; Library of Congress, Prints and Photographs Division, Washington, DC: 10, 12, 19, 49 (Carol M. Highsmith Archive), 50, 51, 56; from *The Literary Digest*, LVII/5 (4 May 1918), photo Robarts Library, University of Toronto: 57; from *Le Littoral*, no. 6448 (9 February 1905): 96; from Lieut.-Col John McCrae, *In Flanders Fields* (New York, 1921), photo University of California Libraries: 94; photo © the Manly Man Company, reproduced by permission: 75; from Maria Sibylla Merian, *Metamorphosis Insectorum Surinamensium, ofte Verandering der Surinaamsche Insecten* (Amsterdam, 1705): 32; from Henry Mayhew, *London Labour and the London Poor; a Cyclopædia of the Condition and Earnings of Those that Will Work, Those that Cannot Work, and Those that Will Not Work*, vol. 1 (London, 1861), photo Digital Collections and Archives, Tufts University, Medford, MA: 63; The Metropolitan Museum of Art, New York: 2, 6, 27 (photo Art Resource, NY), 31, 33, 34, 40, 54, 77; photo Apsara Mokashi (CC BY 2.0): 3; MTVA Archívum: 91; Musée d'Orsay, Paris: 85; Museo Archeologico Nazionale di Napoli (photo Marie-Lan Nguyen): 53; National Gallery of Art, Washington, DC: 29, 41, 42, 87; National Museum of African American History and Culture (NMAAHC), Smithsonian Institution, Washington, DC: 88, 89; The New York Public Library: 4; photo courtesy News Dog Media: 67; photo Krzysztof Niewolny/Pixabay: 20; Norton Simon Museum, Pasadena, CA/© 2021 Banco de México Diego Rivera Frida Kahlo Museums Trust, Mexico, D.F./Artists Rights Society (ARS), New York: 82; Paulo Oliveira/Alamy Stock Photo: 76; from G. Pabst, ed., *Köhler's Medizinal-Pflanzen in naturgetreuen Abbildungen mit kurz erläuterndem Texte*, vol. 1 (Gera, 1887), photo Peter H. Raven Library, Missouri Botanical Garden, St. Louis, MO: 90; photo Halley Pacheco de Oliveira (CC BY-SA 3.0): 95; photo Patche99z: 37; PhotoByte/Alamy Stock Photo: 97; private collection: 9, 18, 25, 58, 60, 62, 72; private collection/© 2021 Banco de México Diego Rivera Frida Kahlo Museums Trust, Mexico, D.F./Artists Rights Society (ARS), New York: 83; photo Ibrahem Qasim (CC BY-SA 3.0): 101; photo Nathana Rebouças/Unsplash: 48; © Marc Riboud/Magnum Photos: 100; from *Le Rire*, no. 25 (8 May 1915), photo Bibliothèque national de France, Paris: 98; Rochester Institute of Technology (RIT) Archive Collections, The Wallace Center, Rochester, NY: 99; from J.H.S., ed., *Floral Poetry and the Language of Flowers* (London, 1877), photo British Library, London: 92; San Francisco Museum of Modern Art (photo Katherine Du Tiel)/© 2021 Banco de México Diego Rivera Frida Kahlo Museums Trust, Mexico, D.F./Artists Rights Society (ARS), New York: 84; photo David Shankbone (CC BY-SA 3.0): 28; from Jane Sharp, *The Midwives Book; or, The Whole Art of Midwifery Discovered* (London, 1671), photo Wellcome Collection (CC BY 4.0): 81; photo Stan Shebs (CC BY-SA 3.0): 69; Smithsonian American Art Museum, Washington, DC/© 2021 Georgia O'Keeffe Museum/Artists Rights Society (ARS), New York): 44; Smithsonian Libraries, Washington, DC: 16; photo Sonning Flowers, Reading: 21; photo Stux/Pixabay: 79; © Tate, London 2021: 103; Tate Britain, London: 22; from Andrew W. Tuer, *Old London Street Cries and the Cries of Today* (London, 1885), photo Digital Collections and Archives, Tufts University, Medford, MA: 64; Dennis Van Tine/UPI/Alamy Stock Photo: 104; from

F. B. Vietz, *Abbildungen aller medizinisch-ökonomisch-technologischen Gewächse, mit der Beschreibung ihres Gebrauches und Nutzens*, vol. X (Vienna, 1819), photo Österreichische Nationalbibliothek, Vienna: 7; Walker Art Gallery, Liverpool: 106; The Ware Collection of Blaschka Glass Models of Plants on exhibition at the Harvard Museum of Natural History, Harvard University, Cambridge, MA (photo Jennifer Berglund)/© President and Fellows of Harvard College: 38; photo Bob Wick/BLM: 8; Wolverhampton Art Gallery (photo Bridgeman Images): 66; Yale Center for British Art, Paul Mellon Collection, New Haven, CT: 78; photo Krzysztof Ziarnek, Kenraiz (CC BY-SA 4.0): 71.

LITERARY PERMISSIONS

Epigraph for Chapter Three reprinted by permission of *The Economist*, 17 December 2014 © The Economist Newspaper Limited, London. All rights reserved.

For excerpts from *Collected Poems 1909–1962* by T. S. Eliot, thanks to Faber and Faber Ltd. and Houghton Mifflin Harcourt Publishing Company (© 1952, renewed 1980 by Valerie Esme Eliot). Reprinted by permission of Houghton Mifflin Harcourt Publishing Company. All rights reserved.

'Sea Poppies', 'Sea Violet', and 'Sea Lily' by H.D. (Hilda Doolittle), from *Collected Poems, 1912–1944*, copyright © 1982 by The Estate of Hilda Doolittle. Reprinted by permission of New Directions Publishing Corp. and by kind permission of Carcanet Press Limited, Manchester, UK.

For an excerpt from *The Complete Poems* by Philip Larkin, thanks to Faber and Faber Ltd. and Farrar, Straus and Giroux, LLC.

An excerpt from 'The Métier of Blossoming' by Denise Levertov, from *This Great Unknowing*, copyright © 1998 by The Denise Levertov Literary Trust, Paul A. Lacey and Valerie Trueblood Rapport, Co-Trustees, is reprinted by permission of New Directions Publishing Corp. and Bloodaxe Books.

An excerpt from 'Tulips' in *The Collected Poems*, Sylvia Plath, copyright © 1960, 1965, 1971, 1981 by the Estate of Sylvia Plath, is used by permission of HarperCollins Publishers and Faber and Faber Ltd.

'Where Have All The Flowers Gone?' Words and Music by Pete Seeger Copyright © 1955 Sanga Music, Inc. Copyright Renewed, All Rights Administered by Figs. D Music c/o Concord Music Publishing. All Rights Reserved. Used by Permission. Reprinted by Permission of Hal Leonard LLC.

Excerpt from 'Under One Small Star' from *MAP: Collected and Last Poems* by Wisława Szymborska. Translated from the Polish by Stanislaw Baranczak and Clare Cavanagh. English translation copyright 2015 © by Houghton Mifflin Harcourt Publishing Company. All rights reserved.

INDEX

Illustration numbers are indicated by *italics*